THE NEW COLLEGE PRESIDENT

THE NEW COLLEGE PRESIDENT

How a Generation of Diverse Leaders Is
Changing Higher Education

TERRENCE J. MACTAGGART
and **EILEEN B. WILSON-OYELARAN**

Foreword by Daniel R. Porterfield

JOHNS HOPKINS UNIVERSITY PRESS | *Baltimore*

© 2024 Johns Hopkins University Press
All rights reserved. Published 2024
Printed in the United States of America on acid-free paper
9 8 7 6 5 4 3 2 1

Johns Hopkins University Press
2715 North Charles Street
Baltimore, Maryland 21218
www.press.jhu.edu

Library of Congress Cataloging-in-Publication Data

Names: MacTaggart, Terrence J., 1946– author. | Wilson-Oyelaran, Eileen,
    1947– author. | Porterfield, Daniel R., 1961– author.
Title: The new college president : how a generation of diverse leaders
    is changing higher education / Terrence J. MacTaggart,
    Eileen Wilson-Oyelaran, Foreword by Daniel R. Porterfield.
Description: Baltimore : Johns Hopkins University Press, 2024. | Includes
    bibliographical references and index.
Identifiers: LCCN 2023029966 | ISBN 9781421448688 (hardcover) | ISBN
    9781421448695 (ebook)
Subjects: LCSH: Educational leadership—United States. | College
    presidents—United States. | Diversity in the workplace—United States.
    | Education, Higher—United States—Philosophy.
Classification: LCC LB2805 .M253 2024 | DDC
    371.2/0110973—dc23/eng/20230818
LC record available at https://lccn.loc.gov/2023029966

A catalog record for this book is available from the British Library.

*Special discounts are available for bulk purchases of this book. For more information, please
contact Special Sales at specialsales@jh.edu.*

We could not have completed this project without the unwavering patience and intellectual engagement of our spouses, Elizabeth M. S. MacTaggart and Olasope O. Oyelaran.

CONTENTS

FOREWORD

DANIEL R. PORTERFIELD

PRESIDENT/CEO, THE ASPEN INSTITUTE

It should be no secret to anyone that American higher education is in trouble. A big part of the problem stems from the flawed or disappearing leadership of our colleges and universities. Presidents who ascended the academic ranks in a more benign era find themselves ill-equipped to deal with today's disruptions. They are departing in droves. Academic deans and vice presidents, who make up the traditional pool of future presidents, are increasingly turning down offers to apply for these precarious roles.

The New College President provides one foundational explanation of why this attrition is happening at the most senior levels of academia. Terrence MacTaggart and Eileen Wilson-Oyelaran assert that we should start at the top by recruiting to the presidency a new generation of powerhouse leaders with the minds, spines, and vision to lead at this pivotal national moment. In this highly readable account, they profile seven exceptionally capable leaders whose talents as college or university presidents developed thanks to their diverse and challenging backgrounds.

MacTaggart and Wilson-Oyelaran's insights dovetail with the findings of a major 2017 report of the Aspen Institute, which I coauthored. In "Renewal and Progress: Strengthening Higher Education Leadership in a Time of Rapid Change," my coauthors and I argue that "to succeed, college and university leaders will need a skillset that is both deeper and broader than ever before." We further assert that "the ability of higher education to flourish will require an expanded and more diverse pool of talented individuals who aspire to and are prepared for the college presidency."* In this book, MacTaggart and Wilson-Oyelaran point the way to recruiting this fresh reservoir of talent.

Higher education is needed now more than ever, but it doesn't seem well positioned to play the same creative and socially enhancing role that it did in previous generations. Enrollment continues to fall at many institutions, especially at community colleges, just as the long-projected national decline in the number of college-eligible young people is about to commence. Virtually everyone laments that college costs too much, even as many institutions struggle to meet their expenses. And then there are the white-hot narratives that college is a left-wing indoctrination factory, or an elitist prestige machine, or an engine of corporate conformity, or a bastion of cancel culture, or a coddler of the fragile, or an overpriced irrelevance . . . or all of the above. Given all of these factors, it's not surprising that public confidence in college education and its value has eroded since the mid-2010s and may yet worsen.

In this period of breakneck change, how can institutions reassert their essential roles and compete confidently for impact and resources? MacTaggart and Wilson-Oyelaran argue that a large part of the answer lies with a new generation of leaders.

Such leaders are out there, they contend, but trustees and search committees will need to widen their apertures to recognize stellar executive talent in its full range and diversity. The authors know from experience that for far too long higher education has selected presidents based on a somewhat narrow set of elite academic credentials. All too often, colleges and universities have missed the opportunity to recruit bold, gritty individuals who have persevered against adversity, broken barriers, and made outsized differences not only in education but also in business, government, culture, nonprofit leadership, and the military. The authors of this book recommend a "forensic approach" to executive recruitment. They believe this is far more inclusive and penetrating than the typical consultant-driven, formulaic processes that myriad institutions have used almost by rote for decades.

---

* https://www.aspeninstitute.org/wp-content/uploads/2017/05/Renewal_and_Progress_CEP-05122017.pdf.

To meet hard challenges when success is not preordained and cynicism and mistrust abound in society, today's campus leaders will need "strengths of character" such as intellect, tenacity, resilience, purpose, empathy, agility, cultural awareness, and a passion to serve others. This "ensemble of strengths," the authors assert, can be found in adults who "have known and overcome adversity from an early age and through the course of their careers." It's an inspiring proposition.

To prove the point that those who scrap and strive often are unintentionally groomed to lead, *The New College President* serves up in-depth profiles of seven high-impact presidents. Each story is deeply compelling. For example, we see how Robert Jones used lessons learned growing up as a sharecropper's son in rural Georgia to equip himself for success as a scientist and eventually as the chancellor of the University of Illinois. We see how Mary Marcy tapped the work ethic and passion for education she developed during her humble Nebraska childhood to fuel her drive to transform Dominican University of California into a student-centered equity engine. And we read about how Freeman Hrabowski III channeled the moral calling of his 1960s childhood in Birmingham, Alabama, into visionary service at the University of Maryland, Baltimore County, where he showed the nation that, with individual attention and academic rigor, underprepared STEM students from underserved communities, especially students of color, can achieve at or above the academic levels of their much more advantaged peers.

Having worked with and learned from all three of these eminent leaders, as well as others whose powerful work is chronicled here, I found these profiles to be both an inspiration and a challenge. MacTaggart and Wilson-Oyelaran make me wonder, what more can I do to make a difference? How best can I see and support the talent of others?

From all seven accounts, readers will take away wise perspectives, creative approaches, memorable anecdotes, and winning strategies. Angela Duckworth might have entitled this book *Profiles in Grit*. With leadership qualities honed by the vicissitudes of life, each of these presidents has navigated the stormy waters of change to help their institutions strengthen excellence, equity, access, and social impact. All are values-driven leaders who've shown the will and the skill with the staying power to succeed in shape-shifting social and institutional conditions that are now more often the norm.

With this book, these experienced authors offer a hopeful perspective at a moment when presidencies are becoming shorter and more tumultuous. No doubt, these profiles will help trustees, faculties, and search committees see that, in turbulent times, our country has a deep pool of can-do strivers ready to lead well if given the chance. Yes, the seven presidents profiled here are exceptional; but the authors want us to know that they're also *representative* of the caliber of future presidents who can be recruited from many communities, fields, and zip codes. The future of higher education, and the country, will be much brighter when our institutions move to recruit and hire more presidents like those Mac-Taggart and Oyelaran present.

"You are only here for show."

The reception for each candidate for president of the college was billed as a "getting-to-know-each-other" experience rather than an official interview. Of course, that was not true. These gatherings were really interviews by other means, this time in a campus lounge instead of a conference room. Lubricated with wine and cheese, members of the search committee would form impressions of the candidate's ability to hold her own in a social setting composed primarily of affluent white people. These major supporters of the institution played influential roles in the search for—and will play an influential role in the life of—whoever becomes the college's next president. The sole African American member of the search committee seemed anxious to speak with the candidate apart enough from the crowd so others could not overhear. She tapped the candidate's elbow, looked squarely into her brown eyes, and said, "You know you are only here for show. Don't get your hopes up."

Was this comment designed to throw the candidate off her stride or to guard her against disappointment? Did it reflect the speaker's perceptions of the search committee? Was she implying that other committee members did not take her candidacy seriously despite her outstanding credentials and demonstrated leadership achievements? Or was it simply a statement of fact: the only person of color in the pool was a token homage to diversity and affirmative action, but not a real contender?

A Reservoir of Talent

You might conclude that we cite the narrative above to excoriate the hypocrisy and unfairness in many searches for college and university chief executives. That would be a justified assumption, but not the correct one. We abhor racism, sexism, and all the other examples of prejudice (conscious and unconscious) that are often present in searches; but adding our voices to the chorus of critics of these social evils is not the chief purpose of this book. Rather, we contend that in this instance and many others, the trustees of the college would be in error if they prematurely set aside a candidate whose life experience, talent, and academic accomplishments might have prepared them to become a superb leader ready to confront whatever challenges the college would face. In bald terms, the trustees would be acting against their own self-interest if they dismissed a high-potential candidate because of the color of her skin.

We argue that an often-overlooked reservoir of talent lies within candidates whose life experience places them at the margins and whose upbringing has included generous amounts of adversity and challenge. Very often these are persons of color, immigrants and their children, people for whom English is a second language, and members of the LGBTQ+ community, although they also may be people who are white who, as one of our subjects put it, spent much of their childhood in "sorrow's kitchen." Because so many challenges abound in higher education today, we believe that candidates for the presidency who have surmounted hardships in their early lives and been forced to cross social boundaries often possess the strengths of character, broad perspectives, and other talents most needed in the academy.

This book profiles seven exceptional presidents who came up the hard way. In so doing, they developed strengths that enabled them to become superb college and university leaders. Boards of trustees and search committees seeking new chief executives, as well as consultants who assist, should go out of their way to recruit candidates such as these. Their leadership qualities make them well suited to take on the rigors of today's presidency. What are the special strengths of these individuals? Courage, resilience, tenacity, mental toughness, and the like are traits they all have in common, but these aspects of grit are far from the only virtues they possess. Their outlier status gives them a unique perspective on the dominant culture and its habits. Our own assessment of their character, which is drawn from extensive interviews, reveals that courage is their dominant trait. An external assessment of their character based on a personality inventory confirms the prominence of courage in their makeup.

These leaders' additional strengths include intercultural competence; compassion for students who, like themselves, come from fraught circumstances; intelligence that is both emotional and practical; and a fervor for a cause greater than themselves.

Our subjects are all accomplished academics. They include an award-winning research scientist, an Oxford-trained student of political theory, and a brilliant pianist, to cite three examples. Their upbringings, which were all peppered with adversity, combined with their academic apprenticeships as researchers and as teachers, bestowed upon them intimate knowledge of the business and culture of the academy.

The presidency today is much more difficult than in the past, as nearly every veteran president will confirm. Beginning with the Great Recession of 2007–2009, the parade of challenges confronting colleges and universities has grown. Today's troubles eclipse even the turbulent days of student unrest in the 1960s, according to those who participated in the turmoil of that heady era. Waves of pandemics, financial distress, increasing competition, enrollment declines, ideological conflicts, emergencies ranging from natural disasters to armed intruders, as well as demanding trustees and angry faculty represent only a short list of current pressures. Omnipresent social media magnifies all of these forces. It is only reasonable to expect that these issues will intensify through the early decades of this century.

To be sure, many presidents born into comfortable and privileged circumstances who ascended smoothly through the ranks to the presidency have stepped up to meet these challenges. Some find the challenges invigorating. Large numbers of incumbents, however, departed in a massive trend known as the Great Resignation and this trend continues. Many presidents from conventional backgrounds who expected a career as a respected leader operating in at least a somewhat collegial atmosphere find themselves unable or unwilling to cope with the new conflict-ridden environment. Turmoil is not what they signed up for. The balance between anxiety-rich events and job satisfaction tilts sharply toward the former. A veteran president captured an attitude shared by many of his peers when he said, "Who would want this job?"

Amid all the Sturm und Drang, however, there is some good news: the reservoir of talent highlighted in this book represents exactly the kind of talent a new generation of leaders can bring to the presidency.

The profiles in chapters 2 through 8 highlight the connective tissue linking each subject's early life experience, growth in a sometimes unwelcoming academic environment, and superior presidential performance. These are extraordinary leaders whose potential might have been lost if they were invited to apply "just for show."

Why We Wrote This Book

The inspiration for this book came from similar though separately experienced epiphanies in our professional lives. Following our stints as a college (in Eileen's case) and a university and system chief executive (Terrence's experience), we became advisors to boards of trustees and their presidents on matters of governance, leadership, and executive performance. We estimate that this work over the course of a decade, beginning in 2012, included over 500 confidential interviews with presidents themselves, as well as with trustees, faculty members, staff members, and students who willingly offered their perspective on the performance of the president. These conversations confirmed our belief that most presidents today work in a fraught ecosystem.

Over the more than ten years of investigation into the performance and often the fate of presidents, we noticed a growing divide between the president's expectations of what their job should be and the outcomes being demanded of them. The image of the president as an esteemed figure presiding over a relatively stable enterprise yielded to that of a harried and occasionally reviled authority figure. Having experienced what several characterized as a "toxic environment," more presidents are choosing or being forced to leave their jobs earlier than in the past. The American Council on Education reports increasing rates of presidential turnover.* Faculty no-confidence votes in their president, once a rare and devastating occurrence, have become as inevitable as the painful changes that bring them about. The life of college presidents had already become more tenuous and uncomfortable when the sudden eruption of the COVID-19 pandemic brought more stress into their lives.

We observed differences between the presidents who thrived in the new environment and those who managed well enough but whose appetite for leadership waned as the disruptions mounted. The president's age, the prospects for an institution's continued financial health and sustainability, and the quality of the board's support and the community's support influenced individual decisions to rise to the challenges or allow someone else to take up the fight. The presidents we advised, coached, or assessed all possessed adequate to superior academic backgrounds, yet academic credentials and accomplishments had little to do with an individual's willingness to continue to lead in the disrupted new normal.

It became clear to us that personal leadership qualities were decisive in determining a president's willingness and ability to engage with the daunting challenges confronting their institutions. Leaders who were viewed as truly exceptional captured our attention. After all, the times demanded not adequate performance but truly extraordinary talent. Our desire to identify the "right stuff" for superior leadership and explain why some presidents had it in abundance and others did not inspired us to write this book.

In late 2020, we decided to combine our efforts on a book that would pursue these questions:

- How does the upbringing of an exceptional leader shape their leadership performance in a challenging epoch such as this?
- What qualities of character and other leadership traits are most characteristic of these high-performing college and university presidents?

---

* Jonathan S. Gagliardi et al., *American College President Study 2017* (Washington, DC: American Council on Education, 2017), https://www.acenet.edu/Documents/American-College-President-VIII-2017.pdf.

- What challenges met and other demonstrable hallmarks separate truly exceptional leaders from run-of-the-mill executive performers?
- How can presidential searches be improved so that candidates with exceptional potential are identified, recruited, vetted, hired, and supported in the challenging work of twenty-first-century presidents?

Chapter Synopses

Chapter 1. The Challenged Presidency: Not for the Faint of Heart

This chapter highlights challenges of the contemporary presidency, then points out five hallmarks of truly outstanding leadership. The chapter also describes the sources of our findings: multiple interviews, document reviews, verifiable measures of performance, and an independently administered leadership assessment.

To test our own conclusions and to discover what strengths these exceptional leaders might share, each participant completed the HU-MANeX In-Depth Leader Assessment, which was developed by Humanex Ventures. We are most grateful for the support of Humanex in this aspect of our work.

Chapter 2. Jeffrey Bullock: Pastor/President

Over the course of twenty-five years at the University of Dubuque, Dr. Jeffrey Bullock has led the transformation of the university from virtual bankruptcy to a robust, prosperous, and mission-driven institution in the reformed Presbyterian tradition. This chapter ties crucible events in Bullock's troubled upbringing, his service to abandoned children on the streets of Seattle, and the influence of a saintly mentor to his search for a vocation in life. The outcome has been the rise of an exceptional leader who is at once a devout pastor and a charismatic president at an institution where the concept of Christian love informs campus strategy.

Chapter 3. Waded Cruzado: The Power of Imaginative Leadership

If Dr. Waded Cruzado's selection as president of Montana State University surprised some, the results she has wrought over a dozen years have defied everyone's expectations except her own. Under Cruzado, enrollment at MSU has multiplied, fundraising has surpassed every previous goal, and the campus itself has grown to become a model twenty-first-century learning and research center. The greatest achievement in Cruzado's mind and heart, however, is its stature as a welcoming land-grant university for the sons and daughters of working-class Montanans. This chapter traces Cruzado's life story as the oldest child in a family "without much money but a lot of love" in Mayagüez, Puerto Rico, to her graduate work in comparative literature. After studying the great magical realist works of Spain and South America, she grew to become a resourceful, imaginative, and hugely respected president in Big Sky Country.

Chapter 4. Mary Dana Hinton: Leadership as Love in Action

None of the messages Dr. Mary Dana Hinton received as a child suggested she would become a transformational leader at two different liberal arts colleges committed to the education of women. Initially at the College of Saint Benedict, and now at Hollins University, Hinton has fostered challenging conversations, resulting in a revitalization of mission and a renewed commitment to building equitable, inclusive academic communities. The result, in both cases, has been increased visibility, reinvigorated curricula, more effective student support, and high-functioning governance. Under Hinton, Hollins received a transformational gift of $75 million, the largest in its history and rare for any women's college. This chapter traces Hinton's journey from rural eastern North Carolina, where the strongest messages she received demanded that she "stay in her place," to the presidency at Hollins. Her upbringing prepared Hinton to became the first African American leader of a historically white Southern women's college.

Chapter 5. Freeman Hrabowski III: Achieving Inclusivity and Excellence

The University of Maryland, Baltimore County (UMBC), was the first institution in the University of Maryland system created post-desegregation. However, in 1987, when Dr. Freeman Hrabowski began his work with the university as associate provost for undergraduate studies, neither the African American community in Baltimore nor the students of color on campus found the university to be a particularly hospitable environment. Today UMBC produces three times as many graduates who go on to earn the MD/PhD as Harvard and the largest number of Black students in the nation who go on to pursue the MD/PhD. The opportunity to serve as president of UMBC for thirty years would have been an unimaginable proposition to twelve-year-old Hrabowski when he found himself in jail during the 1963 Children's Crusade, part of the effort to desegregate Birmingham, Alabama. In this chapter, we will explore the impact of Hrabowski's upbringing in a tight-knit, segregated middle-class Black community during the civil rights era, the role of teachers and mentors, and the impact of both high and low expectations on Hrabowski's development as a nationally recognized educational leader.

Chapter 6. Robert Jones: From the Fields Where Character Grows

The University of Illinois Urbana-Champaign is one of America's great public research universities, though that has proven to be a precarious assignment for many of those who sought to lead the university. Before Dr. Robert Jones arrived as chancellor in 2016, a series of scandals forced two of his predecessors to resign before the end of their terms. This chapter traces Jones's remarkable journey from a sharecropper's shack in rural Georgia, through a distinctly unwelcoming experience in a master's program at the University of Georgia, to his doctoral training as a plant physiologist in Columbia, Missouri. We also touch on what Jones thought would be the apex of his career as a distinguished research professor at the University of Minnesota. To his surprise, Jones was asked to take on a series of administrative posts, culminating in his becoming the University of Minnesota's senior vice president. Yet his life story is most exceptional because of his work in restoring confidence and trust at a troubled university during a state budget crisis, during the national uproar over the murder of George Floyd, and during the COVID-19 pandemic. As one of his colleagues at U of I said, "We knew we would be OK with Robert in charge."

Chapter 7. Kwang-Wu Kim: The College for Creatives

Columbia College Chicago, the gritty art school located in the heart of America's "second city," was a beleaguered place when Dr. Kwang-Wu Kim arrived as its new president in 2013. Declining enrollment combined with budgets out of balance, a faculty union in conflict with the administration, and dysfunctional governance posed serious, potentially fatal challenges. Why would the board of such a place hire a person trained to be a concert-level pianist? Astute judges of character and talent, the trustees knew that in Kim they had found a Chicagoan with an impeccable arts background and the business savvy to restore the college's sense of mission and competitiveness. This chapter follows Kim's outward journey from a Korean American home on Chicago's South Side to the Columbia presidency. We also examine how Kim's inner growth fostered an ensemble of leadership strengths that defined his presidency at Chicago's vibrant college for creatives.

Chapter 8. Mary Marcy: The Intentional Leader

When Dr. Mary Marcy accepted the presidency of Dominican University of California, she was not expecting to orchestrate turnaround. However, during the decade that she led Dominican, the institution pivoted, moving away from its reputation as a relatively unknown California institution without a clear focus to become a nationally recognized and thriving campus with a distinctive educational model. In the process, Marcy strengthened all aspects of institutional governance, rebuilt relationships with the university's founding religious order, and enabled the community to see its diversity as both an opportunity and a strength. This chapter traces Marcy's evolution as a transformational leader, from her rigorous upbringing on a Nebraska cattle ranch to her graduate work at Oxford University, her deep engagement in higher education policy issues, and her determination to live an authentic life as a leader who is a lesbian.

Chapter 9. Recruiting Exceptional Leaders: A Forensic Approach

The culminating chapter offers seven steps for changing presidential search processes to recruit, hire, and retain genuinely exceptional leaders like those described in this book. This fresh approach is "forensic" in that it demands integrating an expanded and more penetrating approach into the conventional search model. It also calls for active recruiting during a quiet phase, well before the official announcement of the interviews, a phase that is better designed to gauge leadership potential. We also advocate for more revelatory vetting of finalists and coaching for traditional and nontraditional presidents alike.

THE NEW COLLEGE PRESIDENT

CHAPTER 1

The Great Resignation Presents a Great Opportunity

The worldwide phenomenon known as the Great Resignation has hit the upper echelons of higher education with a vengeance.[1] Incumbent presidents are bailing out as soon as their contracts expire, and often before. Provosts, academic vice presidents, and deans of large schools within a university and the like are hesitant to apply, having witnessed the cascading pressures that caused the vacancy in the first place.[2] The exit is occurring across the spectrum of colleges and universities, and at both large and small public systems comprised of multiple institutions and presidents. Chief executives are departing early from institutions ranging from community colleges to the Big Ten, public systems, and elite research universities. Even a short list runs long. But there is an upside to the Big Quit if boards and search committees are ready to seize it: the vacancies clear the way for hiring a new generation of leaders equipped to handle the rigors of the job.

There is an untapped pool of resourceful and talented individuals prepared to take on the challenges of the contemporary presidency. They have acquired the appropriate academic credentials and are gifted with the intelligence required to lead complex institutions. Their most important attributes, however, are the several virtues gathered under an old-fashioned heading: strength of character. Personal qualities such as tenacity, resilience, compassion, practical and cultural intelligence,[3] and a passion for or calling to a cause greater than themselves are among their most prominent virtues.[4]

Who are these people, and where can they be found? Like sociologist Georg Simmel's stranger,[5] they are all around us yet distant at the same time, if "us" is defined as the relatively privileged classes who have historically filled the ranks of college presidents. The seven presidents profiled in this book possess these character traits in abundance. They hail from backgrounds hitherto unlikely to lead to a college presidency. Our list features women, people of color, children of immigrants, and a person who identifies as a lesbian. Each of them exemplifies the strengths of "outsiders." They are "misfits" who became the best fits for their colleges and universities.

These people are not quitters. They should have been pursued for presidencies in any era; but during the current exodus of presidents, they and other professionals like them should be among the top picks for the job. They display a penchant for staying the course through both victories and setbacks. Their longevity in office is an important testament to their tenacity. The average tenure of these seven presidents is over fourteen years—more than twice the length of service of conventional presidents.[6]

How did these presidents come to develop the strengths that make them so right for the times? Simply put, they came up the hard way. One had been cast adrift by his family when he was a young teenager. Another grew up in an impoverished community where she was targeted by bullies throughout her childhood. Her vulnerabilities? An impediment affecting her eyes and an interest in reading. A third, at age 12, experienced the unspeakable horrors of a Birmingham, Alabama, jail following a civil rights demonstration. The president of another major research university was born in a sharecropper's shack in one of the poorest counties in Georgia.

In a remarkable paradox, adverse experiences in these people's early experience combined with loving support at critical times in their lives and their native intelligence blended to form them into truly exceptional leaders. More remarkable still, the ensemble of strengths nurtured in arduous circumstances shaped their leadership styles and their sense of mission as college and university presidents. They may have achieved the presidency in spite of their early circumstances, but they achieved so much as leaders because of difficult and sometimes brutal early life experiences.

Hardship in its many forms is what our subjects share. Its origins are quite variable. Some of our subjects have continuous experience with systemic injustice in their lives. We in no way condone the inequitable systems that give rise to these harsh experiences and we recognize—as several of the profiles illustrate—that without the intervention of supportive families, individuals, and often communities, the emergence of their strengths of character would have been thwarted.

We wholeheartedly support diversifying the presidency on the grounds of fairness and social justice. But we also argue that hiring presidents from challenged backgrounds, whatever their ethnic or cultural heritage, increases the likelihood that these leaders will possess the strength of character to effectively lead in these disrupted times. Certainly, there is no guarantee that a challenged upbringing will inevitably produce an exceptionally capable leader, nor is there any certainty that a privileged childhood induces weakness. We contend, however, that "outsiders" often possess underappreciated strengths that are most needed in the upended environment of many colleges and universities today.

Our Five Propositions

Five basic ideas concerning human development and leadership underpin our case for the advantages of "nontraditional" candidates. These notions began as separate possibilities. Gradually, we developed them into hypotheses to be examined, then confirmed these in conversations with successful presidents, reviews of the relevant social scientific research, and explorations of the lives of the seven extraordinary people we feature in this book. Readers familiar with the fraught condition of the academy will find most of these ideas axiomatic. We hope that those less familiar with the troubles facing higher education will regard them as plausible truths based on their experience in other walks of life. Taken together, these premises lay the groundwork for a more fruitful way of thinking about the contemporary presidency and more productive methods for recruiting superior leaders.

We invite you to consider these observations:

- Hundreds of presidents are hastily departing their posts in large measure because the job is far more difficult, conflicted, insecure, and stress-laden than in the past. Aging presidents who in a simpler time might have continued to serve are choosing retirement over the exhausting work before them.

- People brought up in especially challenging circumstances often acquire the appropriate emotional preparation for the rigors of the contemporary presidency precisely because they have experienced and surmounted hardships earlier in life. Those often considered "outsiders" (broadly defined as people of color, people with lower incomes, immigrants and their children, members of the LGBTQ+ community, people with disabilities, and individuals who have faced unique challenges irrespective of class, gender, or race) often develop strengths that those who have less challenging early life experiences never cultivate.

- Among the special attributes of these unlikely higher education leaders are strengths of character, which we define broadly as resilience, tenacity, compassion, and practical and cultural intelligence, among other qualities.[7]

- A formidable barrier to recruiting these individuals lies within the academy itself. Despite a recent uptick in the hiring of African American men as presidents, progress has been slow when it comes to candidates who are women, who are Asian American, or who are from other perceived outside group.[8] Trustees and academics alike tend to choose their leaders from a cadre of the usual suspects while setting aside unconventional candidates whose appearance, language, gender, or identity don't match the legacy image of a college president.

- Finally, a more sophisticated style of identifying candidates' strengths and flaws is required to successfully recruit leaders who are right for the times. We label this fresh approach "forensic" to signal a more penetrating style of analyzing high-potential leaders and attracting them to the modern presidency.

Whether you regard these observations as axioms or hypotheses, we believe you will find that the stories of these seven exceptional leaders illuminate unusual pathways to superior leadership. To be sure, we chose these seven precisely because their stories are archetypal of many more potentially superb leaders. Often viewed as outsiders or underdogs, these leaders, in remarkably frank conversations with us, shared their personal life stories that reveal much about the strengths of character essential to effective leadership in this troubled era.

The Advantages of Disadvantage

In a paradoxical twist of social history, the backgrounds that historically disqualified "outsiders" for leadership positions often nurture some of their most important qualifications for contemporary presidencies. The struggle against the tide of disadvantage—being born a woman or a person of color, growing up poor, speaking with a "foreign" accent, experiencing abandonment as a child, or grappling with other impediments—can produce attributes most needed in today's contested environments.

A complementary paradox is that children born into privileged circumstances who have historically become favorite candidates in presidential searches may be less adept in today's contested world. To be sure, many presidents initially unprepared for the rigors of the job rise to the occasion. Forced by circumstance, they develop or discover the inner resources necessary to address the difficult problems before them. Those unwilling or unable to step in during these critical situations must look for other ways to make a living.

The tough-minded chief of a large public university system told us that administrators accustomed to gentler circumstances often lack the mental fortitude to make frequent hard choices. In a stark recognition of one of those harsh choices, he observed that many former chief academic or student affairs officers probably "never had to fire anyone."

An upbringing in the world of wealth and privilege does not automatically rule out the capacity to assert superior leadership. Theodore Roosevelt, who grew from a sickly youth to a robust national leader, illustrates the point. His cousin Franklin, felled by nearly fatal pneumonia in 1918 and then struck by incurable polio three years later, is another prime example of hardship within a life of privilege. Told that he would never walk again and had no future in public life, Franklin replied, "If you spent two years in bed trying to wiggle your toe, after that anything would seem easy."[9]

"Desirable Difficulties"

Ad aster per aspera (to the stars through adversity) is a venerable Latin phrase that expresses the notion that high achievement comes through difficulty. The potential of adversity to enable individuals to grow in character and capability is a major theme in the works of a gifted essayist, Malcolm Gladwell, and in the findings of scrupulous social science researchers to illustrate that *aspera* is frequently a steppingstone on the path to exceptional performance.

"Desirable difficulties"[10]—a phrase borrowed from social scientists Elizabeth and Robert Bjork—is how Gladwell characterizes early life challenges that nurture superior achievement.[11] In his aptly named *David and Goliath: Underdogs, Misfits, and the Art of Battling Giants* (2013),[12] Gladwell profiles high achievers who came into life with serious impediments. His subjects went on to become brilliant attorneys, financiers, and scientists, Gladwell argues, precisely because of their disabilities. He says that "being an underdog can *change* people in ways we often fail to appreciate."[13] He adds that being the "outsider" can "open doors and create opportunities and educate and enlighten and make possible what otherwise have seemed unthinkable."[14]

The Bjorks, in an intriguing article titled "Making Things Hard on Yourself, But in a Good Way: Creating Desirable Difficulties to Enhance Learning,"[15] distinguish "undesirable difficulties," which impede learning and growth, from "desirable difficulties," which "trigger encoding and retrieval processes that support learning, comprehension, and remembering."[16] The Bjorks acknowledge, and we entirely agree, that there are highly *undesirable* difficulties that stifle learning and growth. Systemic racism is prominent among these, and neither we nor the researchers would argue that it is a good thing just because countervailing forces such as love and support aid in the development of character strengths.

The Bjorks focus on desirable difficulties that deepen and accelerate school-based learning. Gladwell carries their insights further by applying them to human growth and development generally, to learning in the broader sense of applying talents to the competitive world of professions like law and finance.

Strengths Born of Hardship

Impressive social science research based on three independently conducted longitudinal studies goes a long way toward providing a scientific basis for Gladwell's, the Bjorks', and our arguments as well. Three studies on the impact of childhood experience, all involving thousands of children and adults over the course of decades, point to the sinews between adverse backgrounds and the high performance of our seven subjects.

Jay Belsky, a research psychologist at the University of California Davis, and several of his colleagues make the case that "some children prove more resilient to adversity than other children do."[17] Belsky et al. cite three ways that adversity can breed resilience: "supportive parenting, neighborhood collective efficacy, and individual genetic makeup."[18] Belsky and company point to Wordsworth's "child is father of the man" for a summary of the conclusions to be drawn from these independent research studies of the impact of childhood experiences on adult development.

Belsky and his colleagues based their findings on three large and complementary longitudinal studies tracing human development from the early years to several stages of adulthood.[19] Prominent among the three studies "following young lives through time" is *The Dunedin Multidisciplinary Health and Development Study* that followed virtually all 1,000 or so New Zealanders born in the town of Dunedin in a twelve-month period in the early 1970s, with assessment of their developmental experiences during childhood, adolescence, and adulthood.[20]

For those interested, the second study, *The Environmental Risk Study (E-Risk)*, follows "more than one thousand pairs of British twins across their first two decades of life."[21] The third study is the *NICHD Study of Early Child Care and Youth Development*, conducted in collaboration with the National Institute of Child Health and Development, which followed the development of 1,300 Americans growing up in ten locales across the country through age fifteen.[22]

Drawing on the Dunedin research, Belsky and his colleagues observed with appropriate scholarly humility, that there is no certainty in predicting how an individual child will develop based on childhood and family influences. However, they go on to say that "childhood functioning is often a reasonably good prognosticator of future development."[23]

The life histories of the seven remarkable presidents we profile bear out these findings. A level of adversity coupled with supportive and loving parents (in one case, in an adoptive family), joined by inherited strengths, fostered a bundle of talents that offer the potential for truly exceptional leadership.

With all of this evidence supporting the idea that difficulties in early life often represent an advantage when it comes to performance in later life, why is it that "outsiders" who have experienced plenty of *aspera* are so often turned away in the college and university president selection process?

We Have Met the Enemy and . . .

The disproportion between women and people of color employed or enrolled in higher education and their representation in the presidential C-suite invites many explanations. Lack of interest, absence in the ranks leading up to the presidency, and few role models are among the most commonly alleged causes of their relative absence. Bias within the ranks of well-intended academics surely accounts for much of the gap, as well.

The following verbatim statements point to the levees that channel potentially superb candidates away from the presidency:

"This community is not ready to accept a gay president."
—a presidential search committee chair to the search consultant
"I can't bring a man with his accent to this governor."
—rationale for not selecting an Asian American who was the most qualified candidate for president
"A single woman would be an outsider in this conservative part of the state."
—a system trustee rejecting a female candidate for president
"A person with her background won't really be considered for president."
—a search committee member regarding a Hispanic candidate
"I know she is the best, but what if we hire her and she fails?"
—a search committee member at an elite liberal arts college commenting on the top candidate, an African American woman

Two of the individuals who were ultimately hired in these situations lost their jobs within twenty-four months. The outlier candidates rejected in two of these cases received less biased receptions in other searches; both went on to become successful presidents at other similar or superior institutions. In the remaining instance, the minority candidate became president and performed spectacularly.

Politically incorrect and morally objectionable as these comments are, virtually everyone who has worked in an academic environment has heard sentiments like these. Even those who have never voiced a biased opinion and regard themselves as fair-minded and without prejudice have at least overheard more than a few benighted assumptions about "the other" and their lack of suitability for a college presidency. An anthropologist with impeccable credentials who teaches at a premier liberal arts college told us with a straight face that she couldn't assent to hiring a Black candidate "because they just don't seem to fit in."

What can be done about persistent bias in the most liberal of communities? Two remedies present themselves: The first is to encourage boards to appreciate the leadership traits that spell the difference between mediocrity and stellar performance. These touchstones of exceptional leadership are discussed next. The second remedy is to reform presidential searches, which is the subject of the final chapter in this book.

Touchstones of Exceptional Leadership

We had several reasons for developing these criteria. First, as standards of exceptional performance, they provided the filters for selecting the individuals to be profiled in this book. Second, they are major themes in those parts of the profiles dealing with presidential performance. And third, these indicators of superior performance provide essential benchmarks for targeting the right recruits for the presidency, for vetting finalists, and ultimately for choosing the most promising candidate.

In our work of advising, coaching, evaluating, and occasionally supporting the dismissal of presidents, we found that these five standards cut across a wide range of institutional types and situations. They are not exhaustive of all the ways of gauging presidential performance to be sure, yet they have the advantage of being evidence-based and demonstrable. Impartial observers looking at the same data, we found, usually come to similar conclusions regarding the performance of a chief executive. Applying standards like these, we have found, provides a more reliable predictor of candidate potential than gut instinct of committee members or a candidate's skill in schmoozing.

Evidence of Exceptional Leadership

1. Challenges—whether existential or merely problematic, inherited from a prior administration or newly imposed, or well-defined or misunderstood—mark the beginning of every quest for a new president. The new leader's capacity to address these is often the litmus test of the president's performance, and frequently determines the length and happiness of their tenure. Examples of serious challenges that greeted the presidents in this book include

university bankruptcy, racial and ethnic conflicts, scandals derailing prior leaders, dysfunctional shared governance, plummeting enrollment, reputational crises, and the need to sell the campus, among others.

2. Metrics selected as meaningful indicators of performance have moved from the periphery of higher education assessment to center stage for measuring both institutional performance and that of its president. A variety of indicators—including trends in student achievement, enrollment, rankings, financial strength, research productivity, and fundraising—are included with each of the profiles in this book.

3. Signature accomplishments tend to emphasize new construction, major building renovations and repurposing, and innovative and new academic programs. Examples among those profiled include an ambitious and successful fundraising campaign, the initiation of an innovative medical school, and funding being secured for a near remake of an entire campus. Less visible but no less important examples of major accomplishments include a significant repositioning of the institution in the market, enabling the college to recover from a devastating crisis, and restoring trust following ruptures of confidence.

4. Comparisons of the president's performance juxtaposed with the performance of peers from similarly situated institutions in like circumstances is another relevant criterion. The presence of two public research-oriented institutions in North Dakota, Iowa, and, notably for this book, Montana, lend themselves to such comparisons. More general comparisons are available, for example, among tuition-dependent colleges, urban public colleges and universities, and regional institutions within a public system and members of associations of like institutions such as the APLU (Association of Public Land-Grant Universities).

5. Strength of character may be the least tangible attribute, but it is the arch stone that supports the other elements. It includes the virtues of tenacity, resilience, compassion, and practical and cultural intelligence, as well as a deep-seated passion for a mission.

In our own assessments of the seven presidents and in the confirmation provided by the HUMANeX In-Depth Leader Assessment (used with permission of Humanex Ventures), each of our subjects ranked in the upper tenth percentile of high performing executives on their fervent commitment to their institution's mission. Every academic leader is prepared to wax eloquently on their commitment to diversity, excellence, student success, religious values, and any other number of noble causes. What must be sought out is compelling evidence of a truly profound commitment to a larger purpose or to a cause that determined their top priorities and shaped the president's style of leadership.

These touchstones are articulated so they can legitimately be applied to a variety of challenges, problems, opportunities, and expectations facing presidents. With some adjustment to accommodate an institution's resource base, market position, culture, and other variables, they lend themselves to identifying truly exceptional leaders and setting a standard for others to pursue.

Why These Seven Presidents?

Our work as presidential and board advisors and assessors provided the opportunity to closely observe the performance of three of the seven. The others we knew by their reputations, by their publications, through news accounts, and through some quiet conversations with those close to them. We considered approximately fifty potential subjects, then interviewed a dozen to determine their suitability and interest in this project. In addition to gauging their performance in light of the five touchstones identified above, we probed their willingness to be interviewed and to encourage their staff, trustees, and other associates to provide us with confidential assessments of their performance. All readily agreed to take the two-hour Humanex leadership assessment and to share the results with us. A link to the Humanex assessment appears on the last page of this book.

We thought it important to represent a range of institutions across different parts of the country. Our subjects hail from a midwestern, private, religiously affiliated institution that includes a seminary; a western land-grant; a distinctive women's college in Virginia; an urban university within a large public university system on the East Coast; a large, highly ranked midwestern public research institution; a formerly church-affiliated independent college on the West Coast; and a private, urban college specializing in the arts.

Clay Feet and Critics

There is a risk in labeling a currently serving president as "exceptional." Although we conducted multiple interviews with and about our subjects, and reviewed media reports as well as official documents, it is fair to acknowledge the possibility that a hitherto hidden, serious flaw might emerge. What if their ability abruptly changes for the worse? What if their time in office outruns their energy and talent? We do not, nor would any of the presidents themselves, claim to be perfect. Our subjects readily confessed to missteps and decisions they would make differently on another occasion. Like other successful leaders, most professed to have learned from their mistakes.

There is no escaping the criticism that comes with the territory of the modern presidency. If they are leading change, as they all must, then criticism from within the college and externally is guaranteed. Their missteps are magnified in the public arenas in which they operate. Inevitably, the courage they demonstrate in making painful and unpopular decisions can arouse harsh criticism from those affected and from those who simply disagree with the policy. Today's contested environment makes it even more important to recruit presidents who have learned to shrug off, or at least appear immured to, invective of all sorts.

Not for the Faint of Heart

The work life of a contemporary president is not for weaklings. A short list of the challenges facing today's presidents includes a demographic cliff in which the numbers of high school graduates and thus potential first-year college students drop precipitously, especially in the Northeast and Midwest; ideological and partisan conflicts that disrupt campuses and boardrooms alike; sharply diminished public confidence in the value of a college education; and an unforgiving strain in contemporary culture exacerbated by social media that is captured in words of one president who said he felt one allegation away from a forced resignation. The most serious consequence among these and other forces confronting the president is the leadership vacuum resulting from rampant presidential departures.

The Great Resignation is especially acute in a disrupted industry like higher education, where the demands for expert leadership are rising while interest in the job wanes. In recent years, two presidents from the two-year College of Northern Idaho departed early and under pressure from trustees. Ohio State's president stepped down under ambiguous circumstances. The first Hispanic head of the California State University System, as well as individual presidents within that twenty-three campus system, have departed under pressure related to Title IX violations. Ivy League and elite college presidents—including leaders at Harvard, Dartmouth, Columbia, Tufts, and MIT—have recently left or announced their departures.[24] The headlines are dominated by presidential departures that have been triggered by sexual misconduct at brand-name schools, but the huge wave of departures includes sinners and saints across higher education. Many of those leaving have performed well and without major controversy but are just tired of the unrelenting pressures of the job.

Miscreants who are convicted of ignoring or covering up blatant cases of sexual misconduct and other serious offenses need to go. The avalanche of highly publicized charges filed under Title IX[25] has led some male presidents to examine their past behavior and their vulnerability to accusations of inappropriate conduct. The highly publicized turnover of presidents, however justified the departures, both forced and voluntary, underscores just how precarious the job has become. In a remarkably frank observation, one highly regarded president, speaking to his male colleagues, said that they are all only a sexual harassment case mishandled or a Title IX complaint away from losing their jobs.

Mishandling of sexual harassment allegations or being the target of such complaints are among the most visible but are far from the major factors driving presidents out. Veteran presidents tell us that their job has become more difficult and more perilous especially since the Great Recession. The challenges have increased, while the vaunted satisfactions of the job lag far behind. Angry and fearful faculty members are producing no-confidence votes or threatening them in greater numbers. A censure vote may no longer guarantee a rapid presidential departure, but it all but eliminates the chances of securing another presidency elsewhere.

If lost confidence motions signal a breakdown on the administration/faculty side of the shared governance equation, then relationships between presidents and their boards of trustees are troubled, as well. Governing boards have become more demanding, more divided, and less patient with the pace of change. Highly publicized divisions within boards seem to be on the rise. A long-serving president who previously enjoyed a generally positive relationship with trustees told us, "I'd like to believe the board has my back when I make an unpopular call." He added that he needed to count the votes more often to confirm their support.

Partisan political and ideological conflicts that wrack the nation also play out in boardrooms, classrooms, and public spaces on campus. Culture war skirmishes and pitched battles endanger presidents, as well. One veteran executive begins the list of woes with contention erupting over critical race theory, then moves to "safe spaces on campus, to free speech and speech codes (for students and faculty and visiting speakers), to transgender rights, to affirmative action, to academic freedom in the classroom, to renaming buildings, to removal of statues, to apologies and reparations for an institution's complicity in slavery." He sums up the plight of current president with the question: "Who would want this job?"[26]

A former president turned head of a fast-growing executive search firm recognized the emotional impact of the pandemic on sitting presidents. Sitting presidents are tired, he says. His executive search business is booming in part because the stress induced by two years of the COVID wave equaled "four or five years of normal times."

With the acceptance of viruses as unwelcome but long-term visitors, preexisting campus conflicts have returned in full force. To be sure, many stalwart or phlegmatic leaders cope with the problems, conflicts, and animosities that have become more common. Even these stalwarts, however, are less inclined than their predecessors to seek longer terms of employment. "A toxic ecosystem," is how one veteran characterized his current campus environment. Hans Selye, the pioneering researcher on stress response, named exhaustion as the final stage in the typical three-part response to stress.[27] Simply put, mental and physical exhaustion is driving many presidents from their posts. Vince Lombardi, the legendary football coach, might have been speaking for college presidents when he said, "Fatigue makes cowards of us all."

The New College President

The litany of challenges speaks to the tough aspects of the presidency. It also underscores the need for exceptionally experienced and talented individuals like those profiled in this book to lead institutions across very rough terrain.

Of course, not every presidency is imperiled by this host of threats; but many are. And no presidency is free of a goodly number of serious, potentially career ending, challenges. All of this prompts the question: where will higher education find individuals with both the academic know-how and strengths of character to take on these conflict-ridden assignments?

A large part of the answer lies in candidates who have known and have overcome adversity from an early age and through the course of their careers. Our experience suggests that the adversity they have experienced produces a high level of equanimity in their lives. They do not seek conflict and disruption within their institutions, but they are not intimidated by criticism and opposition, having known worse challenges in their lives. With this unique combination of strength of character and academic experience, these individuals are precisely the right kind of leaders that higher education needs most now.

CHAPTER 2

Jeffrey Bullock
Pastor/President

F ew people who knew Jeffrey Bullock as a young man would have predicted he would become a Presbyterian minister, much less a university president. An optimist might have imagined a foreman's job at a seed company, or that maybe he would apply his athletic skills to becoming a high school football coach if he ever finished college. Others probably saw him as one of those capable guys who moved around a lot, picked up jobs easily, and just as easily left them when other opportunities beckoned.

For over twenty-five years, however, Bullock has led the transformation of the University of Dubuque from virtual bankruptcy to prosperity. Most important in Bullock's eyes, Dubuque has become a purposeful Christian university along the way. Bullock describes the outward transformation of the university as the fruit of an inner renewal of its mission as an exemplary Christian college in the Reformed Presbyterian tradition. His personal transformation foreshadowed and indeed shaped the school's eventual metamorphosis. Turning points in Bullock's life as well as in the university's have been marked by difficulty, gradual progress, and a commitment to practicing Christian love in what the school's website terms a "diverse and equitable faith-based community."[1] These words capture Bullock's personal faith and the university's pledge to each of its students.

Bullock did not work alone to transform the university, although most would agree that he was the animating force behind its resurgence. A handful of determined and generous board members joined him in the work of reviving the University of Dubuque's Christian identity. During Bullock's tenure, these board members and others inspired by Bullock's vision have contributed more than $250 million. In doing so, they have moved Dubuque from an institution that retained only vestiges of its Christian heritage to one fully committed to actualizing its calling to support the growth and success of students who have few other options for a good education.

The University of Dubuque's transformation rivals those of more widely known schools such as Elon University.[2] Dubuque's enrollment has grown from 600 students to over 2,500. Its endowment stands at $250 million, up from $13 million when Bullock arrived. The once run-down campus with grim, ill-maintained buildings, moldy dormitories, and halls mothballed for lack of students has become, to echo Puritan leader John Winthrop and later, Ronald Reagan, a shining city on a hill. In this case, the hill overlooks the historic city of Dubuque, Iowa, and the Mississippi River.

Born in "Sorrow's Kitchen"

The story of UD's transformation begins with Bullock's own journey from a tough, streetwise kid to pastor, seminary dean, and eventually, college president. His personal experience in fact mirrors the twists and turns that resulted in the university's transformation under his leadership.

Troubled best describes the tenor of life in the home into which Bullock was born in Ames, Iowa, in 1959. Bullock never knew his biological father. The oldest of the four siblings, Bullock was abandoned to his own devices, along with his younger brother, with the abrupt departure of their mother. Bullock was fifteen at the time. His two sisters were sent to live with relatives in South Dakota, and he became the virtual guardian of his younger brother. The two brothers lived on their own for several years. Family members now share a positive relationship with one another, but that was not the case in Bullock's formative years.

Whatever grit he may have inherited from his forebears, his resilience in the face of adversity grew even stronger in response to the challenges of his early years. "I grew up in sorrow's kitchen," Bullock says, "and that probably made me especially sympathetic to others who came up the hard way."

"Rough around the edges but smart" would have been a good description of Bullock in those early years. When confronted with serious challenges—poverty, abandonment, personal attack—he learned to take care of himself. "You can choose whether you want to survive or be crushed by your circumstances," he recounts. Bullock was not prone to fighting; but with the physical bearing of a quarterback who also played free safety, he didn't have to worry about many of his peers having the will to take him on. Football fans know that the free safety is the strong, agile player whose job is to tackle the opponent's ball carrier in order to prevent him from streaking downfield. In keeping with that, later in his life, a friend described Bullock as being "incentivized by challenges; Jeff doesn't back down."

At a few inches over six feet and all of 220 pounds, Bullock is an imposing though not especially threatening figure. With a ready smile and an easy manner that seems to embody Midwestern character, Bullock's public persona is that of a friendly pastor—even a fatherly one. But no one at the University of Dubuque doubts that he is the man in charge.

Bullock's toughness served him well during his arduous early years as university president. "Losing is not part of my DNA," he said later, adding, "Every day is a battle" to do better in realizing what God called upon him to do at the University of Dubuque. Bullock's tenacity fortifies his commitment to the success of students who, like him, took their meals in sorrow's kitchen. Reflecting on the ties between hardship and leadership both in his life and in the lives of others, Bullock says, "None of us would want to go through it again." However, he adds that in those tough times, "we learned the most important lessons of our personal lives and our lives as leaders."

Religious Stirrings

Bullock moved with his family from Ames, Iowa, to Omaha, Nebraska, when he was about eleven years old. Once they arrived, his mother enrolled him in Vacation Bible School "probably just to get me out of the house," he recalls. Bullock loved the Bible stories he heard there, the smattering of Christian doctrine, and, most of all, the welcoming atmosphere that was in short supply at home.

Frequently on the move, his family next migrated to the small town of Jackson, which is located on the Iowa border in a stretch of rich, southwestern Minnesota farmland. Corn and soybean farming, along with a large farm implement manufacturer and distributor, provided what employment there was in Jackson. Coming from a family with few resources, Bullock learned from a young age that anything he wanted would need to be paid for by the sweat of his brow. From the age of twelve on, he worked in the fields, sold newspapers, and cleaned hotel rooms, among other hourly paid jobs. High school football and hard work were cultural cornerstones in Jackson and in Bullock's early life.

Bullock started eighth grade in a school that released students for an hour each week for religious confirmation studies. When asked for his religion, Bullock said Presbyterian because that church supported the Bible school he had attended in Omaha. His family had never been churchgoing, but Bullock embraced the welcoming spirit of the Bible teachings in his confirmation classes. He kept attending church on his own after completing his confirmation. He felt that the church's youth programs were "kind of goofy," but he admired the pastor and loved the sermons. Looking back, he believes that his faith orientation began with those almost haphazard experiences in Omaha and Jackson.

Football, Beer, and a Girlfriend

A star football player in high school, Bullock was both athletic and bright. To the surprise of his contemporaries, his high school grades were strong enough to get him accepted to Macalester College in Saint Paul, Minnesota. Mac, as it is known, was recognized as a good school at the time but had not yet begun its climb to distinction as a nationally acclaimed liberal arts college.[3]

However, in the 1970s, Mac did achieve national recognition for losing football games. When Bullock enrolled in 1977, the Scots were best known for their forty-one-game losing streak. It was 1980 before the Scots finally broke a record fifty loss streak by squeaking out a three-point win over a now-closed college in rural Wisconsin. Lily Denehy, editor in chief of the *Mac Weekly*, the university's student newspaper, reported on a 1978 *Sports Illustrated* article that "poked fun at the disinterest and outright heckling of the football team by Macalester students."[4] Apparently, the few students who attended the game with the Minnesota rival spent more time playing backgammon than cheering on their team.

It is not surprising that Bullock never felt at home at Macalester, although the coaches were happy to attract a smart kid who could play quarterback or free safety. Many of Macalester's students leaned left politically and came from upper middle-class backgrounds. They enjoyed generous allowances and the time to pursue their studies and other interests without part-time jobs. The civil rights movement, and in earlier years, the escalating war in Vietnam, were among the causes that preoccupied the undergraduates. Football and its players were not of great interest to them. With his blue-collar background, Bullock felt he had little in common with Mac's more privileged students.

Dreaming of playing in the Big Ten and feeling out of place at Macalester, Bullock left to try out for the football team at Iowa State. The university readily accepted him as a transfer from a reputable liberal arts college, though his potential as a football player may have helped. In any event, his football career at Iowa State never developed. When Bullock talked about dropping out again, his friends cautioned him that another departure would probably end his chances of ever earning a college degree.

Meanwhile, Bullock had taken a job on the loading docks of a major company. Before long, he was offered a promotion to full-time work that paid more than he had ever earned in his life. He said later, "I knew if I took that job I would never go back to school." Bullock sensed that life should offer something better than a good job and a steady paycheck. He was seeking something more, but what exactly that something was continued to elude him.

Dissatisfied with college and unfulfilled by the work available to him, Bullock says his life at the time revolved around beer, football, and his girlfriend. Yet he also experienced a calling, however faint, to a purpose in life beyond the immediate pleasures that young men often pursue.

A Chosen Family

Bullock was better at leaving than staying the course up to that point in his life. He had dropped out of Macalester College and Iowa State and turned down a steady job with a reliable employer. A Presbyterian pastor in Jackson had taken an interest in this young man so clearly at loose ends. When the pastor joined a congregation in Seattle, he offered Bullock a place to stay should his wanderlust take him to the Pacific Northwest. Subsequently, in the fall of 1979, with just $40 in his jeans and a $500 car with dubious brakes, a twenty-year-old Bullock headed west. To stretch the little money he had, Bullock camped out in a flimsy pup tent along the way. Bullock showed up on the pastor's doorstep, intending to stay there for a few weeks until he found work. Ultimately, that stay would last six years, and Bullock's relationship with the pastor would endure for their lifetimes.

Henry Eli Fawcett, the pastor who was so influential in Bullock's growth as a leader, was a member of the Tsimshian, a coastal indigenous people of the Pacific Northwest. He was born in the small enclave of Metlakatla on an island on the southeast Alaskan coast. A commercial fisherman turned Presbyterian minister, Fawcett was a short, rugged man marked by prodigious upper body strength obtained from hauling nets and traps weighted by hundreds of pounds of fish from the deep Alaskan waters. Those who knew Fawcett well remember his ready smile, limitless supply of optimism, and abiding faith in a loving God.

Fawcett eventually left work on the salmon trawlers to become a fisher of men. According to a fellow minister who knew him well, Fawcett was especially gifted at "encouraging people to seek their highest calling." The warmhearted pastor could also engage in "hard conversations when they needed to be had." On one occasion, Bullock returned to the Fawcett household with a few beers in him and some rough language on his tongue. He became an unwitting participant in one of those hard conversations. Fawcett announced in no uncertain terms, "If you want to live with us, you can't drink." This admonition ended Bullock's interest in alcohol.

Bullock's years with Fawcett built his own capacity for hard conversations—a skill that would prove very useful to a young president at a strife-ridden university. Life with the Fawcetts also helped develop the softer side of Bullock's leadership. Simply put, he came to experience and appreciate the values of love and compassion.

Living with Henry Fawcett and his wife, VeNita, gave Bullock his first experience with a truly loving family. Bullock recalls that it was the first time in his life that he encountered a couple "openly in love with each other." They and their extended family were part of a close-knit native community that lived at the margin of Seattle's dominant white culture. Though routinely shunned by the larger society, the native community brimmed over with love, joy, and good humor. "Paradoxically," Bullock says, "these people so oppressed in life became so joyful while together." The Fawcetts, who had no children of their own, symbolically adopted Bullock. He still regards the members of their extended family as his aunts and uncles. "These people became my real family," he says.

Today, a model of Fawcett's fishing boat, the *Top Notch*, rests prominently above Bullock's desk in the president's office. The Alaskan fisher of men passed in 2019 at the age of eighty-six. But the virtues of self-discipline, Christian love, and dedication to serving others nurtured in the Fawcett household remain tenets that Bullock continues to pursue.

Growth Through Adversity

Bullock recognizes that his tough upbringing bred a thick skin and an appetite to take on all comers. Crises that might intimidate others brought out his competitive temperament. He tells the story of a professor in graduate school—a "truly brutal man"—who so excoriated his class over a mishandled assignment that some students collapsed in tears. Bullock encouraged his distraught classmates to buck up. Vitriolic and unjust personal attacks might hurt, he told them, but they should not keep you from pursuing your goals. For someone like Bullock who has faced much adversity in life, harsh criticism from a mean-spirited professor was small stuff. His resilience in the face of personal attacks would serve Bullock well during his initial years as president in Dubuque.

"Hardship teaches you how to survive, but it doesn't prepare you very well to give or receive love," Bullock says. The meaning of love and commitment to family were lessons he had to learn at the dinner table in the home of his surrogate parents, who themselves were no strangers to rejection. Fawcett once told Bullock that shortly after Fawcett had joined a new parish as its pastor, a member of the nearly all-white congregation had painted "dirty Indian go home" on the church wall. Bullock asked how the pastor had responded. "Oh, I just painted over it and went on with my work," he replied.

Similarly, personal attacks, no-confidence votes, and threats of violence would greet Bullock and his family during his first months as president of the University of Dubuque. But life experience and lessons from his Native American mentor provided the right preparation for his arduous early years there.

Streetwise in Seattle

The famous Pike Place Market in Seattle attracts tourists and locals alike who come to buy freshly caught salmon, halibut, and other fruits of the sea brought in from the frigid waters off the northwest coast. Multimillion-dollar condominiums with spectacular views of Puget Sound rise up off streets near the market. Sadly, the price of a few pounds of salmon might also buy the services of a teenage boy or girl working the sex trade just a few blocks away. Abandoned by their parents, young boys and girls have been known to eke out a living as thieves, bullies, and prostitutes under the scrutiny of their pimps—and occasionally, the police.

Bullock came to know these lost children firsthand when, at age nineteen, he landed a job as an adult monitor in a group home for delin-quents. These emotionally damaged, streetwise teenagers traveled be-tween the group home and various crash pads in abandoned buildings. Bullock worked with some of the same fourteen- and fifteen-year-olds depicted in Martin Bell's award-winning 1984 documentary, *Street-wise*.[5] The film captures in searing images and dialogue the lives of nine teenagers who alternated between bonding with and preying upon each other.

"Tiny," whose real name is Erin Blackwell, is a central figure in the documentary. A fourteen-year-old prostitute, Tiny was afflicted with several varieties of venereal disease and had an alcoholic mother. Tiny says in the film that she never knew her father. She speculates that he may have been one of the many men she "dated."

Abandoned at age fifteen, Bullock could relate to these street kids. *But for the grace of God*, Bullock thought, *my brother and sisters and I could have wound up on the same streets as these destitute kids*. His commit-ment to "people who never had a shot" lives at the heart of Bullock's personal mission and that of the University of Dubuque and surely stems from his own upbringing and from this harsh experience with Seattle's lost children.

The gap between Christian love experienced with the Fawcetts and the savage existence of these children precipitated a dramatic change in Bullock. He says that it was not a single crucible or numinous moment but rather an accumulation of moments across his life, and especially in Seattle, that brought about his conversion experience.

William James, psychologist, philosopher, and brother to the famous novelist Henry James, defines conversion as "a process, gradual or sud-den" that permits the converted "to be regenerated, to receive grace, to experience religion, to gain an assurance." He goes on to say that this process transforms the self "hitherto divided . . . inferior and unhappy" to a state that is "unified and consciously right superior and happy." Bullock's conversion seems to have been something like the experience James describes.[6] The persistent if uncertain calling he had experienced from his early years became clearer as his life centered on the pursuit of further education and the ministry.

The Education of a Pastor

When Bullock returned to college in 1980 at Seattle Pacific University, he majored in philosophy. He excelled in discussions of the great ideas from some of the West's most brilliant minds. Called to pastoral service like his mentor and surrogate father, he subsequently enrolled in the Pittsburgh Theological Seminary. This time, he focused on homiletics, the art of rhetoric applied to delivering sermons, before graduating in 1985. At the seminary, he met Dana, the woman who in 1988 would become his wife. When asked what she saw in Bullock, she replied, "He seemed like such a good man."

Bullock returned to Seattle in 1991 after serving a church in Pennsylvania for four years. Once back on the West Coast, he became minister to two small Presbyterian churches. Bullock deferred sleep to find time to honor his commitment to furthering his education. Accepted to the University of Washington, Bullock earned a master's degree and then a doctorate in speech communications. No stranger to long hours and hard work, Bullock completed both graduate degrees in five years—a remarkable achievement for a three-quarter-time minister. He proved to be an adept student of philosophy, theology, Bible study, and the art of communication.

In 1996, Bullock visited Dubuque to spend time with his old friend and mentor Henry Fawcett, who was serving as pastor of the University of Dubuque Theological Seminary, which is a major unit of the university. By chance, Bullock learned that the seminary was seeking a new dean. He applied and got the job.

At the time when Bullock was hired, the University of Dubuque had not yet recovered from the recession of the early 1990s. Enrollment had yet to stabilize at 600. The campus was tired and in need of repairs that the school could not afford. Two other small, religiously affiliated colleges in town competed for many of the same students, as well as for local donors. A thirty-minute drive took students to the much less expensive and larger University of Wisconsin branch in Platteville. One longtime trustee not prone to exaggeration described the attitude of the board as the University of Dubuque approached the turn of the century in stark terms: "We really didn't know if the university would survive."

A Presbyterian minister founded the college in 1852 to train clergy for the burgeoning numbers of Protestant migrants seeking a new life and rich farmland in the Upper Midwest. Over the years, the school expanded its curriculum to include liberal arts, accepted women, and in 1920, adopted the name it bears today. By the time Bullock arrived, the university had drifted far from the ecclesiastical mission of its founder.

"We Don't Celebrate Christmas"

Many of the faculty, supported by an amenable president, envisioned the University of Dubuque as a secular institution tied more by history than current practice to the Presbyterian church. They aspired to join the ranks of more highly regarded Iowa liberal arts colleges that retained only a vestigial link to their Christian origins. As a practical matter, some felt that branding the college as Christian would drive students away. "We don't celebrate Christmas," a staff member once said to a deeply shocked trustee, thus underscoring how far the university had moved from its Reformed Presbyterian roots.

The trustees intended the university to "fly the Presbyterian flag," as one of them put it. But what that banner represented in a modern university and who would lead it remained undecided.

Plagued with internal dissent, weak management, and the absence of a distinct mission, the school operated in the red for years prior to Bullock's arrival. According to one report, the administration carried two sets of books: one presented a rosy picture of the finances to the board of trustees. An internal set painted a more realistic picture of an unsustainable decline in enrollment and tuition income.

At War with the Faculty

Employed by a university that was failing on the financial side and distrustful of the board of trustees, the faculty sought the protections of a union. Following the layoff of a tenured faculty member in the early 1970s, the remaining faculty had formed a bargaining unit under the umbrella of the National Education Association. Although understandable in the circumstances, unionizing did nothing to improve relations between the administration and the faculty. Moreover, it gave its members a sense of job security that proved illusory.

Following a series of legal battles pitting the board against the faculty, the National Labor Relations Board decertified the union. The stream of well-publicized disputes eroded what faith remained in the university's reputation. Fewer parents felt inclined to entrust their children to a school in such obvious disarray. Football coaches from rival colleges warned high school prospects that the University of Dubuque was about to go under. Potential donors were embarrassed when a former Dubuque president on a fundraising tour promised to start any program they desired if they would only "give us a gift."

"We Should Become What We Were Created to Be"

Monetizing vacant property that now supports student housing was on the table. Perhaps a developer could entice Walmart or Red Lobster to purchase the land. In a room crowded with trustees, faculty, and others, the board's resolve gradually coalesced around one uncompromising proposition that stated this: "We should become what we were created to be or go out of business." But where would the university find a new president with the ability to redeem it?

Dedication to Dubuque's mission and dogged Presbyterian determination were about all that stood between the board and closing or selling the university. The board's experience with career academics as president did not breed confidence in conventional candidates, and past national searches had failed to uncover a leader who could reverse the school's decline.

The board offered the job to their seminary dean, whose experience as an academic leader spanned all of two years.

Death Threats and Armed Protection

At the age of thirty-eight and in his first year as president, in 1998, Bullock had inherited a university on the brink of closure, bankruptcy, or selling itself if a willing buyer could be found. He and his wife and their firstborn son lived in a leafy neighborhood a few blocks from the University of Dubuque campus. His neighbors were flattered to have a university president and his family reside on their block. But the police car regularly parked outside the new president's home was perplexing. Students and teachers might have wondered why armed guards so often spoke into their shirt cuffs while walking beside the new president around campus. As it turned out, death threats greeted Bullock and his family during his first year on the job. The new president went so far as to wear a bulletproof vest under his purple and gold regalia at the university's 1999 commencement.

Upon leaving his job as dean of a well-functioning seminary, Bullock said he knew the university was challenged, but he had no idea just how life-threatening the challenges were. He and his wife discussed his and the university's future. They expected that Bullock would be forced to take such drastic actions that he would be forced to leave after two or three years when a conventional peacemaker might take over.

"God Has a Purpose"

The new president believed that taking on the Sisyphean task of redeeming the failing university was a mission he was called upon to try, at least for two or three years. "A sure career killer" is how Bullock and his wife initially regarded the offer. However, they agreed that redeeming Dubuque was worth their best efforts because, as she said, "God has a purpose" for the failing university. Bullock felt that the painful actions required to save the school would leave him "radioactive" as a candidate for any other presidency.

Board members who had worked closely with Bullock when he was dean of the seminary saw in him intelligence, strength of character, and a commitment to the school's Christian mission. But some were doubtful. "Who ever thought that a pastor would make a good president?" asked one skeptic. "The last place I would look for a president is a young Presbyterian minister," opined another some years later. As it turned out, that trustee partnered with Bullock to redeem the university's Christian identity. He, along with a dedicated board chair, made truly transformational gifts that powered UD's revival.

Some faculty members were dismayed at Bullock's appointment. They were aghast that a Presbyterian minister and seminary dean would be chosen to lead what many hoped would be an increasingly secularized school. The seminary and the academic side of Dubuque, often called "the college," had long been isolated from each other with different leadership, professors, and students. The college professors didn't really know Bullock when he became their president. True, he held a doctorate from a top research university, but he had never held a tenured academic position. To the academics, he was just not one of them.

In retrospect, Dubuque got what it needed most: an empathetic pastor, a toughened soul who had experienced the rough edges of life, and a man who could articulate what turned out to be an inspiring and marketable vision of a Christian university dedicated to students with few other good educational choices.

Radical Restructuring and Cost Reductions

Bullock and the trustees supporting him knew they needed to act quickly if they were to save the university. They embarked on a program they described in a board resolution as "radical restructuring and cost reductions." The innocuously titled *Plan for Transformation* became the text for restoring Dubuque's identity as a competitive Christian institution in the market for students and resources.[7]

Closing academic programs and dismissing both tenured and untenured faculty were considered essential stepping stones on the university's path forward. Only about fifteen of approximately forty majors were to be retained. In May of 1999, fourteen faculty members, including ten men and women with tenure, received termination notices.

There is no minimizing the stress experienced by faculty members and their families and the rest of the university community during the ensuing months. Getting fired from any job is disturbing, but for academics, the loss of a tenured position is a devastating experience. In the minds of most academics, tenure ensures lifetime employment in the profession they labored years to achieve. Of the tenured Dubuque professors who were dismissed, three accepted severance packages offered by the university, and another was hired elsewhere. Except for those ready to retire or the fortunate ones who were able to land other teaching jobs, the loss of tenure cast an academic into a market with only modest interest in their services at best.

Bullock recalls walking from a board meeting room across campus through a gauntlet of angry professors during that first year, some hoisting banners, others simply turning their backs on the new president. One professor distributed a pornographic cartoon depicting Bullock in a compromising position that circulated around faculty offices. Twenty-five years later, hostility to Bullock and his family persists in a few quarters in Dubuque.

As painful as the cutbacks and dismissals in the *Plan* were, it is difficult to imagine that Dubuque could have survived, much less become the vital institution it is today, without first undergoing a painful restructuring. Restoring financial stability is "*always* a necessary first step" in restoring vitality to a distressed college facing imminent closure, merger, or sale, according to a study of academic turnarounds.[8] As another president of a small, troubled college said, fixing the finances was job one, or no one at the college would have a job. The painful dismissals and program eliminations paved the way for more marketable programs that, along with philanthropy, have put the University of Dubuque on a secure financial footing.[9]

Parallel Conversions

The conversion of the University of Dubuque from a failing institution to the vibrant university it is today parallels to an uncanny degree its president's personal journey and his growth in character, intellectual breadth, and faith. When the board chose Bullock to be president, in part because he was the available candidate, those staunch Presbyterians were unaware of the degree to which Bullock's life had prepared him to lead a remarkable transformation of the university they cherished.

Bullock describes his gradual conversion without drama or pretense. "A calling describes just about everything I do," he says. His words come across as facts of his life that have become clearer to him over the years. Sunday school in Omaha, confirmation classes in Jackson, life with the saintly native pastor and his family, work with the abandoned teenagers in Seattle, and theological and academic training are all milestones in Bullock's pilgrim's progress.

As the president of the University of Dubuque, Bullock is realizing his life's mission as Christian practice in the here and now. Just as he found a welcoming spirit and love not in his family of origin but in the churches of his youth and his "real" family in Seattle, he sees the university as a welcoming place for those who otherwise might not have a shot at a better life.

Douglas Schuurman describes what seems to be Bullock's calling in the spectrum of Protestant vocations as embracing virtually all aspects of human endeavors. "The power of vocation," Schuurman writes, "is to infuse all of life with religious meaning and to extend its range into all relational fields." He finds the origin of this "expansive, religiously rich understanding of vocation in the Bible and the Reformation."[10]

Bullock says that his own sense of calling has been heavily influenced by his life experiences, both searing and supportive. In theology, he leans toward the mystic existentialist Martin Buber, especially his personalistic interpretation of God's will embodied by the title of his influential book *I And Thou*. In the book, Buber describes the "I–Thou" relationship between people as one that respects and cherishes the other as a human being worthy of love. He contrasts this with the "I–It" relationship, which treats the other as an object to be subjugated, controlled, or exploited. When Buber writes that "the relationship of a genuine educator to his pupil" is of the I–Thou type, not the I–It configuration, he captures much of what Bullock has tried to shape in the culture of the university.[11]

Character Building and Student Success

Two signature initiatives figure prominently in Bullock's attempt to instill Christian principles into the life of every student. The first of these is the Wendt Character Initiative, funded by a substantial gift from the Wendt family. The second is the Student Success Commitment, a contract that Bullock himself signs with every undergraduate student. The Wendt initiative underwrites several programs, including funding for Wendt Character Scholars, lectures, support for faculty course design, and an online journal titled the *Wendt Center Journal*. The director of the Wendt Center for Character Education gets at the heart of the Dubuque project with these words: "Living out of a strength of character where virtues such as perseverance, integrity, and compassion contribute to the lens of hopefulness, turning that hopefulness into its own virtue."[12]

Dubuque's Student Success Commitment is intended to be Bullock's practical implementation of the I–Thou relationship between the university and its students. Bullock commits on behalf of the university to, among seven other promises, "model a diverse and equitable faith-based community where Christian love is practiced." In addition to a list of promises to engage in a variety of academic and student life pursuits, each student declares that "I will exhibit positive moral and ethical character through my words and actions" and "practice behaviors that contribute to my mental, physical, and spiritual well-being."[13]

The Best Small Christian University

Midway into his tenure, Bullock and the board engaged in heated debates over what it would mean to aspire to become "the best" small Christian university. By this time, the university had emerged from the desperate straits it was in when Bullock was hired. Enrollment had tripled, the endowment was growing, and the school's reputation had been largely restored. With its newfound affluence, to which trustees were major contributors, some board members believed that the time had come for the college to advance in the ratings as well. While somehow honoring its high-access mission, they argued, more selective admissions would boost the college's reputation and its attractiveness to better-prepared students and their middle-class families. They interpreted "the best" in conventional terms, where selectivity is equated to quality and value.

Bullock demurred. He argued that the rankings "tell you which schools have the wealthiest alumni base, recruit students from the best school districts, provide the best-paid teachers, and offer the widest range of extracurricular activities." He added that while there was nothing wrong with that aspiration, "I am interested in kids who never had a shot." He went on to say that these kids came from high schools "where the teachers were tired and worn out, the textbooks outdated if available at all, the students don't get enough healthy calories," and their safety may be at risk as well.

That debate has subsided in recent years as the university continues to prosper. Bullock readily admits that his own biography shaped his intentions for Dubuque and what it really means to be "the best." A troubled childhood spent in sorrow's kitchen, work with abandoned kids on the streets of Seattle, life in the home of a loving couple, responding to a calling to serve, and academic training at a demanding university were all crucial elements in the formation of his character and intellect. These experiences combined to provide Bullock with the courage, empathy, and vision to transform a failing institution into a shining city on a hill in America's heartland.

CHAPTER 3

Waded Cruzado
The Power of Imaginative Leadership

The dark-haired woman lowered the microphone and paused long enough for the chatter among the two hundred or so in attendance to soften then fade away. Clearly at ease in front of a crowd of strangers, she allowed the silence to linger a few seconds longer. Her story of the transformative effects of a land-grant university in her own life enthralled the audience at Montana State. Her fervor in calling up the language of the Morrill Act of 1862, which provided federal land to finance higher education opportunities for, in Cruzado's words, the "sons and daughters of the working classes," struck a chord. The words were not new to this group of professors, students, and others associated with the university, yet they possessed a powerful emotional quality when spoken by this five-foot-tall woman with an accent. A person in the audience said later that this was the moment when they began to imagine that this woman from Puerto Rico with an infectious smile and steady gaze could be their next president. The wife of a board of regents member later told her husband, "If you don't hire her, you're crazy."

But not everyone was crazy about Waded Cruzado's bid to become the next president of Montana State University in 2009. Some regarded her presence at the podium as homage to affirmative action. She would not be the first token minority candidate not seriously expected to get the job. Earlier in the search, a faculty member questioned the likelihood of someone from "her background" becoming president. A skeptical rancher doubted the suitability of "that English lady from New Mexico," referring to her doctorate in literature and service as provost and interim president of New Mexico State University. (He later acknowledged that she was the right choice after all.)

Judging by her academic degrees in comparative literature, one might conclude that Cruzado would be more at home at the University of Montana, Montana State's rival for attention and resources some 200 miles northwest of Bozeman. During the 1960s and 1970s, the University of Montana had acquired a reputation as a bastion of poets, playwrights, and philosophers. This reputation as a mecca for the liberal arts and humanities lingered, despite the fact that the school had developed programs in business and the STEM disciplines like those of Montana State.

"Do You Have a Green Card?"

A serious obstacle to Cruzado's candidacy arose when a local reporter posed two markedly unusual questions: "Do you have a green card?" and "Wouldn't you fit better in Florida or California?" While all three candidates were peppered with predictable questions during their public interviews, only Cruzado was asked to clarify her immigration status.

Some who heard the questions speculated that the reporter may simply have been too busy to research Cruzado's background. Then again, she may have been unaware that Puerto Rico's commonwealth status makes its residents full-fledged US citizens. Green cards grant work rights to permanent residents from other countries.

"Aghast" is how one observer described Cruzado's reaction to the ill-informed questions. As a woman of color, Cruzado knew that she "had to pay a price to open the door for others to follow." However, she wondered if a presidency in Montana would be worth the cost. Would she be welcome in this predominantly white state where a journalist didn't seem to know that Puerto Ricans are US citizens?

At the time of Cruzado's interview, individuals who identify as Hispanic represented about 2 percent of Montana's population. The Commonwealth of Puerto Rico, where she grew up, was over 90 percent Hispanic and Spanish speaking. (Cruzado spoke Spanish before she gained fluency in English.) The population of New Mexico, where she was the highly regarded provost of New Mexico State University, was about 50 percent Hispanic. Were the reporter's questions typical of Montana's insularity regarding not only Puerto Ricans but also those of Hispanic heritage in general?

The faculty chair of the Native American studies program, an MSU graduate and prolific author in the field of Native American history, approached the topic in a more respectful way. "If offered the job," he asked, "will you come, and if you come, will you be happy here?" Perhaps he knew what it felt like to be an outsider. But Cruzado still wondered if Montanans would welcome her—or at least give her a chance to show what she could do. Other universities were seeking her services. Would a more diverse state be friendlier to this child of a tropical island proud of its centuries-old tradition of Spanish language and culture?

Cruzado put her misgivings on hold, thanks in part to the encouragement she received from members of the search committee. Eventually, she was offered the job, and she accepted. Their confidence in her ability to gain the support of Montanans and to advance the university has proven to be well placed over the dozen years since the search for a new president began. In the opinion of virtually everyone interviewed, Cruzado's performance over her twelve years has been nothing short of spectacular.

"There Was Nothing Logical about Choosing Waded Cruzado"

The story of Cruzado's recruitment to Montana State offers a bounty of lessons for trustees and search committees seeking exceptional leaders. The saga leading up to Cruzado's presidential appointment speaks to the crucial importance of having committee and board members with the wisdom and courage to buck conventional assumptions. The Montana State search committee was populated with members astute enough to discern the special strengths that separated Cruzado from more traditional applicants.

Cruzado's candidacy would not be universally embraced by Montanans, though. The university had never chosen a woman—much less a woman of color—as its chief executive. Members of the search committee appreciated her enthusiasm for the egalitarian mission of the land-grant, but they could only hope that she possessed the practical skills to realize that progressive vision in Montana's conservative political environment. Responding to Cruzado's obvious commitment to students and their success, a skeptic observed that she would make a good dean of students. One committee member said, "We knew there was nothing logical about choosing Waded Cruzado."[1]

Cruzado's doctorate in comparative literature (the literature of Spain and the Americas in particular) did not align with the university's signature programs in engineering and agriculture. A degree in the humanities, however, did not categorically rule her out. For all its strengths in the STEM disciplines, Montana State had a history of welcoming presidents with degrees in the humanities and social sciences. Geoffrey Gamble, Cruzado's predecessor, was a respected linguistics scholar. The president before Gamble, a well-respected historian, authored the definitive history of the state. Cruzado's academic pedigree was not a litmus test of her qualifications, except temporarily for the few skeptics her advocates have described as "old cowboys."

As it happens, far from being irrelevant to the practical work of a modern president, her discipline underpins one of Cruzado's greatest assets: her imaginative style of leadership. Her appreciation for magical realism[2] in Spanish literature reinforces her capacity to shed customary thinking as a prelude to imagining more expansive futures for the university. Of course, early in her tenure, her ability to deliver on her vision of the great potential of the state's land-grant university remained a matter of speculation and hope.

Cruzado enjoyed a solid apprenticeship as an administrator on her way to the presidency. She served as a tenured faculty member then dean of the College of Arts and Sciences at Puerto Rico's land-grant university in Mayagüez; dean of arts and sciences at another land-grant, New Mexico State University; and acting president for eleven months in New Mexico as well. Despite this traditional path upward, some still questioned how Cruzado would fit in this western state of cattle ranches and ski resorts, far from the tropical island where she grew up.

Conventional wisdom dictated that one of the two white males competing with Cruzado for the job would become the top candidate, and the search committee regarded both as strong candidates. They held doctorates from highly ranked US public universities—the University of California, Irvine and the University of Illinois. They carried the imprimatur of degrees in chemistry and plant science—two disciplines prominent at Montana State.

During the interview process, Cruzado attracted particular attention as she made her way through the gauntlet of large and small group forums. Scholars sought to evaluate the purity of her intentions regarding research in agriculture and the STEM disciplines. Her willingness to champion academic freedom and low-demand disciplines as well as her ability to persuade legislators in Helena to loosen the purse strings were topics of great interest. Women were pleased to see one of their own among the finalists for the first time, but they did not give her a pass on questions of equal pay and fair standards for promotion.

She Was "The One"

Steve Barrett, chair of the board of regents when Cruzado was hired, wrote about the experience ten years after Cruzado's appointment. Barrett says that there were a lot of reasons not to hire her.[3] He knew that choosing one of the two white men with degrees from prestigious universities in STEM disciplines would have been the less controversial decision. But Barrett and his colleagues Clay Christian, vice-chair of the board, and Sheila Stearns, commissioner of higher education and Cruzado's would-be boss, were willing to set aside traditional political ideas. They favored the person they sensed possessed the right temperament and experience to lead the state's land-grant university.

The instincts of Stearns, Barrett, and Christian, honed in Montana higher education and its politics, told them that Cruzado had the right vision and personality for the job. They were taken with her energy, poise, imagination, and almost religious commitment to the land-grant mission. They also knew that, initially at least, the choice of an outsider would raise eyebrows in Montana. They agreed that Cruzado was "the one." They didn't want to lose her due to some off-putting questions from a harried reporter.

Cruzado expressed her concerns triggered by the green card question, so Barrett and his like-minded colleagues set out to persuade Cruzado to stay in the hunt. They stressed the university's strengths achieved under earlier presidents. "It ain't broke," Barrett assured her, referring to the fiscal health and basic functionality of the university. Convinced by the arguments and the sincerity of the three Montanans, Cruzado agreed to remain a candidate. But staying in the hunt did not mean she would accept the position if, in the end, she still felt Montana was not right for her.

Green Chilis and the Moment of Truth

Presidential searches turn on a dime when the process narrows to the top candidate. Up until that point, candidates are supplicants seeking to impress the search committee and the larger community if the search unfolds in public. Power in the candidate–search committee relationship resides with the institution in the early stages. The power of choice shifts to the finalist once the position is offered. Searchers then need to negotiate a pay package and persuade the finalist to accept it. (Candidates with a presidency already under their belt tend to be cagier in this negotiation phase, while first-time presidents are much less so.)

In Cruzado's case, she held the high cards. Comfortable and respected in her current position, she had other attractive opportunities. The choice to accept, reject, or negotiate a better deal with Montana State was hers. It's fair to say that at this point, the success of the search was in doubt from the committee's standpoint; a laissez-faire attitude toward securing this candidate would not do.

After seeing Cruzado in action during the interview scrum and then getting a closer read on her temperament at a private dinner, Barrett, Stearns, and Christian set aside the established calculus and bet on their instincts. Not content to merely offer the job and await her response, they recognized they needed to sell Cruzado on the advantages of Montana and Montana State University. And although Montanans are not prone to offering rich compensation packages for their public officials, the search leaders knew that their offer needed to at least match what competing institutions would bid for a top-notch president. They wasted no time in borrowing a plane from a friend to fly to Las Cruces, where Cruzado remained provost at New Mexico State. She greeted them at the airport with gifts of locally grown hot peppers. In a Las Cruces café, she offered still more hot peppers—green chilis this time. Maybe Cruzado was testing their stomachs for the vigorous brand of leadership she would exercise.

The visitors from Montana reiterated the very case Cruzado had made to them during her interviews. Land-grant universities like Montana State opened unheard of possibilities for the daughters and sons of Montanans equal to the vast landscape of the state of endless plains and towering mountains. Cruzado had already demonstrated her dedication to the democratic land-grant mission. Now, these university leaders were offering her the chance to transform her faith into action. Cruzado accepted their proposition. At the end of the search, Stearns said that Montana was Cruzado's first choice, and Cruzado was Montana's first choice as well.

Cruzado later said that she decided to accept Montana State's offer despite the tension during the search because she "felt so comfortable" in a state that prized informality, hard work, and honesty.

Early Tests of Her Leadership

"Challenges are us" is how one college president, echoing the name of a famous toy company, characterized the life of today's college and university presidents. The ability to meet, overcome, and achieve positive outcomes from serious problems is the first criterion for identifying the truly exceptional leadership described in chapter 1. Challenges confronting a new president include unresolved conflicts, stalled projects, and angry stakeholders looking for redress that the previous president failed to provide. Cruzado faced all these challenges and more.

Tests of leadership come early in the tenure of most new presidents, and such challenges present opportunities to establish a brand that, for better or worse, will define the public's perception of the president's character throughout their tenure. Cruzado received several opportunities to establish herself as a quick-witted, gutsy leader.

Cruzado's first significant challenge came from what is a third rail for many presidents with strong academic credentials and loyalties: intercollegiate athletics and their enthusiastic boosters.[4] Coaches and athletic directors frequently complain that academic presidents just don't get football. However, Cruzado appreciates the power of athletics to engage students and bond the university with the larger community. Additionally, college sports appeal to another of her strengths: her hugely competitive spirit. An experienced coach described this virtue simply: "She is the most competitive person I know."

"She Showed Her Mettle and Her Brilliance"

The Quarterback Club, a group composed of mostly male boosters, had long sought university support for additional skyboxes in Bobcat Stadium. The club existed for "the sole purpose of enhancing the Montana State Football program," according to its own publicity.[5] Club membership required an annual gift, and the higher the donation, the closer the booster could get to the team and its coaches. The skyboxes, sometimes called luxury boxes, would be reserved for significant donors and potential benefactors. Although criticized elsewhere for their elitist tinge, skyboxes, suites, and other opportunities to purchase a degree of exclusivity at sports events had become the rage across the country, promising another revenue stream to feed the quest for more money for athletics.

Cruzado saw the wisdom of supporting an initiative dear to one of her more skeptical constituencies, but she strenuously objected to the elitist aspect. Exclusive seating for wealthy donors was inconsistent with her vision of a university that put its students first.

"Are you with me or is this all talk?" is how one observer recalls Cruzado's challenge to the boosters. Instead of raising millions to build more luxury skyboxes, she countered with the idea of creating a facility at the south end of the field that would attract more students to the games.

She also insisted that the donations to cover the cost of the facility be in hand before a shovel ever penetrated the hard Montana soil. Cruzado's stance was clear: she was ready to move forward with or without the club's support.

Initially nonplussed by her challenge imbedded in an ultimatum, club members soon agreed to join Cruzado's crusade. The new building was completed within ten months of Cruzado's appointment as president. The end zone addition, coupled with Cruzado's "Go Cats!" enthusiasm, sparked fresh support among fans. The stadium that used to be sparsely populated on cold Montana Saturdays is now regularly sold out. Avid fans who cannot secure seats in the arena with a capacity of 17,777 come anyway to stand and stomp their feet, warding off the Montana chill while the Bobcats compete.

The drama that led up to the construction of this new student facility offered early signs that the new president was engaging, tough-minded, and shrewd in equal measure. "She showed her mettle and her brilliance" with that one play, according to a person close to the action. She earned the respect of the boosters by challenging them, she demonstrated her support for Bobcat football, and she bolstered student interest in athletics. Furthermore, she put to rest any lingering doubts among football fans about the audacity of the woman from Puerto Rico.

Skirmishes with the Faculty

"Nothing is more perilous to conduct . . . than to take the lead in the introduction of a new order of things."[6] Machiavelli's famous dictum applies to university presidents as it did to Renaissance princes. Presidents who ignore, or appear to ignore, faculty concerns court deteriorating relations at best and no-confidence votes at worst. Early in her tenure, Cruzado experienced an inevitable contretemps with the faculty over the potential conflict between burgeoning enrollment and MSU's research mission. According to one professor, three of his colleagues orchestrated an off-campus meeting of about a hundred faculty members in order to air their concerns with the university's directions under its new leader.

Cruzado's response displayed logic, her deft hand at the politics of the academy, and a disarming willingness to engage personally with the most concerned academics. She pledged to seek more resources, especially for research, and to ensure even more transparency. She also employed diplomacy. She met personally over a meal with each of the three faculty members responsible for organizing the meeting.

Cruzado regularly navigates tensions with the faculty over two issues: enrollment growth and rival claims to funding for student services and research. The university's current strategic plan lists "transformational learning experiences creating outstanding educational outcomes for all students" as the top priority, with improving "lives and society through research, creativity, and scholarship" second. The fact that enrollment has increased substantially during her tenure, and research funding has grown to merit R1 status in the Carnegie classifications speaks to her ability to address both priorities. A longtime faculty member described these periodic dissentions among faculty as "skirmishes" on a field of overall satisfaction with their president.

Cruzado Crosses the Line

The trifecta of important relationships for any president consists of the faculty, the community (including athletic boosters), and, for those in the public sector, politicians. Politicians can be tireless advocates or vociferous critics (and sometimes both) as the political season demands. Early in her tenure, Cruzado got another opportunity to show her determination in an encounter with an influential local legislator. This drama involved an antiquated gymnasium, a long-delayed building project, and speaking truth to power to a local politician who claimed credit that he had not earned.

The fifty state senators and one hundred members of the Montana House of Representatives, the majority of whom belonged to a resurgent Republican party,[7] were not shy about inserting themselves into the affairs of the university. (Democrats take equal interest in university affairs.) When Cruzado became president, state sources supplied about a third of Montana State's operating budget. Securing support from the legislature and the governor in maintaining or increasing that subsidy is essential to the success—and sometimes the survival—of public university presidents.

Romney Hall, the original campus gymnasium, was built in 1922, nearly thirty years after the founding of the university. The distinctive building, with its massive curved roof, rose to iconic status when the 1928 Bobcat basketball team won the national championship under George Romney, the coach whose name adorns the building.

By the time Cruzado took office, a modern field house had replaced Romney Hall, though the venerable building still occupied a prominent place on campus. "I thought it absolutely gorgeous, until I went inside" is how Cruzado describes her earliest visit to the building. However, tearing down Romney Hall would mean saying goodbye to a beloved chapter in the university's history and inviting the wrath of nostalgic alumni and donors.

A signature building when viewed from the outside, the inside of Romney was a hodgepodge of antiquated rooms and vacant spaces. The goal of the Romney project was to transform this eyesore into a high-functioning educational showpiece. Today, its warren of tired rooms has been eliminated, and Romney has been redesigned to serve one thousand of Montana State's burgeoning student population an hour. Prior to Cruzado's arrival, there had been much hand-wringing over what to do with the old fieldhouse. Cruzado took action that eventually led to the creation of a very attractive locus for student learning.

After two attempts to secure funding, in 2015, the Romney project finally reached the top of the regents' request list. The funding bill failed by one vote in the legislature, partially in response to criticism from Democrats that Republicans failed to support university priorities. Bozeman Representative Art Wittich later claimed that he supported MSU's budget request and criticized Cruzado for taking issue with him.

Cruzado says that she could not remain silent while the university's priorities were misrepresented by regional legislators. She had no objections to legislators disagreeing with the university system's priorities. However, Wittich exaggerated the cost of the renovations as well as the educational uses of the refurbished Romney Hall. A Montana newspaper supported Cruzado by opining that "her job is to promote and protect her school," and if that meant calling out hypocritical legislators, so be it.[8] There was no dramatic denouement to this drama, although in part due to campaign finance violations unrelated to Romney Hall, Wittich never held legislative office again.

Publicly criticizing a sitting politician, especially one of some influence in the majority party, is perilous for any chief executive of a university that receives even a fraction of its funding from public coffers. It requires the courage of one's convictions and the willingness to hold politicians accountable. An intuitive sense of just how far a president can go in calling out politicians is also essential. There are precious few examples of presidents willing to speak truth to power in this fashion and fewer still of cases where the president didn't pay a political price. Cruzado is one of the exceptions.

Measures of Effectiveness

Montana State has become a more competitive institution under Cruzado's leadership. Enrollment has climbed to well over 16,000 during her tenure, a nearly 40 percent increase that displaces the University of Montana as the largest in the state. Part of the increased enrollment picture is a remarkable first-to-second-year retention rate of over 78 percent achieved before the COVID era. Other measures of student success include an 80 percent increase in four-year graduation rates over the past decade. MSU doctoral degree production rose from 53 in 2012 to 90 in the fall of 2022, a 70 percent increase. Successful fundraising has fueled the university's ability to attract and retain students, as well as to erect a more modern and attractive campus. The university raised nearly $222 million in 2022, an astounding sixfold increase over the amount it brought in only ten years earlier.[9]

Grizzlies vs. Bobcats

When Cruzado interviewed for the Montana State University presidency, some thought she would be a better fit in Missoula, the home of MSU's rival, the University of Montana. Montanans take an outsized interest in the fortunes of both their research universities. To outsiders, the two look like close siblings. Montana State is best known for its STEM programs, while the University of Montana has the state's only law school and remains prominent in the humanities. Both are ranked in the middle of the pack in the *U.S. News & World Report* 2022–2023 rankings of national universities. Outsiders might see more similarities than differences between the state's two eponymous universities, but in Montana, the prevailing sentiment is that "you are either a Cat or a Griz."

The University of Montana claims flagship status, though both universities are sometimes described as the state's flagships. Since Cruzado's arrival, the University of Montana has been steadily losing ground to its rival. Enrollment dropped steadily from a high of over 15,000 in 2010 to just over 10,000 in the fall of 2021. During the same period, Montana State's climbed above 16,000. Jon Krakauer's 2015 exposé of an epidemic of rapes and subsequent mishandling of the victims' cases further damaged the reputation of the Missoula institution.[10]

Presidential turnover is also a critical factor in the University of Montana's woes. During the twelve years that Cruzado has been at the helm of State, four presidents (including an interim appointment) have served in Missoula. The 2018 arrival of Seth Bodner, a top West Point graduate and former executive at General Electric, suggests a turnaround may be taking place. The enrollment picture is brightening, and there seems to be an uptick in research success. However, the opposite trajectories of the two schools underscore the competitive advantages of hiring and retaining an able president for the long term, especially if that president is as adept as Cruzado.

Promise over Prestige

When asked to enumerate Cruzado's more significant accomplishments, her senior staff repeats the expected litany of construction projects, advances in research funding, initiatives in support of student success, and her remarkable popularity with the people of Montana. The rebirth of Romney Hall from a decrepit building long past its prime into an education building with attractive and highly functional space is a striking example of such changes. The stunning architecture of American Indian Hall is another. The campus has become a splendid venue for twenty-first century education. Investment in major renovations, repurposing, and new construction has exceeded $180 million in philanthropic and public funding since Cruzado came to town.

Cruzado's most significant accomplishment, according to many, is enabling this research university to commit to choosing promise rather than chasing prestige. Student success, especially for the sons and daughters of working Montanans, is truly the North Star in Cruzado's journey, and it has risen to the top of the agenda for the university. It is the lead objective in the current strategic plan. Initiatives like the Freshman 15, which enables students to complete their degrees in four years, and the Hilleman Scholars, which serves promising students nominated by their county extension agents, are making a difference in retention and graduation rates. In her introductory comments to new students and their families, Cruzado welcomes them "to your university" and invites them to tour the campus "which the people of Montana built."

Fervor for Children of the Working Class

The deeply personal commitment to a noble cause lies at the core of Cruzado's personality and practice of leadership. She brings a religious intensity to the ideals of the Morrill Act, which established universities that would educate sons and daughters of the working class. This 1862 act, sponsored by Senator Justin Morrill of Vermont, provided financial resources through land grants to support what have become the nation's great public research universities. She featured the land-grant mission in her inaugural address on September 10, 2010, and repeats that theme in virtually all of her important communications. "You could hear a pin drop," recalls one member of the inaugural audience, until riotous applause erupted as Cruzado finished with "we will build, together, an even better and stronger Montana State University that will empower the people and transform the world."[11]

The transformative power of her land-grant university is an article of faith for Cruzado. It also connects this practicing Roman Catholic to Montanans of all classes, but especially to Justin Morrill's working classes. To make their mark in Montana, as in many other rural states, a president needs to show a presence not just in the university towns of Bozeman and Missoula, or the capital, Helena, but across this largely rural state of just over a million inhabitants. Rural Montana remains a major political power in the state. A public university president needs to speak to the constituents who keep politicians in office. Cruzado's elixir of hope through education speaks to the heartbeat of Montanans, as one resident put it. According to a university system regent who sometimes accompanied Cruzado on her listening tours across the state, strangers in small-town Montana approach her just to shake her hand. To many citizens in rural Montana, he added, "she is a rock star."

Growing Up in Mayagüez

Where did this remarkable leader develop the strength to achieve what she has and earn the trust of her fellow academics and Montanans alike? The answer lies in the university town of Mayagüez, Puerto Rico, some three thousand miles away.

When Cruzado was born in January 1960, her mother was still a teenager, soon to be divorced. Cruzado characterizes her mother, Daisy, as "that force of nature." Two of her aunts, her maternal grandmother, and her stepfather made up their household. Cruzado's father visited periodically, though her maternal uncle who visited regularly played an influential role in her upbringing. She credits him with expanding her horizons and introducing experiences she might have missed in her mostly female household, including playing basketball and how to win at 500 Rummy. By far the oldest child, Cruzado played a dominant role among the youngsters in the family. She says she was "something more than a big sister" who played a major part in managing the household from age fourteen onward.

Family responsibilities were thrust upon her from an early age. She was charged with preparing dinners of rice and beans, a staple of family dining, beginning at age ten. Her grandfather worked a coffee farm, cultivating the beans that produce the robust beverages for which Puerto Rico is famous. "The Coffee of Popes and Kings" reads the tagline of a popular brand. When her mother totaled the income and expenses from coffee sales "down to the last penny," Cruzado was by her side. She helped her grandfather, beginning when she was five years old. The business of growing, packaging, and selling coffee sustained the family. This early experience in the competitive coffee business helps explain Cruzado's comfort with the business side of the academic enterprise.

"We didn't have much money, but we had a lot of love," is how Cruzado summarizes her early life. The children were expected to work, although there were times for storytelling and play as well. Cruzado remembers sitting on the porch swing enthralled by her grandmother's imaginative stories. This experience, she says, sparked her interest in literature, including magical realism. Playing teacher to a classroom of stuffed animals and dolls as a preteen, Cruzado believes, demonstrated that she was meant to be a teacher. Being the oldest child with family responsibilities, working from an early age in the family coffee business, and growing up surrounded by strong women all contributed to her ease with taking on the role of the person in charge.

When she was ten, Cruzado enrolled in the Catholic school for girls in Mayagüez. Nuns from Spain taught all the classes, including English, which itself was taught in Spanish. No student took second place to a boy or needed to compete for attention. Each year, the school held a contest in which students recited poetry before a sizeable group of students and teachers. Cruzado regularly won the contest. She attributes her mastery in addressing audiences to her early experience on stage in Mayagüez.

Cruzado is convinced that being multilingual gives her an edge. Being fluent in two Latin languages (she also speaks Portuguese) and one with Germanic roots, she believes, gives her special sensitivity to the expressions of people from many cultures. A member of her staff recounts that she also speaks the languages of research scientists, government policy-makers, parents of students, and students themselves. Her cultural fluency helps explain why so many Montanans respond favorably to her.

The Catholic nuns who taught Cruzado in her early years instilled in her a love of learning, self-discipline, and a sense of a higher calling. Her devotion to the land-grant mission that opens the door to higher education for children who might otherwise be denied shows something of the spirit of those Spanish nuns who dedicated their lives to Christ and their students. Catholic nuns with vocation in teaching take the vows of poverty, chastity, and obedience as other sisters do, but they also embrace teaching as their prime calling in the world. Cruzado remains a devout Catholic.

A Garden of Forking Paths

The presence of Puerto Rico's land-grant university in Mayagüez reinforced Cruzado's family's faith in the importance of higher education, and she was the first in her family to get a college degree. Like many parents of first-generation college graduates, Cruzado's mother always regretted that her life circumstances prevented her from going beyond high school. Already interested in literature, Cruzado majored in comparative literature with a special emphasis on the Spanish language writers known for their magical realism.

After graduating from the University of Puerto Rico, Mayagüez, Cruzado enrolled in the University of Texas at Arlington to complete her graduate studies in comparative literature, specializing in the literature of Spain and Latin America. When asked her favorite author, Cruzado places Cervantes at the head of the list. His most noted work, *Don Quixote*, is a seventeenth-century example of satire that traverses the dimensions of fantasy and reality. It anticipates modern magical realism.

Cruzado also studied modern South American writers like Nobel Prize winner Gabriel García Márquez and Jorge Luis Borges. These authors are among the major exponents of magical realism, which, like *Don Quixote*, luxuriates in the porous space separating the realm of the everyday from fantasy. The celebration of the art of imagination, Cruzado says, is what attracted her to this literature.

To understand both the literature of magical realism and the complexities of Cruzado's own views of reality, she recommends a brilliant and perplexing short story by Borges titled "The Garden of Forking

Paths."[12] Written in 1941, the story "invites the reader to imagine what else, other than the world we know, might be possible."[13]

At the risk of stretching the metaphor between imaginative literature and the art of the presidency, it seems safe to say that Cruzado's pursuit of the possible at Montana State owes something to her love of a literature that is at once magical and realistic.

It may come as a consolation to English majors that the literature of magical realism fortifies Cruzado's own willingness to break with conventional thinking when it comes to her professional life. She abhors the "we've always done it this way" excuse for not envisioning alternatives. She encourages her senior staff members to think of their work as an ongoing narrative in which they explore different versions of the next chapters in the university's story. Cruzado realizes that in literature and in life, great things can happen when imagination is combined with realism. It is difficult to capture the genius of a multitalented leader like Cruzado in a few words, but *imaginative realism* comes close in acknowledging her pragmatism and creativity.

"She Speaks to the Heartbeat of the University and the State"

Academics are a notoriously difficult bunch to please. Administrators from the president down are often suspect, even when they share academic credentials and profess to hold the same values. Experienced presidents, it is said, need an implicit vote of confidence from the faculty every day to accomplish anything of importance. Cruzado earns her implicit vote of confidence by radical inclusion of disparate voices and players in decisions large and small. Her warm, personal style of engaging with others and her ability to deliver the goods in student success, funded research, and a remarkable building program all contribute to her success. Like the other presidents portrayed in this book, Cruzado enjoys a deep reservoir of confidence from most of her faculty, who also profess to like her.

A special bond has developed between the woman from Mayagüez and the people of Montana. Cruzado says that she experienced an unexpected sense of comfort with the state even as she was interviewing for the presidency. Several multigenerational Montanans have said that the state's harsh physical environment breeds common traits that they characterize as "Montana grit" and "Montana kind." They added that Montanans give strangers a chance to prove their worth before levying judgment on their character. As one observer noted, "She speaks to the heartbeat of the university and the state." Hard work, honesty, and delivering on promises are virtues Montanans cherish most. These are also some of Cruzado's most prominent qualities.

CHAPTER 4

Mary Dana Hinton
Leadership as Love in Action

Every message Dr. Mary Dana Hinton received in her childhood, except those from her mother, Mrs. Susie Hinton, reinforced the notion that she had no right to be in the room where things happened. Growing up in rural eastern North Carolina as a self-described "poor, brown-skinned, cockeyed girl who spoke differently and read too much," Hinton was not expected to be or do much of anything except "stay in her place." And yet, forty years after a school counselor informed her that "Black girls do not go to college, they go to the military," Hinton is widely recognized as both a higher education thought leader and a transformational college president.

In many ways, Hinton represents the ultimate outsider at each of the institutions she has led: first, the College of Saint Benedict, a Catholic institution for women in the Midwest, where she was a non-Catholic and the first African American leader; and, second, Hollins University, an independent historically white Southern women's college with a legacy steeped in the Old South, where she was the first African American president. Each of these presidencies represents a bold, even risky, career choice. Yet, each seemed to place Hinton exactly where she was needed at a particular moment. As she observes, "My superpower is helping people be seen and heard. I know how to honor and to hold their concerns." In fact, President Hinton does more than hold their concerns. With intentional focus coupled with fierce determination and kindness, she has enabled each institution to address its unique concerns in a manner that affirms and reimagines the mission while enhancing community.

Any way you parse it, African American women are significantly underrepresented among American college and university leaders. According to 2021 census data, African American women represent 10.2 percent of higher education enrollments. They constitute 8 percent of all graduate students.[1] According to the 2017 American Council on Education Study of the American College Presidency, African American women constitute approximately 2.7 percent of all college and university leaders.[2] Although African American women are making gains as leaders of private colleges and universities (most recently, Harvard University, Mount Holyoke, and Harvey Mudd College, among others), they represent less than 3 percent of this cohort.

Selecting the "Outsider"

After a nationwide search, Hinton's selection as the president of the College of Saint Ben's, as it is fondly called, could easily be seen as counterintuitive. She was a non-Catholic who had not progressed through the faculty ranks with its expectations for scholarly productivity. Hinton had served as a chief academic officer for only three years and had no record of garnering significant gifts from major donors.

Neither the search firm nor anyone on campus recognized the name Mary Dana Hinton when the review of candidates began. However, as members of the all-white search committee read her cover letter, they were taken by the ways in which her words resonated with the College of Saint Benedict and its values. "The language she chose seemed to capture the essence of the institution," one member of the search committee observes. Undoubtedly, her previous professional experience in Catholic higher educational institutions was a plus.

Hinton herself questioned whether she should apply for a job at a Catholic women's college in rural Minnesota. She decided to apply at the *insistence* of Father Kevin Mackin, the president at Mount Saint Mary College in Newburgh, New York, where Hinton was serving as the vice president of academic affairs. In fact, a reluctant Hinton had waited until the last day to submit the letter. But as she wrote, something happened. "I can often tell if something is going to work if I can write something that is flowing from my heart," she reveals. "I could write that cover letter. It just made sense to me."

During the off-site interview and the subsequent campus visit, the members of the search committee and those on campus became intrigued by Hinton's capacity to connect, by her deep appreciation of Benedictine values, and by her detailed knowledge of the college and of higher education in general. To the delight of many, during her on-campus presentation she recognized the basketball coach and congratulated him on the team's performance, correctly citing his win/loss record. The campus security officer charged with transporting her in the middle of a snowstorm, which completely disrupted her campus visit, reported that Hinton seemed more concerned about him and his safety than about the various demands of the day. He had nothing but praise to offer. Her presentations and interactions on campus confirmed that she was a mission-centered, people-focused, and compelling communicator who valued students, championed the liberal arts, and understood issues related to the bottom line. In other words, she was "eminently presidential."

However, as the search committee received feedback from the campus and began its final deliberations, concerns emerged related to her non-traditional background. She had not gone through the faculty ranks. She did not have a record of fundraising with individual donors. While there was no question that she had the capacity to present the institution's vision compellingly, had she ever had to make the "big ask"? Could she?

Her racial identity also entered the mix, but not in relation to her readiness for the role. Rather, the search committee was keenly aware of the lack of diversity in central Minnesota and sought to discern the readiness of those in the region to recognize and accept the talents and skills that a possible President Hinton might bring to Saint Ben's and to the area. How effective would she be at garnering resources in central Minnesota, where the perspectives of potential donors might be quite different from her own? How would her children adjust to a new locale? While identifying these types of considerations has the potential to become a slippery slope, the search committee was brave in honestly facing these issues at the potential inception of her presidency rather than later. The committee was wise in its recognition that race did matter. Despite these concerns, on July 1, 2014, Dr. Mary Dana Hinton became fifteenth president of the College of Saint Benedict.

Coordinate Leadership

A unique aspect of the presidency of the College of Saint Ben's was its "coordinate relationship" with the all-male Saint John's University. For over fifty years, the two Benedictine institutions had maintained a close relationship, offering a common curriculum and appointing faculty jointly. Each institution operated independently, with its own president and its own board of trustees, but the provost, the vice president for enrollment, and the chief planning officer held joint appointments. Other members of each institution's senior leadership team, including the chief financial officer, were hired by the respective president. Hinton acknowledges that the relationship provided efficiencies. On occasion, however, she found the arrangement cumbersome, and even problematic. If the two presidents had different priorities or the boards had differing perspectives, negotiating a uniform way forward was time-consuming. The relationship limited the strategic agility of both institutions. Members of the senior leadership team report that Hinton navigated this relationship with "patience and grace, even when she found it frustrating." One vice president comments, "She was sensitive to the challenges the relationship posed for jointly appointed senior leaders and tried to be as supportive as possible."

Members of the College of Saint Benedict leadership team describe her tenure as "transformative." As part of an initiative funded by the Mellon Foundation called "Becoming Community," the institution revised the core curriculum, expanded academic programs, and embraced a student-centered focus. President Hinton used her personal experience with exclusion and marginalization to educate her colleagues as she positioned the work of diversity, equity, justice, and inclusion (DEJI) as central to Benedictine values. She opened a space for the hard and difficult dialogues that were much needed on the campus, and she forged a deep relationship with the Benedictine Sisters.

A Potential Opportunity and a Potential Risk

In 2020, Hollins University enticed Hinton to become its president after she had served successfully at Saint Ben's for seven years.

The Virginia institution faced a series of challenges at the time of Hinton's recruitment. In the fall of 2017, Hollins had welcomed Dr. Pareena G. Lawrence as its twelfth president. The search committee had been impressed with Dr. Lawrence's experience as an economist who possessed a distinguished record of scholarship, teaching, and academic leadership. After serving two years, Lawrence stepped down to pursue her interest in international education and development. Her abrupt departure left the university community unsettled. Many among the faculty, staff, and administration felt that the board had not been appropriately attentive to the various challenges facing the institution. Like many institutions of higher education, Hollins experienced ongoing concerns about enrollment and retention. Issues related to campus culture, gender expression, and racial equity required attention.

In the midst of searching for President Lawrence's permanent successor, COVID-19 began to sweep across the nation. The pandemic further damaged morale and ignited additional concerns about enrollment and campus health and safety.

Consistent with its practice in several previous presidential searches, the Hollins University presidential search committee prioritized the need to hire a sitting president. Several members of the committee admit that the desire to identify a sitting president may have taken precedence over the need to clarify the specific leadership skill set that the university needed at that time. Despite this oversight, the university was fortunate that Hinton, in addition to the requisite presidential credentials, brought a unique capacity to lead effectively in an environment where love and healing were needed. A member of the search committee, commenting on Hinton's first two years at Hollins, notes, "Mary has brought so much more to us than we realized she would. She seemed to know what Hollins needed better than the committee did. She has been a mentor to many of us."

A conjunction of personal and professional factors made the leadership opportunity at Hollins intriguing to Hinton. She had deepened her commitment to the education of women and to women's institutions during her Saint Ben's presidency. Hollins University's commitment to the liberal arts and to humane values resonated with her. She recognized that she could advance the institution's efforts to become more inclusive. Additionally, its location in the Roanoke Valley would place Hinton closer to her ninety-three-year-old mother who was in ill health. She had not resided in proximity to her mother since the tenth grade. The quality of the Hollins leadership team energized Hinton. As she interacted with the senior leadership team, she could envision what might be accomplished without the challenges inherent in the Saint Ben's and Saint John's coordinate leadership structure.

All the same, accepting the presidency of Hollins University could be considered potentially risky. If she accepted, Hinton would become the first African American leader of a historically white Southern women's college. Such an appointment would be particularly significant (and, to some, surprising) given the institution's antebellum origins and its enduring legacies.

Founded in 1842 during an era when most women were denied the opportunity to earn a college degree, Hollins University was established on the principle that young women (white and of means) required an education similar to that afforded to young men. Unlike its Virginia "sister" institutions Sweet Briar College (founded in 1901) and Randolph Macon Women's College (founded in 1891), Hollins University, along with Mary Baldwin College, was founded in the antebellum era when slavery was the bedrock of Southern economic and social systems. The legacy of these inequitable systems endured at Hollins well into the twentieth century.

Hollins's early leaders, trustees, and financial supporters were slaveholders. Enslaved individuals, commonly referred to as "body slaves," often accompanied faculty, staff, and students to the institution to ensure that their various needs were met. Although Hollins did not own enslaved persons, when the need for additional labor was required, the college leased enslaved people from others in the region.[3] In the post-bellum period and well into the early twentieth century, jobs at Hollins were considered "good jobs" in comparison to other employment opportunities that were available to African Americans, and the institution continued to depend on the services of formerly enslaved individuals and their descendants.

Most of these employees resided nearby in what is now called the Hollins Community. The long-lasting legacy of inequitable economic and social systems is reflected in the relationship of Hollins University to the Hollins Community. Despite its proximity to the university and the significant role many of its residents played in sustaining the college, the community did not have access to running water until 1988. By the turn of the twenty-first century, only one young woman from the Hollins Community (Paula Meade '84) had graduated from the university. Ethel Morgan Smith, when writing about the Hollins Community, noted, "One hundred and fifty years after the founding of the college, 27 of the 124 Hollins Community residents are still employees of the college performing many of the same tasks their ancestors had: cooking, cleaning, painting, mowing, serving the college rather than being served by it."[4]

Hollins enrolled its first African American student in 1966. In the intervening years, the student body has become increasingly diverse in terms of race/ethnicity and socioeconomic status. In September 2022, the Hollins student body was 63 percent white, 16 percent African American, and 10 percent Latina; and 40 percent of the undergraduates were eligible for Pell Grants.[5] Galvanized by the actions of students, the university has taken a courageous step to confront its history. Under the auspices of the Working Group on Slavery and Contemporary Legacies, faculty members and students have collaborated to unearth the stories of those individuals whose significant contributions had been excluded from the institution's history. Widely revered traditions are being re-imagined to reflect a more inclusive institutional story.[6]

With full knowledge of the institution's history, its current needs, and her own strengths, Hinton accepted the presidency of Hollins University in August 2020. A few months earlier, George Floyd and Brianna Taylor had been murdered. By the time of her arrival, the COVID-19 pandemic had erupted in full force. These were only two of the challenges Hinton would need to address. She would also have to attend to multiple concerns about campus climate, as well as declining morale of faculty and staff.

As Hinton assessed the state of the institution and the country, she observed: "At Hollins our call must . . . be . . . to reconcile our institutional past with enslavement; to ensure all of our students—including the voices and concerns of students of color—are heard, seen, and valued, on campus today; to create an environment of inclusive excellence that supports rigorous teaching and learning in the liberal arts tradition; and to develop a plan that guides our efforts to be an inclusive community."[7]

After only three years, the university's trustees, senior leaders, faculty, staff, and students affirm the veracity of President's Hinton's proclamation of "I see you." As Hinton entered the DuPont Chapel for her installation on April 22, 2022, the audience let out a deafening roar of appreciation. It felt as if the roof might collapse. As she exited the chapel, duly installed as president, the equestrian team mounted on horses stood at alert. The pride, anticipation, and excitement within the Hollins community were palpable.

Entering through the Side Door

Hinton never aspired to become a college president. In fact, she argues, "I came to it through a side door." A series of intersecting and somewhat contradictory forces created the crucible in which Hinton's leadership style and commitments developed. She faced rejection by childhood peers, low expectations from K–12 educators, and continuous messages reinforcing the limited opportunities available to Black women. The mantra from her mother that she *must* attend college militated against these experiences, as did the intervention of mentors who saw more in Mary than she saw in herself. Hinton also nurtured a fierce conviction that more was possible, along with the determination to find it.

Vance County, where Hinton grew up in the 1970s–80s, remains one of eastern North Carolina's poorest counties. According to *Opportunity Atlas*, based on data from 2014–15, the average household income for adults aged thirty-five years who grew up in Vance County is $23,000. Seventy-one percent of these individuals have completed high school, but only 15 percent are college graduates. Based on 2014–15 data, over 50 percent of African American women aged thirty-five years who grew up in Vance County report giving birth between the ages of 13 and 19.[8]

Hinton received limited positive affirmation and endured considerable bullying growing up in the community of Kittrell Estates in Vance County. An avid reader whose eyes were crossed and whose hair was often unkempt, she defied the expectations of her peers and her teachers. By so doing, she opened herself to ridicule and disappointment. Simultaneously, she began to germinate seeds of resistance and not a little bit of shame.

North Carolina public schools had been forced to desegregate in the 1970s. A decade later, white teachers continued to maintain limited expectations for African American students. White parents were reluctant to have their children associate with Black people, and cross-racial friendships were discouraged. In the 1970-80s, no one in Vance County prohibited the Klan from marching through town if it wished, and the "N" word was common parlance.

Many African American children unconsciously absorbed the limiting expectations they encountered on a daily basis, resulting in a narrow definition of what it meant to be Black in a white world. A young Black girl who lacked a Southern accent and "had her nose in a book all the time" was a prime target for unrelenting teasing. How dare she break the mold? Was she trying to "act white"? Did she think she was smarter than the rest of them? Reflecting upon her elementary and teenage years, Hinton surmises, "You know, I got bullied more than my fair share. We didn't call it bullying back then. It was called 'riding the bus to school' and 'walking down the highway,' but today, I'm sure someone would be in jail for the things that happened. But that just was not the case then."

In stark contrast to this negativity, Hinton's mother recognized her daughter's talents and stressed the importance of college. She often remarked, "Mary, you have a good working brain. You need to use it to support others." After Hinton's father died when she was ten, the importance of meeting her mother's expectations and of becoming self-sufficient reached epic proportions for the youngster. Her widowed mother supported the two of them and a sister in college on a maid's salary. Hinton did not want to be an additional burden.

Given her limited understanding of the college admissions process, Hinton sought guidance from her tenth-grade counselor, who quickly responded, "You're not going to go to college. Black women go into the military. You don't belong in college." Looking back on that moment, Hinton confesses, "This felt like one of the worst moments of my life." It represented one more affirmation of her inadequacy, of the narrow confines in which the lives of African American women were envisaged. It was an assault on her humanity.

If the counselor's advice was meant to destabilize the aspiring student, then it had the opposite effect on Hinton's mother. In an uncharacteristic act, she reported the incident to her employers, Mr. and Mrs. Cooper. Aware of the young scholar's intellectual abilities, Mrs. Cooper offered to pay Hinton's tuition at Saint Mary's High School, a private all girls boarding school in Raleigh. Hinton and her mother readily accepted this generous offer.

Mrs. Cooper was one of several individuals who would see in Hinton what she did not yet see in herself. Her teachers at Saint Mary's guided her through the college application process, and she enrolled at Williams College, where she was advised and mentored by Dr. Laurie Heatherington. Although she often felt like an outsider at Williams, Hinton found a home and a sense of belonging through her interactions with Professor Heatherington. "She recognized my intellect and trusted my academic skill. She saw me," Hinton recalls. The power of being seen after years of discouragement helped crystallize Hinton's sense of purpose. "I wanted to do that for others: to see people when they were afraid to be seen."

Hinton's purpose was clear, but she had not determined how she would act upon it. After completing a master of arts degree in clinical child psychology, she spent seven years devoted to the improvement of public education. In the process, she further clarified her calling to ensure that a liberal arts education be available, affordable, and effective for students who, much like herself, had grown up at the margins, with their humanity and their potential unrecognized. She wanted to make sure their talents were seen and honored. Hinton had not yet linked this mission to higher education.

Although it paved the way to an academic career, her decision to pursue a doctoral degree was not driven by professional interest in teaching or research. Ever curious, Hinton sought to explore and understand the perplexing issue of how the humanity of Black women was acknowledged within the context of the African American church. Following graduate school, she was intrigued by the opportunity to teach and opted for a two-year contract at Misericordia University in Dallas, Pennsylvania. Hinton fell in love with teaching, with students, and with higher education.

President Michael A. MacDowell of Misericordia recognized that Hinton was well suited for higher education leadership. He encouraged her to assume responsibility for institutional planning and diversity initiatives at the institution. MacDowell invited Hinton to accompany him on fund-raising trips. During a development meeting at the Teagle Foundation, then CEO Rich Morrill remarked that he thought she could be a college president. Hinton notes, "I filed it away but didn't think much of it." Although Hinton had not yet come to grips with her potential and was (perhaps) still working through the debilitating impact of potentially destructive childhood messages, many of her colleagues saw her as "presidential" material. "Many people at Misericordia saw her as presidential," says her husband, Robert. "I saw it also," he admits with a smile.

Father Mackin, president of Mount Saint Mary's College where Hinton served as vice president of academic affairs for three years, both recognized and developed her potential. He strategically invested in Hinton's professional development, exposing her to various aspects of presidential responsibility, including fundraising and executive management. As he did so, he never admitted to Hinton that he was preparing her for the presidency. Instead, he observed that these were things he thought she "needed to know."

Hinton admits that before she could fully manifest the qualities that have led everyone with whom she interreacts to describe her as an "extraordinary, authentic" leader who possesses a "balance of exceptionally high IQ and EQ," she had to confront stereotypical views of leadership and discard the self-limiting impact of the messages she had encountered throughout her life's journey.

At both Saint Mary's and Williams College, Hinton had found herself in the midst of abundant wealth. The implication was clear. She did not belong. Hinton obtained an outstanding education at both schools, yet she admits that in each environment she felt like an outsider and experienced a "deep sense of shame."[9] As an African American student who was both from a lower income household and a first-generation college student, she lacked the social capital and economic security of her peers. She notes these destabilizing feelings began at Saint Mary's and were solidified at Williams. "When you see the wealth at Williams, and you know your mom is a maid, you just develop a healthy sense of shame. I didn't know about social capital back then. I just knew that sometimes my friends would have conversations about going to museums and places. I had no idea what they were talking about."

The liberal arts education she received at Williams College and the spirit of resistance she developed in response to her childhood experiences were critical factors in helping Hinton confront those demons. Her experiences instilled the spirit of fierce hope and resilience that remain the bedrock of her strength of character. Reflecting on her childhood, she notes that in the face of persistent bullying and low expectations, "you learned how to keep on. I had to learn how to keep moving on with this belief that there was going to be something better." Her liberal arts education broadened her definition of what it meant to be fully human, providing new ways of being in the world that challenged the confining box allocated to Black girls who grew up poor in Vance County, North Carolina.

In addition to facing the impact of poverty and racism, Hinton had to meet head-on persistent stereotypes regarding leadership and gender. Who is capable of leading and how is leadership exercised? The majority of leaders Hinton had been exposed to during her life were white men who acted decisively and carried themselves as if they were the smartest people in the room. This was highly inconsistent with her way of being in the world. If Hinton was going to lead, then she would need to discern how to do so in a manner consistent with her experiences as an African American woman.

Leading from the Margins

Hinton acknowledges that she was a tentative leader as she began her presidency at the College of Saint Benedict. In many ways, this is not a surprise because she was a first-time president at an institution with a cumbersome leadership structure. Although she identified strongly with the missions of the college and the Benedictine Sisters, she was an outsider in terms of geography, religion, and race. The new president carried the burden of being the "first." She was keenly aware of the potential impact that stereotypical conceptions of leadership might have on how she was perceived. It was a lot to carry.

Hinton was well into the second year of her presidency at Saint Ben's before she was confident and comfortable enough to liberate herself from the baggage of other people's perceptions of her as a viable leader. She was sensitive to the ways the intersection of her race, gender, and background might make it difficult for some people to see her as capable. She consciously and subconsciously felt the need to defy stereotypes. Consequently, Hinton strove to satisfy others even at her own expense. In the process, she reflects, "I became increasingly aware of the fact that the emotional demands of anticipating and responding to perceived expectations, of controlling one's behavior, tone of speech and presentation of self, do not come without a physical and spiritual toll."

Through a process of self-reflection Hinton recognized that her capacity to persist and to lead effectively required that she "embrace her multiple identities and use her experience with multiple forms of marginality as a source of strength." She would need to relinquish the standards and expectations of leadership that were based on a monocultural world view. A recalibration of her leadership was required.

In 2020, as she began her presidency at Hollins University, Hinton had fully embraced the power that comes from leading as her authentic self: a Generation X, African American woman who is no stranger to poverty, racism, sexism, and just plain meanness. She is finally comfortable wearing what she wants to wear ("No St. John suit for me. I'm a ruffles woman"). She gracefully calling out microaggressions and disrespect, and using the power of her story to connect heart to heart with each individual she encounters in the course of exercising her duties. Hinton can say definitively that she leads with authenticity, confidence, and intent. That does not mean she won't make mistakes. In fact, she acknowledges this and says, "Of course I will get some stuff wrong. My promise to this community is not that I won't ever fall, but it's that we will get back up together."

Authenticity and love are the foundation of Hinton's philosophy of leadership. During conversations with trustees and members of her leadership teams, the words "love" and "authenticity" were used consistently. Hinton believes that an authentic leader displays a commitment to mission, the drive to succeed, and a willingness to accept feedback. She adds trustworthiness, reliability, and discipline as essential features of effective leaders, which her colleagues say are characteristics that define her.

Hinton believes self-awareness is particularly critical for leaders who are women. She declares, "It has been the unearthing, knowing, revealing, and leveraging of my identities that has enabled me to persevere and excel as a leader."[10] And, indeed, Hinton has excelled as a leader. She has used each aspect of her life's journey to galvanize institutions. She has assisted faculty, staff, and students at Hollins and Saint Ben's with developing ecosystems in which the marginality that has accompanied her journey ceases to exist. The power of her narrative and moral imagination inspires donors to support her vision as she invites them to be co-creators of more just and inclusive communities.

Hinton uses the word "love" more often than is common in conversations with institutional leaders. One member of her leadership team opines, "When she says she loves you, she means that. It is borne out in her actions, in the way she relates to each member of the community both personally and professionally."

For "President Mary" as she is fondly called at Hollins, embracing and supporting each individual she meets is essential to good leadership. She emphasizes the importance of being in relationship with almost everyone she encounters. "You've got to bring your full self and be present to and with other human beings who are going to bring their full selves to you," she says.

Members of her senior leadership teams provide multiple examples of the way in which she operationalizes being "in relationship" with others across the campus. Shortly after her arrival, Hinton began observing the talents of various individuals on campus. When she perceived that their talents were underutilized, she tapped them for new roles. In many cases, this presented opportunities that the particular individuals may have never envisioned for themselves. Another colleague notes, "Mary has an astonishing way of paying attention to what matters to people." On a development trip in New York, she ran into a Catholic church and purchased a gift for an incoming student because through their conversations she had learned that religion was important to this young woman. "I thought it would matter to her," she said to her colleague, with a smile.

While intentionally working to bring those students who have often been invisible into the circle, Hinton is very cognizant of making sure that the student body knows that she is everybody's president. "I want to show up for everything our students do." This summer she began taking riding lessons at the Hollins stables to honor the university's highly regarded equestrian program. With a twinkle in her eye, she confesses, "I've got the chaps and the boots, but it's so darn hard learning new things."

Hinton is particularly fond of praising her leadership teams, and the sentiments are reciprocal. Members of the senior leadership at Hollins and Saint Ben's laud the way that she invests in them personally and professionally, serving as a mentor and recognizing what motivates each person individually. "President Hinton is the most transparent CEO I have ever worked for," a long-standing administrator observes. At some institutions, information is a form of currency to be guarded and closely held.

Hinton has a different perspective: information is currency; however, the more you share, the better it is for all involved. One vice president comments, "By candidly sharing the challenges and opportunities facing Hollins and by inviting us to problem-solve collectively, she has opened a space in which we can work to ensure that all members of the team succeed. We can be open, honest, and vulnerable together because she is."

Hinton admits that she had to intentionally develop the capacity to work effectively with a team. "After my father died, I was very conscious of the heavy burden my mother was carrying. I learned to fend for myself and not be dependent on others. I had to learn how to develop and support a team." Hinton recalls that she once sat in a meeting where the president of the institution berated every member of the leadership team. She vowed that she would not follow this example. Instead, she would focus on enhancing each member's performance and nurturing their capacity to work as an interdependent team. She invests in her senior team's development by inviting facilitators to work with the group on a semi-annual basis.

While Hinton centers genuinely connecting with those she leads, over the years she has also developed some boundaries for her interactions. She observes that she is no longer willing to sustain relationships with people who choose to assault her humanity and call her competence into question. She no longer feels it is her responsibility to try to prove her worth. Recently, she received a letter from an alumna who challenged her intelligence and competence to lead. Earlier in her career, Hinton admits she might have spent time trying to convince this individual of her worthiness. Now, instead of "wasting" her time trying to convince someone of her humanity, Hinton has learned to ignore these individuals. Instead, she focuses on her mission by tending to the needs of people who want something better for their lives.

Loving the Balance Beam

Leading with love sounds rather mushy. Does it really work? Does it enable one to move the institution forward? If measured by the impact Hinton has had on two liberal arts colleges, the answer is definitely yes.

Trustees, faculty, staff, alumnae, and students uniformly cite five major accomplishments when they describe Hinton's tenure as president of the College of Saint Benedict: reputation enhancement, strategic planning, renovation of facilities, fundraising, and generation of a commitment to the creation of an inclusive student-focused ecosystem.[11] The president's success in these areas illuminates her leadership strengths and her readiness to face risks head-on in service of the mission.

A compelling communicator, Hinton is a formidable fundraiser and a savvy negotiator who generates enthusiasm among campus constituents. She surpassed the campaign goal of one hundred million dollars by 7 percent, completing the most successful campaign in Saint Ben's history. She negotiated with trustees, the faculty, and the Benedictine Sisters to reimagine the master campus plan. Instead of constructing a new (and very costly) academic building, she garnered consensus for a more cost-effective plan to renovate three historic buildings. In the process, Hinton had to persuade the Benedictine Sisters to sell a beloved but underutilized building to the college. Members of her leadership team described the endeavor as "walking a tightrope."

Early in her tenure, Hinton led the first joint strategic planning process for the College of Saint Benedict and Saint John's University. Although the two institutions had a long history of collaboration, each surprisingly had its own strategic plan. Her presidential colleague at Saint John's was less excited about the initiative. According to those involved in the process, Mary handled this difference of opinion "with equal parts grace and determination." She engaged the relevant campus leaders and the two boards of trustees (independently and collectively) to craft a joint vision and strategic plan accompanied by mutually agreed upon metrics of success. Hinton faced some risk when she assumed this responsibility as a new president without the enthusiastic support of the Saint John's president. However, she believed a joint plan was mission-critical for both institutions. Hinton attributes the success to the strong support of both boards and the strategic engagement of the jointly appointed administrators.

Trustees, faculty, and staff praise Hinton for the ways in which she advanced the reputation of Saint Ben's nationally and internationally, a factor of critical importance for a small midwestern liberal arts college. Hinton established the biennial *Liberal Arts Illuminated* conference at the College of Saint Ben's. Administrators and policymakers from across the globe gathered to discuss the major challenges, opportunities, and imperatives facing liberal arts education. "These were shining moments for Saint Ben's. The participants' respect for Mary was palpable," one of her colleagues recalls. The institution's standing in the US News Ranking of National Liberal Arts Colleges improved from ninety in 2015 to eighty-two in 2019.

Hinton's love-informed leadership is also very powerfully on display at Hollins University. In the summer of 2020, immediately after her arrival, she launched the "Culture of Care," designed to nurture a sense of collective responsibility and mutual accountability in response to the COVID-19 pandemic. In a very short time, the Culture of Care quickly moved beyond a COVID-19 protocol to become an institutional North Star, guiding the entire community to assume responsibility for the university's collective success and for mutual care for one another. A manifestation of this culture of care is the university's shift from a traditional student affairs model to a divisional structure focused on every aspect of student success. This reimagining has sharpened the institutional commitment to inclusion and equitable student success throughout all divisions of the university.

Whether it is a faculty or staff member, a trustee or alumna, a senior administrator or student, those familiar with Hollins are amazed at the way Hinton has come to know and to heal a broken community while managing a pandemic. Shortly after her arrival, she held a series of virtual meetings with alumnae and donors, as well as faculty, students, and staff. These conversations were particularly important because the search had been closed and the new president had only interacted with the campus representatives on the search committee.

As Hinton listened to the concerns expressed during the virtual meetings, she encouraged participants to imagine a more inclusive and engaging Hollins University. Inspired by the conversations, alumnae and donors contributed over $8 million to support the "Imagine Campaign," designed to move Hollins forward immediately. The campaign provided a vehicle for leveraging the talents within the Hollins community while generating hope and engagement. By the fall of 2021, fifty-two proposals developed collaboratively by faculty and staff had been submitted. Eighteen of those had been funded and fourteen others were conditionally approved. Momentum and hope had returned to Hollins.

To support her vision that a high-quality liberal arts education should be accessible to those at the margins, Hinton secured a gift of $75 million to support scholarships for traditionally underserved and limited-income students. At the time, this was the largest donation ever received by a women's college and the largest single gift in the history of Hollins University. She also launched the HOPE Scholarship (Hollins Opportunity for Promise through Education), which provides full tuition scholarships for young women who come from families with limited economic capacity and have graduated from a Virginia high school within forty miles of the campus.

While generating these new initiatives, Hinton has worked with the trustees, administration, faculty, and staff to deepen their capacity to understand and address the needs of an increasingly diverse student body. As part of this effort and ever conscious of the importance of representation, she has significantly diversified the Hollins senior leadership team. With grace and determination, she provides inspiration as the community confronts past policies and practices courageously and in a spirit of reconciliation while moving forward to create an equitable and inclusive community.

Her consistent focus on the metrics is infused with a deep concern for the human beings behind the numbers. A trustee observes that Hinton's combination of empathy, compassion, and focus on the metrics "must be exhausting." Hinton acknowledges the challenge of bringing head and heart to the decision-making, particularly when the decisions have significant impact on individuals. "The choices are hard, and it makes my heart ache," she says, "but I watched my mother make much harder decisions almost every day."

When you talk to Hinton about metrics, she diverts to love. She simply states, "We have no option but to meet the metrics, whether these are related to enrollment, student success, finances, or fundraising. There are simply too many lives depending on it. If we fail, someone on the grounds staff may not be able to feed their family." She firmly believes that nothing is impossible if you have the right people who are committed to the mission and to one another in the room. If you care about those you lead, then lack of success is not an option.

Hinton's commitment to leading when days are hard and decisions are difficult is informed by a deep faith that is the foundation of her existence and her source of strength. During her early years, she would often accompany her father to church. She loved the rituals and the music of the African American church. Several years after her arrival at Saint Ben's, she felt called to Catholicism. She entered a year of discernment with the Benedictine Sisters prior to converting and now describes herself as a "Holy Ghost, spirit-filled" Catholic. Her love-informed leadership is the outgrowth of her religious convictions.

Hinton claims that she does not fit into a "presidential type." In fact, she rejects such typologies. "I'm the human president. In all my imperfection, somehow I sit in this presidential seat. When I say love, I actually mean love. I don't use the word lightly. I think my leadership gift is a willingness to love the people around me, which I think is a very human thing. And as I express this love and further the mission, I may be called to all types of presidential descriptions: the fund-raising president; the liberal arts defender; the diversity, equity, and inclusion president; the campus construction president." What is most important to her is that she moves the institution forward in a way that is supportive of everyone in the community regardless of role or background.

Leveraging the Margins

Hinton leads authentically because she has confronted and resisted messages that assaulted her humanity. She has embraced the marginal spaces from which she leads and would encourage any person aspiring to be a leader to do the same. Her perspective is clear: affirm who you are and resist fitting in the box that anyone else may have crafted for you. She cautions that the cost of failing to do so is injury to your body and your spirit. It is an unsustainable place from which to lead.

Hinton never set out to be a college president. Somewhere along the way, she forged a mission to ensure that students who have been marginalized by poverty, race, or gender, or all three have access to a liberal arts education in an environment where their potential will be recognized and their talents will be seen and honored. Her commitment to this vision and the manner through which she transforms institutions to achieve it have been forged by her faith, by the positive and negative experiences of her childhood, by her knowledge of what it means to live in marginal spaces, by her understanding of the impact of being seen, and by a fierce belief in the power of re-imagination. In many ways, the ultimate "outsider" has entered the room, and two institutions are better for it.

CHAPTER 5

Freeman Hrabowski III
Achieving Inclusivity and Excellence

The unconditional love of family and community, the compelling call of a civil rights leader, and five days in a despicable jail cell. These are among the seminal forces that developed Dr. Freeman Hrabowski III, president emeritus of the University of Maryland, Baltimore County. Hrabowski looks back at his professional career with gratitude and humility, and observes, "When I was a twelve-year-old boy in jail in Birmingham, I kept wondering what my future would be. I had no idea it was possible for this little Black boy from Alabama to one day be the president of a university that has students from 150 countries who are there not just to survive but where they love learning, where they strive to be the best, where they plan to change the world."[1]

Nor could he imagine the accolades he would receive from the scientific community. In 2022, in honor of his extraordinary career, the Howard Hughes Medical Institute (HHMI) would launch the Freeman Hrabowski Scholars Program, a $1.5 billion initiative geared toward the development of a more diverse scientific workforce. And, less than a year after his retirement in June 2022, the National Academy of Sciences (NAS) would honor him with its most prestigious award, the 2023 Public Welfare Medal, in recognition of his distinguished contributions applying science to public welfare.

True to fashion, Hrabowski repeatedly acknowledges that the honors he has garnered are the result of the collective body of work co-created with his colleagues at the University of Maryland, Baltimore County (UMBC). Ever appreciative, those at the university note that without Hrabowski's passion and vision, without his unflinching focus and hard work, these achievements would not have been possible.

The Compelling Call

In May 1963, in the midst of efforts to desegregate Birmingham, twelve-year-old Hrabowski found himself in a back pew at Sixth Avenue Baptist Church doing math problems and listening to a young preacher from Atlanta. The minister passionately urged parents to allow their children to join the campaign to desegregate Birmingham.

A young Hrabowski perked up as he heard Reverend Martin Luther King Jr. suggest that involving children in the struggle could result in their gaining access to the best schools in the city, something the precocious student wanted desperately. Looking back, Hrabowski acknowledges that King's message, his call to action and his vision of a different reality, signaled a profound turning point in his life.

Black parents in Titusville, the segregated section of Birmingham where Hrabowski grew up, provided a singular message as they socialized their children: "Life is not fair. If you are Black, you must work twice as hard and be twice as good." In contrast, Reverend King was suggesting that a new, more equitable world was possible. Creating that new world would be difficult, the young pastor cautioned; it would take time, but it was within their grasp. Equally compelling, the Atlanta preacher saw a role for children in bringing that world about. Hrabowski remembers King telling the congregation, "What we will achieve by marching will impact the lives of children yet unborn." This was a powerful message for a young child.[2] Much to his parents' dismay, young Hrabowski left the church that day determined to participate in the Birmingham Children's Crusade.[3]

When the coalition of civil rights organizations proposed using children to demonstrate against racial injustice, many Black people in Birmingham found the tactic troubling. Most parents believed that children belonged in school, not on the dangerous streets of Birmingham where they might be subject to violence and arrest. Residents of the Black middle class in Birmingham, many of them teachers in segregated schools, were particularly vulnerable. The local school board threatened to fire any teachers whose children were involved in the marches. Banks implied they would withdraw the mortgages of participants. Domestic workers faced the threat of termination by their white employers.

What parents feared most, however, was what would happen to their children inside the Birmingham jails, which were filling up with youngsters. The brutality of the city's racist police had become national news. Evening newscasts featured Sheriff Bull Connor, Birmingham's staunchest advocate for segregation, ordering the police to set dogs on the children. Television stations across the country broadcast clips of firehoses drenching little boys and girls as they marched for civil rights. Birmingham's Black parents had reason to fear for their children's safety.

The Hrabowski family shared these fears and were disinclined to allow their young son to participate. After a night of soul searching and prayer, with tears in their eyes and no small measure of trepidation, his parents decided to give Freeman their blessing to participate. Hrabowski admits that once his parents agreed, he realized the weight of his decision and was, in fact, quite fearful. Would he be okay? Did he have the stamina and fortitude for this undertaking?[4]

Hrabowski's participation in the Children's Crusade represented a formative moment in his personal development. This was the start of his lifelong journey to embrace improbable dreams, foster inclusion, speak with clarity and impact, and lift others up no matter the challenge.

Hrabowski was put in charge of a small group of students assigned to march to Birmingham City Hall to kneel and pray for the rights of full citizenship. The youngest child was eight years old; the oldest was fourteen. Despite his own fear, a young Hrabowski led the children to city hall. As they reached the steps, he encountered Sheriff Bull Connor. Hrabowski still recoils as he describes his meeting with a red-faced, enraged Connor.[5]

"Nigra, what do you want?" the sheriff barked.[6]

"Sah, to pray for our freedom," the frightened but well-prepared child replied.

Connor then spat in his face, picked him up, and threw him in the paddy wagon.

In jail for what he describes as "five unspeakable days," Hrabowski was responsible for protecting his charges from the older delinquents with whom they shared the cell. He was shocked when the jailers laughed as the older boys treated them like "slaves and animals." Hrabowski recollects reading the Bible and encouraging the frightened children to recite Psalm 23 in an effort to keep the older cellmates from accosting them. Sometimes it worked. Sometimes it didn't.

Reflecting on his prison experience, Hrabowski says it had opened his eyes to the plight of Black people experiencing poverty. While he found the living conditions in the cell unbearable, he was shocked when some of the boys claimed that even with the urine stench, the cell was tolerable because it was warm. "I had never experienced the type of discomfort I experienced in jail and these kids were saying that it wasn't that bad. Here I was only worried about being able to go through the front door. I had no idea of what poor Black people had to go through."

Although not yet a teenager, Hrabowski came to the realization that within the context of the racial caste system, he was privileged to have many more opportunities and creature comforts than other Black children. In that "eureka" moment, he came to understand that his own view of the world might be limited and that he would need to listen carefully to the voices of others before making judgements or resolving issues. The importance of full inclusion in the process of problem-solving would become a central tenant of his approach to leadership.

The five nights in Birmingham's jail was an emotionally searing experience. But no event was more jarring to Hrabowski and his peers than the bombing of the 16th Street Baptist Church in September of 1963, a few months after the Children's Crusade. Members of the Ku Klux Klan planted multiple sticks of dynamite that exploded on Sunday, September 16. The explosion killed four young girls. Given the tight-knit nature of the community, everyone knew someone who attended the church. For Hrabowski, it was his friend Cynthia McNair. The pain is still evident as he remembers the incident. "I had seen her the Friday before the bombing. As we were leaving school, she said to me, 'Bye, Freeman! I'll see you Monday.' " His voice softens and trails off as he repeats, " 'I'll see you Monday.' "

While the bombing pricked the conscience of the nation, it traumatized Black children in Birmingham. Many were left with the question, "Will we be okay?" Hrabowski recalls, "The father of one of the girls had given her a ring that morning, and she wore it to church. They found her severed hand with the ring. Many of us had nightmares about that hand for years."

Hrabowski attended the funeral of three of the girls where Dr. King's eulogy had a significant impact on the teenager. To this day, King's words have informed his sense of purpose. Speaking about their tragic deaths, King extolled, "So they have something to say to us in their death . . . they say to each of us we must substitute courage for caution . . . . Their death says to us we must work passionately and unrelentingly to make the American dream a reality."[7] Every day Hrabowski has carried the responsibility to ensure that his friend did not die in vain.

Faith, Education, and Hard Work

Hrabowski's philosophy of leadership, as well as his passion for action, willingness to dream big dreams, and occasional bouts of uncertainty were shaped by the contradictory messages he received growing up in Titusville, a Black middle-class "bubble" in segregated Birmingham at the height of the civil rights movement.

Within the confines of Titusville, Black children had models of excellence at home, from the pulpit, in the classroom, and in the entrepreneurial arena. However, when they ventured beyond their supportive and tight-knit community into other sections of Birmingham, messages of devaluation and exclusion abounded. Birmingham schools were segregated, and the Black schools were poorly equipped. Access to restaurants was via the back door. Separate and unequal bathrooms and water fountains were standard. Movie theaters demanded that Black people sit in the balcony. African American children were barred from the Kiddie Land Amusement Park, a circumstance they found particularly disheartening. Moreover, acts of white violence were so prevalent in Birmingham that a section of the community became known as "Dynamite Hill."

Young Hrabowski's upbringing, like that of all children in Titusville, was grounded in faith, education, and hard work. Middle-class Black parents believed that the combination of education and hard work represented the key to success, and, hopefully, a buffer in a hostile world. Nothing less than excellence was acceptable. The mantra from everyone in the community, whether at church, school, or home, was, "You are a child of God. Don't give anyone else the power to take your humanity away. Work hard and be twice as good. Above all, don't be a victim."

Hrabowski describes his home as a site of unconditional love. As the child of college-educated parents who were trained as teachers, he learned the importance of education at an early age. Reading was highly prized in the Hrabowski home. Already reading at four, the precocious child accompanied his mother to school and entered the first grade before he was old enough to enroll formally. His parents conscientiously exposed him to those aspects of culture often associated with "refinement," like poetry, art, and music. He quotes Langston Hughes and Emily Dickinson in casual conversation and continues to study classical music today.

Hrabowski has vivid memories of how parents and teachers attempted to counter negative messages while simultaneously conveying high expectations. He reports that the first time he realized other people saw him as "second class" was in the second grade. His teacher was distributing textbooks, and as she did so, she instructed the students not to remove the covers. A curious child, Hrabowski peeled back the cover only to discover a tattered book with a label from the white school. Young Hrabowski queried the teacher. "Why would they give us their raggedy books?" After initially scolding him for removing the cover, the teacher looked at her curious student with a pained expression and speaking with contained emotion responded, "Don't you *ever* forget, you are a child of God, and *no child of God* is second class. The book may be second rate, but the knowledge in the book is first rate. Get the knowledge. Get the knowledge, and let it go." The message was clear. Life may not be fair, but do not be a victim.

The church, the one institution where Black people were seen in their full humanity, played a central role in the socialization of Birmingham's Black children. Reflecting on his upbringing, Hrabowski notes, "In my parents' minds the only thing that superseded my education was my spiritual development." The Black church was a venue for the acquisition of faith and civic education, a place for addressing critical questions of the day. Children were taught that their talents were not of their own making. These were gifts from God that must be fully developed and used wisely in support of others. To whom much is given, much is required.

"It seems we were always in church—Sunday school, Vacation Bible School, youth choir, and youth fellowship. We didn't want to be there, but it was expected," Hrabowski reflects. Faith remains central to Hrabowski's identity and informs the way he leads. "I ask God to help me every day," he admits unapologetically. Those who know Hrabowski say his faith is the source of his hope and resilience.

Leadership Lessons

In the aftermath of the Children's Crusade, a young Hrabowski garnered several leadership lessons: the importance of having a clear message and delivering it compellingly, and, equally important, what a leader does may be less important than how they do it.

During the desegregation efforts in Birmingham, Hrabowski observed leaders who inspired others through well-crafted, powerfully delivered oratory. After the Children's Crusade, he was tapped by the Southern Christian Leadership Conference (SCLC) to serve as one of the child spokespersons. This provided a unique opportunity for him to hone his rhetorical skills. As a child he had a pronounced lisp and could not pronounce the letter r. Staff from the SCLC and his local pastor, Reverend Porter, worked with him on various aspects of public speaking including enunciation, brevity, pacing, sincerity, clarity of message, and eye contact. Often when you listen to Hrabowski speak you hear the cadence of a Baptist preacher. His colleagues note he has an uncanny capacity to use data to craft an inspiring narrative.

Mr. George Bell, Hrabowski's school principal, taught him that sometimes what you do is less important than how you do it. Bell was instructed by the Birmingham School Board to suspend all children who had participated in the crusade. Given the importance of education to members of the Titusville community, the suspension was an effort to further disgrace the youngsters and their parents. Bell did not wish to comply but had no choice. So, he carefully crafted his actions to ensure that the students were lifted up as heroes rather than disgraced.

Principal Bell called an all-school assembly much like the Honor Society assembly, one of the most prestigious events of the year. He explained to the gathering that sometimes a person may be forced to do things he does not want to do. When this happens, it is important to stay true to one's values. He talked about the appropriateness of children standing up for the rights that every American should have. As he would have at any Honor Society assembly, Bell called each child who was to be suspended to stage. The hall erupted in a standing ovation. "Everyone in the audience was crying; we were crying. I can't even say it without tearing up. It was so powerful, so powerful," Hrabowski recalls with emotion. To prevent the students from falling behind during the more than week-long suspension they received, Principal Bell worked with teachers to ensure they received their books and homework assignments.

Crafting an Educational Philosophy

Hrabowski began thinking about teaching and learning at an early age. These considerations and his own experiences in varied educational settings significantly influenced his educational philosophy. Conversations about teaching and learning were a staple during dinner conversations in the Hrabowski home. In addition to her responsibilities as a classroom teacher, Mrs. Hrabowski assisted her husband in preparing Black workers to obtain their GEDs. It was not unusual for a young Hrabowski to listen as his parents discussed various approaches to enhancing the reading and math skills of these workers. By high school, Hrabowski was tutoring his classmates in math and chemistry, and he began to perceive a link between effective reading skills and success in mathematics.

Hrabowski had a series of personal experiences that underscored the important role teachers play in student achievement and the development of a learner's self-confidence. Black teachers in Titusville set high expectations and demanded that all students perform to their potential. These educators did whatever they could to advance the students intellectually and personally. "They had a way of making us feel seen, valued, and cared for even when they had to give us the hand-me-down books or were using their own money to buy supplies. They had a way," he says, as his voice trails off in reverie and respect.

However, when he went to Springfield, Massachusetts, to study chemistry and literature the summer after tenth grade, Hrabowski found the behavior of teachers quite different. For the first time in his life Hrabowski was the only Black child in the class. He recalls that throughout the summer he was never called upon to answer a question. His teachers made no effort to engage him academically. "Even if my hand was the only one in the air, the teachers would look straight through me. It was as if I was invisible," he explained.[8] "It may have been rich academically, but it was painful." In contrast to the pain engendered by his Springfield experience, the affirmation Hrabowski received from his teachers in Birmingham, whether it was a teacher who reminded him he was a child of God or a principal who orchestrated a special assembly, left him with a sense of deep responsibility to live up to their expectations. Failing to fulfill his potential would dishonor their sacrifice.

During undergraduate and graduate school, Hrabowski had similar encounters with faculty and staff who either invested in him or harbored low expectations regarding his capabilities. As an undergraduate at Hampton Institute, Hrabowski encountered, for the first time, white professors who were invested in the learning and the success of Black students. The high-achieving scholar was forever impacted by these professors who encouraged students to ask questions and seek additional help if they were having difficulty. According to the Hampton philosophy, smart students sought help.

Conversely, at the University of Illinois (UIUC), where he pursued a doctorate in mathematics, Hrabowski was one of only three African American students in the program. He was often the only Black person in his classes. Hrabowski experienced a sense of deep isolation, which was exacerbated by several faculty members' low expectations of his abilities. Some professors were quite supportive, but others expressed surprise at his outstanding performance. Despite his love for mathematics, without the tight knit, competitive, high-achieving community of learners that had been a hallmark of his Hampton education, his experience in the Illinois mathematics department was not fulfilling.

Hrabowski's personal experiences at the University of Illinois intersected with his professional work in the UIUC Division of Student Affairs and as the director of the Upward Bound program. He began to appreciate the broad range of factors that influenced student success, including academic preparation, motivation, social integration, family issues, and finances.

In the late 1960s, like many institutions across the country, Illinois was attempting to diversify. Many students of color were performing quite well. In contrast, those students who had come from under-resourced schools with less rigorous academic programs, although academically capable, had not been well prepared for college level work. In many ways, the keys to academic success had been stolen from these young people. They lacked sufficient understanding of the level of effort that was required to achieve academic success. Society bombarded these students with negative messages about their capabilities. Consequently, they lacked confidence in their own ability, which diminished their motivation.

As he distilled these various experiences, Hrabowski identified components of an educational philosophy, which he would continue to refine throughout his career. He asserts that institutions have a responsibility to develop the structures and processes that will enable academically capable students to succeed even if their preparation is lacking. Students learn best in diverse communities that are characterized by high expectations and appropriate support from teachers and peers. Building such communities may require faculty to elevate their expectations regarding the performance of students of color. Likewise, students must understand the level of discipline and hard work required for success.

Energized by the opportunity to further refine his understanding of student success, particularly minority student performance in science, technology, engineering, and mathematics (STEM), Hrabowski elected to change his academic focus. Rather than spend five years completing a doctorate in mathematics, in a department where he felt particularly isolated, Hrabowski enrolled in the University of Illinois doctoral program in higher educational administration with a focus on statistics and evaluation. As part of his doctoral study, he would continue to investigate how students of color might live up to their full potential in a world that was not fully welcoming.

After completing his doctorate at University of Illinois, Hrabowski assumed the role of associate dean of the graduate school and associate professor of statistics and research at the Historically Black Alabama A&M University. He served for only one year before being appointed professor of mathematics and dean of arts and sciences at Coppin State University, a Historically Black institution in Baltimore. Within five years he was promoted to vice president of academic affairs. At both institutions Hrabowski remained focused on the issue that had informed his graduate study: how to enhance the academic achievement of minority students, particularly those studying in the STEM fields.

A Promising but Unlikely Candidate

While serving as vice president at Coppin State University, Hrabowski caught the attention of Dr. Michael Hooker, then president of the University of Maryland, Baltimore County. Founded in 1966, UMBC was the first institution in the university system of Maryland established after the US Supreme Court *Brown v. Board of Education* decision, making it the first public institution in Maryland to enroll students of all races from its inception. A relatively young institution founded during a period of social turmoil, UMBC was unencumbered by tradition and, therefore, better positioned for innovation.

The identity and mission of the university fluctuated in its early years. When the late Dr. Hooker arrived as president in 1985, he found a rather somnambulant institution still attempting to clarify its purpose. President Hooker proposed a new vision of UMBC: an institution committed to economic development, community engagement, and the resolution of societal problems. This would be achieved by improving academics, growing research, and partnering authentically with the local community.

Consistent with this vision, Hooker sought to diversify the leadership at UMBC. Hrabowski was widely respected in Baltimore for his commitment to the academic preparation and success of African American students, and Hooker thought the young, accomplished administrator could play a significant role as UMBC worked to realize its vision.

In many ways, Hrabowski was an unlikely candidate for UMBC. Except for his graduate studies in higher educational administration at the University of Illinois and one year of administrative work in the UIUC Division of Student Affairs, Hrabowski had spent his entire professional career at Historically Black institutions. He had not progressed through the faculty ranks before taking on significant administrative roles. Hrabowski had remained intellectually engaged with the issues related to the academic achievement of minority students, particularly those studying in the STEM fields. However, the demands of academic administration at institutions with limited resources did not leave much time to publish the kind of research expected by an institution like UMBC.

During his tenure at Coppin State, Hrabowski had refined his understanding of student achievement and grappled with the paradigm shift inherent in moving faculty from a focus on teaching to a focus on student learning. He provided considerable support for faculty who were female and addressed the many complex administrative issues that dominated the academy. Reflecting on his tenure at Coppin, Hrabowski admits, "I was young. Undoubtedly, there were situations I might have handled better, but I was always focused on the students." After a decade at Coppin, Hrabowski was ready for a change. He was eager to find an institution where faculty and staff were willing to try new approaches to foster student success and where he could impact the culture. Several higher education leaders in the African American community were urging him to consider a presidency at a Historically Black institution.

Hrabowski admits he was captivated by President Hooker's charisma. He was inspired by the president's openness to innovation and commitment to serving all students, especially first-generation students and students of color. The young administrator unexpectedly found himself confronted with a consequential career decision. Should he assume the presidency of the Historically Black institution from which he had an offer, or should he assume the role of associate provost for undergraduate studies at UMBC? Where could he have the most impact? Where might he have the freedom to innovate? Where could he have the biggest dreams?

Hrabowski was drawn to the UMBC opportunity and to the substantial challenges it posed. Black students at UMBC found the institution unwelcoming and were actively protesting the racial climate on campus. In fact, they had been doing so for years.[9] Members of the Baltimore African American community also questioned the institution's commitment to African American students.

Hrabowski's wife, Jackie, played a pivotal role in his decision-making, as she had on many previous occasions. She had worked with UMBC faculty and staff in an early childhood education program in Baltimore. She advised her husband to seriously consider the opportunity, noting that the faculty she had worked with were "good people who really want to make a difference." She believed the problem was that they were unsure about how to do so. It was clear to her that her husband could make a significant impact. As he would often do throughout their more than fifty-year marriage, Hrabowski followed his wife's counsel. He turned down the opportunity for a presidency at a Historically Black institution and cast his lot with UMBC.

Two months before he was to assume his new role, Hrabowski received an anonymous letter indicating that the UMBC faculty senate had deliberated upon a proposed vote of no confidence in President Hooker because it objected to the selection process that had resulted in

Hrabowski's appointment. Although the resolution did not pass, Hrabowski recalls thinking, "This is not very promising." He understood that Hooker had taken a professional risk to bring him to UMBC.

To his credit, President Hooker was realistic enough to recognize that it might be challenging for many UMBC faculty to transcend the prevailing academic hierarchy by acknowledging that talent can be found anywhere, including right down the road at Historically Black Coppin State University. The president also suspected that Hrabowski's rather thin publication record might concern some faculty. Hooker, a charismatic figure who was unafraid of risk, decided that he would ignore the accepted UMBC academic search processes. He established a "select" search committee composed of individuals he thought had the capacity to look beyond potential biases and recognize the young administrator's unique potential. He invited Hrabowski for a series of meetings confined to this select group.

The selection process placed the new associate provost at a distinct disadvantage. Within his first month on campus, a well-respected faculty member came to his office to inform him that the selection process represented a breach of shared governance. He told Hrabowski, "The faculty are not happy that you are here. It's not personal. It's about process." In recollecting this encounter, Hrabowski smiles, "After ten years as a dean and VP, I had been knocked down many times and I knew how to be humble, and to say, I get it." He thanked his colleague for his honesty and offered the following challenge: "Watch what I do and how I do it. If it's not working out, I won't want to be here. You won't have to tell me to go. All that I ask is that you treat me fairly now that I'm here."

Hrabowski's awareness that he was not uniformly endorsed did not prevent him from beginning to engage the faculty in thinking deeply about better serving UMBC students. As any mathematician would, he began by examining the data, which revealed a dismal graduation rate of 35 percent and an African American graduate rate of 25 percent. The data clearly indicated that while UMBC was admitting some students who lacked the academic preparation to be successful, it was also admitting many students with strong academic profiles. These well-prepared students experienced success in the humanities, arts, and social sciences, but they were not succeeding in STEM courses. The conclusion was evident: capable students were being underserved.

Equipped with this new information, the new associate provost invited faculty, staff, and students to join him in thinking creatively and critically about how to address the findings. He reminded them that improving academic performance for *all* students aligned with the institution's mission to conduct research and implement strategies to address societal problems. He appealed to the faculty's desire to be data-informed problem-solvers and effective educators, thus recognizing and reinforcing their own commitment to students. Hrabowski's approach exemplified his commitment to shared governance, which was still a sensitive issue in light of the hiring process that brought him to UMBC.

From Birmingham Jail to University President

The associate provost, whose selection the faculty members questioned five years prior, became their favorite choice for president when Michael Hooker departed. A few years after Hrabowski's arrival, Hooker informed him that he thought he would be president at UMBC someday. In 1992, when Hooker announced he was leaving UMBC, Hrabowski was serving as executive vice president. He was by then a well-respected campus leader and had established a reputation for working effectively with faculty, staff, and students. All the same, Hrabowski was surprised when the same faculty messenger who had been delegated to convey the faculty's displeasure at his hiring, returned to report that many at UMBC wanted him to be the next president. Influential people outside of UMBC, including the governor, shared this perspective. After serving as interim president for one year, Hrabowski was appointed president in 1993. Hrabowski became the first African American president of a predominantly white campus in the Baltimore area.

It is no surprise that Hrabowski could not imagine leading a predominantly white public university. Serving as president of a Historically Black College or University seemed a more likely destination. In 1993, when Hrabowski officially took the reins of UMBC, African American leadership at predominantly white public comprehensive and doctoral universities was rare. According to the American College President Survey in 1990, only fifty-seven African Americans served as presidents or chancellors at predominantly white institutions. Of that group, only one was employed at a public doctoral-granting institution, and fewer than a dozen provided leadership at predominantly white public comprehensive institutions. The majority of African American presidents were serving at community colleges. Additionally, the median age for college presidents in 1990 was fifty-four, and only one in three were younger than fifty. At forty-two years old, Hrabowski was one of the youngest college and university presidents in the country.[10]

Transforming UMBC

Hrabowski spent thirty-five years at UMBC, with thirty of those as president, before retiring in 2022. During the course of his tenure, Hrabowski and his colleagues transformed the institution from a sleepy commuter college into a well-respected research university with an undergraduate honors college and remarkable evidence of student success. Among its notable accomplishments with Hrabowski at its helm,[11] UMBC:

- developed and implemented an educational model to improve performance in STEM fields for all students, particularly women and students from underrepresented groups,
- became the undisputed leader in producing graduates who enroll in joint doctoral programs and obtain the MD/PhD inclusive of the largest number of Blacks who complete this joint degree,
- has been recognized since 2017 by the *Chronicle of Higher Education* and the organizational management consulting firm Modern Think as a "Great College to Work For," achieving honor roll status for several years,
- increased graduate enrollment by 40 percent and undergraduate enrollment by 20 percent while simultaneously improving academic standards and expanding the diversity of the student body,
- improved the six-year graduation rate from 35 percent to 65 percent,

- boosted research and development expenditures more than eightfold to $84 million annually, putting UMBC among the country's top 100 public universities in federal research funding, and
- earned the Carnegie Foundation Community Engagement Classification, which recognizes an institution that invests its time, assets, and expertise in strengthening communities and dismantling the barriers to opportunity that have calcified over time.

Though these institutional accomplishments are impressive, Hrabowski's expansive smile broadens and his eyes twinkle as he recites the names and accomplishments of UMBC graduates and highlights the work of the faculty and staff who have served as their mentors. As one of his mentees notes, "Talking about the accomplishments of UMBC graduates gives him goosebumps."

How does someone transform a "little backward institution in Catonsville, Maryland with a 35 percent graduation rate, less than a third of students in residence, and a Black population guaranteed to fail in most STEM programs" into an innovative R1 university lauded for the development of a model of inclusive academic excellence? How does one transform a culture in such a manner that African American males, a group historically marginalized and underserved in higher education, become standout performers in STEM? The answer is multifaceted, but the leader is critical to such transformation. Someone who can inspire constituents and garner support for a compelling vision; who brings focused attention to strategy and assessment; who exhibits a values-based leadership style characterized by a deep sense of responsibility, a passion to make a difference, and a commitment to inclusivity. This is the type of leadership modeled by Freeman Hrabowski III.

When Hrabowski discusses the transformation at UMBC, the first thing that he says is, "It's about US not me." A member of the UMBC leadership team who has worked closely with him for many years, confirms that this is more than a mere slogan. "Freeman may have had a vision, but he did not impose it on the university. Instead, he identified the values the UMBC community shared. We aspired to be an institution characterized by inclusive excellence. We believed in supporting students and faculty."

Hrabowski, an insider who understood the aspirations of the community, crafted a vision that aligned with these aspirations. He facilitated, guided, and led the university to these goals. When he faced resistance for particular projects that aligned with the agreed upon goals, he called the institution back to the values it held in common.

"Thirty years later," his colleague continues, "we know who we are: a diverse institution that values inclusiveness and excellence; a university that offers a challenging experience to all of our students. We sense that we are part of something bigger than UMBC, that we have significantly impacted the national discourse on the STEM education."

Equally significant, the culture of UMBC has shifted during the course of Hrabowski's presidency. The institution has become unapologetically aspirational. The mantra "success is never final" permeates the university and serves as a reminder that innovation must be continuous, and that everyone can lead. An alum who graduated early in Hrabowski's tenure highlights a particularly unique change in the culture. "Everyone on campus recognizes that African Americans at UMBC are really, really smart," she says. "Faculty and staff have high expectations for their performance and are invested in their futures."

Hrabowski's efforts to spearhead the Meyerhoff Scholars Program, which was established in 1988 prior to his presidency, provide an excellent example of his approach to leadership. Hrabowski played a critical role in articulating its components, ensuring its implementation, and in obtaining the financial support that undergirds the program.

Initially envisioned as a program designed to improve the performance of African American men in the STEM fields, the Meyerhoff Scholars Program is now open to all high-performing students interested in diversifying the STEM fields. The program's emphasis on high expectations, building community, faculty engagement, and early exposure to research are reflective of Hrabowski's educational philosophy.

At its inception, the Meyerhoff Scholars Program generated skepticism and opposition from multiple constituents. In the late 1980s there was little distinction between the concepts of equality and equity. A cohort of highly regarded faculty argued that any race- or gender-conscious program, regardless of intent, was *ipso facto* antithetical to justice. Some white students saw it as reverse discrimination. There were rumblings about a protest petition, although this never occurred. Students of all races raised questions about the program, particularly the fact that a cohort of students was getting a level of academic support and educational mentorship not available to the rest of the student body. Faculty questioned the focus on African American males. Would they have the motivation to study science and engineering? The program's financial aid strategy posed another point of tension. Some questioned the wisdom and fairness of providing financial support to talented students who had financial capacity instead of targeting aid only to students of limited financial capacity.

Hrabowski responded to the angst regarding the Meyerhoff program by listening carefully. He took people's concerns seriously. In small group discussions, focus groups, and faculty meetings, he explained the rationale for the admission criteria, program design, and pedagogical approach. Thirty years later, a faculty colleague still remembers how Hrabowski countered the concern about giving scholarships to smart Black students regardless of the family's financial capacity by comparing it to giving scholarships to the best athletes regardless of family income. Everyone agrees that Hrabowski has a gift for "getting things done."

Hrabowski was president in 1993 when the first cohort of Meyerhoff Scholars graduated. By that time some of the program's earliest critics had become converts. The outcomes demonstrated that with high expectations, appropriate support, and early immersion in the laboratory, students from all backgrounds had the potential to become adept in the STEM disciplines.

Faculty and staff continued to assess the outcomes and refine the program. Based on its success, UMBC set a goal of leading the country in producing African American graduates who pursue and successfully complete the MD/PhD. By 2018, data from the Association of American Medical Colleges (AAMC) provided evidence that this goal had been realized.[12]

Based on the demonstrable success of the program and the lessons learned through its continuous assessment, the institution has been able to attract the financial resources required to develop similar opportunities in other divisions in the university. UMBC now boasts the Sondheim Scholars in Public Service, the Humanities Scholars, the Linehan Artist Scholars Program, and the Sherman STEM Teacher Scholar program.

Explaining Success

Hrabowski cautions that changing culture is hard. It does not happen overnight. Realizing improbable dreams requires institutional consensus, careful implementation, and assessment. A conductor can do nothing without the orchestra.

Possessed with considerable self-awareness, Hrabowski is grateful for what he and his colleagues have been able to accomplish. He readily admits that his colleagues and students have greatly contributed to his effectiveness. "My colleagues and students have made me much better than I thought I could be. They have slowed me down at points when I was moving too fast. They have suggested that I allow others to speak and give the point because sometimes when the president makes the point it's dead on arrival. They have critiqued the approach I wanted to take and said, 'We can find a better way.' They have made suggestions that go far beyond what I had been thinking about. And in the hard times, and every president has those, they have said, 'We can get through this; we can get through this together.'"

Although the transformation at UMBC during his thirty-year tenure has been dramatic, Hrabowski brings a gradualist approach to change. When advising presidents at the Harvard New Presidents Seminar he cautions, "Carefully assess how much change is possible without weakening the presidency. I'm willing to take certain risks, but before I take risks, I socialize the idea with individuals at the institution and identify allies." Hrabowski understands the impact of racial representation and the power of unconscious bias. This awareness may partially explain his measured approach to change. He concedes that Black presidents are often under greater scrutiny with less margin of error than their white counterparts.

Hrabowski believes that people are the most important factor in realizing a bold vision. Throughout his presidency he has invested in building and sustaining relationships with internal and external constituents. "Dr. Hrabowski understands that you can't move people to do remarkable things if you don't know what matters to them," an alumna observes. She adds nuance by explaining that Hrabowski's focus on getting to know people is not to ensure that they do his bidding. "He wants to know their dreams so he can help people realize these," she explains. Hrabowski is a skilled networker and has leveraged connections in the Baltimore/Washington corridor to recruit partners for the institution's research park, to identify financial resources to enhance scholarship and research opportunities, and to obtain mentors for students and faculty.

Hrabowski walks the campus like a "rock star," engaging with everyone at UMBC irrespective of institutional role or disciplinary affiliation. He seeks to make authentic connections throughout the institution and wants to know people personally and professionally. He recognizes the important role that human connections can play when an institution faces difficult choices. "The chemistry on our campus comes not only because of our love of ideas but because we are connected as human beings, and we go through problems with our children, illnesses of our parents, and challenges in our homes. The trust we have built in the community through human connections enables us to handle a disagreement about an approach or an idea because we know each other. We know we want what's best for our students and we can have different perspective regarding how to get there."

Members of Hrabowski's senior leadership team note that he possesses an "astounding" work ethic. His energy level is legendary. Although he struggles with work-life balance himself, he stresses its importance for each member of the team. "He trusts you to get your job done and does not micro-manage, but if you ask for help, he is there to assist," a senior leader says. "He has created an environment in which it is safe for us to take risks and this risk tolerance has permeated the community, creating conditions conducive to innovation."

Hrabowski thrives best in community with others. His investment in building authentic relationships at UMBC is valued and reciprocated. When his mother died in 1997, students, faculty, and staff from UMBC traveled to her funeral in Birmingham. Hrabowski was deeply moved by that act of support. When he returned from Birmingham, he received an eight-foot-tall sympathy card with thousands of comforting messages from students, faculty, and staff. It's important for Hrabowski not to feel alone. Acts of support such as this contribute to his resilience.

Will I Be Okay?

It may surprise those familiar with Hrabowski's successes to learn that, although he was no stranger to UMBC, he assumed the presidency with some measure of apprehension. As he contemplated his new leadership role, the recurring question from his childhood reemerged: will I be okay? Hrabowski confesses, "I knew I would give it all I had, but I still wondered would it be enough? Until you are successful, you wonder every day will it be enough?" He acknowledges there are multiple dimensions to that question. Will it be enough to meet the expectations of his parents and mentors? Will it be enough for those who might question his ability? Will it be enough to assuage his own sense of responsibility?

Hrabowski no longer has to worry. It was, indeed, enough, and then some.

CHAPTER 6

Robert Jones
From the Fields Where Character Grows

The bright yellow school bus stopped alongside the cotton field, standing out like a patch of marigolds against the acres of white and green. Two young African American brothers scrambled off the bus and onto the red Georgia clay. The boys bantered as brothers do when they walked through the fields lush with crops ready for harvesting on a warm autumn afternoon. The two, not yet teenagers, would spend hours in those fields until it became too dark for them to see.

Robert, later to become Dr. Robert Jones, the younger of the Jones boys, lagged a little behind his brother in gathering his quota of cotton. He paused often to examine the white fluffy bowls, pulled them apart, rubbed the green leaves between his fingers, felt the soil, and looked up at the remaining sunlight. What miracle made it grow, this simple yet mysterious plant that represented so much of his family's time and constituted most of its livelihood? Why were some fields bursting with cotton while others produced only a little? His older brother, and sometimes his mother and sister when they too worked the fields, would hide Robert from the overseer during those moments when he stopped picking.

Young Robert's curiosity surrounding the dynamics of growth would remain a lifelong interest. The study of plant physiology would dominate his career as a scientist. Later, his curiosity and powerful intellect would be applied to the research universities he led.

It was not unusual in the 1950s and 1960s for Black children and their families (and some whites) to spend days in Georgia's cotton fields for weeks or months at a time. Youngsters missed what they might have learned in the classroom. Their chances for the better life that education could provide also slipped away. For their families, earning a living was a necessity, and school was a luxury that could be foregone. These two brothers and their sister were exceptions. They entered the fields only after the school day because their strong-willed father told the man who owned the fields, "My children will not miss a day of school harvesting your cotton."

Some fifty years after picking cotton in the fields of southwest Georgia, Robert Jones took charge of one of the nation's leading research universities. His rise from a sharecropper's shack in Terrell County, then and now one of the poorest counties in the state, to the top job at Illinois's flagship public research university truly defied the odds.

However, Jones's story is more meaningful than overcoming poverty and racism to achieve career success, as inspiring as that narrative is. An even more important story is how this sharecropper's son proved so adroit in leading a major university in the perilous environment that derailed his predecessors. His upbringing in a sharecropping family in rural Georgia, his personal growth in the face of race-baiting and discrimination, his tenacity in the study of what makes plants grow, and his apprenticeships in academic leadership all contributed to the formation of an exceptional leader.

A "Hot Mess" in Illinois

This narrative begins with Jones's arrival at the University of Illinois Urbana-Champaign (UIUC) in September 2016 at a time overripe with crises and challenges for a new president.

Scandals had forced his two immediate predecessors out of office, leaving the community disillusioned and the university adrift. Moreover, the university's problems did not end with the chancellors' departures. A two-year impasse between the Illinois governor and the legislature had led to a massive cut in state funding. Anger over the misuse of

Native American imagery in the university's athletics mascot, Chief Illiniwek, persisted, coupled with sharp resistance to changing that imagery. Charges and countercharges of anti-Semitism and anti-Muslim behavior on campus fueled further conflict between advocates of Israel and Palestine. In 2020, the COVID pandemic interrupted the academic and research enterprise. The murder of George Floyd by police in Minneapolis in May of that year threatened to disrupt the campus as it ignited demonstrations across the country. A longtime university staffer described the state of the institution that Jones inherited as a "hot mess."

Caught up in crises not entirely of their own making, the two chancellors who held office prior to Jones were forced to resign before their contracts ended. The rough-and-tumble world of Illinois politics created plenty of casualties during that time. State politicians regularly traded their offices for prison cells after convictions for crimes ranging from kickbacks and bribery to perjury. Governor Rod Blagojevich was sentenced on multiple corruption charges, including monetizing the appointment of a US senator. Four recent Illinois governors served time in federal prison.[1]

The porous borders separating the academy, statehouse, board of regents, and state power brokers had proven to be dangerous territory for previous chancellors. Chancellor Richard Herman, a distinguished academic and onetime provost at UIUC who served from 2004 to 2009, found himself enmeshed in an admissions scandal that anticipated another similar debacle ten years later. Varsity Blues is how FBI agents with a flair for irony labeled the investigation of the later scandal, in which well-heeled parents bribed their children's path into elite universities on both coasts. However, in Illinois, clout (not cash) was the leverage needed to get an underqualified child or friend into the state's flagship public university—in some cases, after their applications had been formally rejected. Chancellor Herman was forced to resign. The head of the University of Illinois system, though not personally involved in the scandal, as well as several regents, suffered the same fate.[2]

Following a scandal-free period under the interim chancellor, Robert Easter, Phyllis Wise became head of the Urbana-Champaign campus in 2011. Another well-regarded academic and seasoned administrator, Wise was caught in the crosshairs of a series of conflicts that overshadowed her achievements.[3]

Crises piled upon crises during Wise's four years as chancellor. Football players and soccer players sued Wise and the university over alleged mistreatment. In a widely reported case that brought on a censure by the American Association of University Professors, Wise was forced to withdraw a job offer to Native American studies professor Steven Salaita, whose anti-Israel Twitter messages before accepting the position led to accusations of anti-Semitism. Wise was accused of using a personal email account to avoid compliance with open records requests. She received no-confidence votes from several academic departments. Upon her departure, Wise defended her administration, saying she only agreed to step down "at the board's and the president's request that I tender my resignation."[4]

Seeking a "Highly Ethical and Transparent Chancellor"

"We simply lost confidence in our leaders" is how one professor described UIUC's response to the scandals and forced resignations. Considering the hot mess surrounding former chancellors, it is not surprising that several faculty members repeatedly told the chair of the search committee seeking a new chief executive that UIUC needed a "highly ethical and transparent chancellor."[5]

If there was ever a time for a steady and experienced leader at the helm, this was it. After two strikeouts in the chancellor's office, the flagship campus and the University of Illinois system could not afford a third. Clearly, Illinois higher education leadership is not for the faint of heart or those who surrender their principles to curry favor from venal politicians. A senior faculty member characterized the decade before Jones arrived as a "convulsive lost decade."

A Tough First Day on the Job

Would Jones be the one to redeem the university? The search committee was looking for a leader who could restore the school's reputation in the minds and hearts of the thousands of Illinois residents who cared about their beloved school.

The University of Illinois is a globally recognized research university enrolling over 50,000 students. Its budget is greater than those of several small countries. Nevertheless, many faculty and others in the state felt that UIUC had never quite received the respect it deserved. Berkeley and Michigan should have been its natural peers, but instead, Illinois seemed mired a few rungs below those top-ranked public universities. "We believe we are fabulous," one professor said, "but we lack a narrative describing how fabulous we are." The scandals and early departures of its chancellors did nothing to advance the university's standing with its many supporters, or even with itself.

Jones's experience on the first day of his new job, September 26, 2016, was anything but auspicious. A murder near the new chancellor's home interrupted Jones and his wife, Lynn, as they unpacked their belongings. It happened in the early morning hours when shots were fired at an off-campus party nearby. One was killed, and three were wounded.

Setting aside his immediate plans for the day, Jones issued a thoughtful, reassuring message to the university community. Then he calmly went about the business of a newly arrived leader. He greeted students, chatted with his staff, and responded to a reporter's questions about the budget crisis afflicting Illinois. Clearly, the new chancellor could handle tense situations with aplomb while also advancing the work of the university.

"Being Black in America"

UIUC hired Jones, at least in part, in the hope that a Black chancellor would be better equipped to navigate the racial and ethnic divides that dominate politics in Illinois, and indeed, in much of the rest of the country as well. To be sure, Jones brought strength of character and other leadership traits to the table beyond his ability to deal so effectively with crises of racial conflict and injustice.

However, his sensitivity and courage in addressing the murder of George Floyd reveals much about Jones's leadership abilities. This most striking example came four years into Jones's tenure at Illinois, when a uniformed Minneapolis police officer killed Floyd. The policeman drove his knee downward onto Floyd's neck and held it there for over nine minutes, cutting off his ability to breathe. Video recordings of the event quickly flooded social media, setting off sometimes violent demonstrations in major cities and on university campuses.[6]

In his widely distributed testament titled "Being Black in America," Jones responded to the murder by describing his own dangerous encounters with racial violence:

> Jogging while Black and dogs let loose by unwelcoming neighbors. Strangers shouting, "Get out of the road N——!" from car windows as they drove by. Sitting in the pew for the funeral of a cousin whose innocent life was cut short by the use of excessive force by police. Being summoned to an aunt's house in the middle of the night, the dwelling bullet-riddled only because two of her sons were actively engaged in the civil rights movement and marched with Dr. Martin Luther King Jr., John Lewis, and others. The sadness in seeing them feeling compelled to move to another state.
>
> Driving by smoldering ashes of three Black churches burned to the ground. The grandfather I'd never met because he was shot dead in his front yard of his sharecropper's shack by a racist landowner, on the day of his eldest daughter's wedding. And there is something about the sound of a pump shotgun being cocked that I'll never forget—especially when I turned and found it leveled over the hood of a pickup truck and aimed at me, only because of the color of my skin.[7]

Jones struck an eloquent and somber tone in his response to the murder of George Floyd at the hands of police. Where many college and university presidents offered expected and no doubt sincere lamentations over Floyd's death, few could offer testimony drawn from their own firsthand experiences.

His next steps went beyond words. Jones had already hired the university's first chief diversity officer. In July 2020, he launched a call to action "to dismantle systemic racism and injustice that are both measurable and accountable by the end of the coming academic year." Jones committed $2 million annually to support actions to enable the university "to intervene in institutional disparities, structures of violence, and over-criminalization to fundamentally address the root of causes that continue to create inequality, inequity, and lost opportunities for too many in our society."[8]

Jones makes no apologies for his commitment to racial justice, diversity, equity, and inclusion. His own harsh childhood in the rural South and the discrimination he faced at the University of Georgia reinforce his fervent dedication to fairness. Jones has hired more African American senior staff than his predecessors, as he says, because "I sought out the best candidates for the job."

However, like many high-profile Black and minority leaders, he continues to receive more than his fair share of hate mail. A staff member who viewed some of this vitriol said that reading the racist rants that come Jones's way "hurts my heart." Knowing Jones well, she went on to say that although these vicious attacks must distress him deeply, he displays "resilience, grace, and class."

"The Past Is Never Dead. It's Not Even Past."

"The past in never dead. It's not even past." These famous words from one of William Faulkner's characters in *Requiem for a Nun* (1951) are widely taken to describe the persistence of old beliefs, passions, interpretations, and misinterpretations of history indigenous to the American South.[9] Likewise, according to writer Michael Gorra, the durability of the past in the land where Jones grew to manhood contradicts the pious hope that time heals all wounds. Jones is all too familiar with the intransigence of inherited prejudices and the durability of cultural symbols. His experience with the enduring past helps explain why he manages conflicts with racial dimensions so well. It is far beyond the authority of Jones, or anyone in his position, to resolve these conflicts. Yet he does not allow them to define his presidency or derail whatever progress can be made.

Jones is adept at responding to instances of racial and ethnic discord when neither side sees any value in compromise. The misuse of Native imagery in the persona of Chief Illiniwek, the university's storied sports icon, and the campus hostility spurred by the Palestinian-Israeli conflict both illustrate two especially intractable scenarios. Ronald Heifetz, in his aptly named *Leadership Without Easy Answers* (1994), captures the complexity of situations like these, in which deeply held values remain obstacles to necessary change. In circumstances that admit no quick or easy solutions, Heifetz writes, "To make progress, not only must invention and action change circumstances to align with values, but the values themselves may also have to change. Leadership will consist not of answers or assured visions but of taking action to clarify values."[10] Jones approaches the aforementioned conflicts with the subtlety that Heifetz describes.

Chief Illiniwek was the mascot of several UIUC athletic teams from 1926 until 2007, when he was officially retired under pressure from Native American advocates and a threat from the NCAA to deny UIUC participation in postseason competition. It should be noted that the mascot's headdress resembled that of a Sioux chief, thus representing a tribe that never resided in or near Illinois. None of this has gone down easily with fans of Chief Illiniwek and his legacy as a colorful symbol of Illinois athletics.[11]

Jones chose language that would both lower the emotional temperature surrounding the issue and contextualize it as part of a larger quest for racial justice. He set up the Commission on Native Imagery: Healing and Reconciliation, which issued its report in May 2019 calling for a variety of initiatives ranging from in-state tuition for students of any federally recognized tribe to repatriation of Native American collections to tribal communities to increasing the number of Native American faculty members.[12]

By defining the problem in the more neutral language of Native American imagery rather than calling attention to the colorful—and to some, beloved—icon of Chief Illiniwek in full headdress, Jones created a broader context for understanding. The term *reconciliation* echoed the Truth and Reconciliation Commission founded by Nelson Mandela and Archbishop Desmond Tutu (a personal friend of Jones) at the end of apartheid in South Africa. Jones reframed the issue over the mascot in terms of respect for Native Americans and a commitment to justice.

Thus, in Heifetz's terms, he set the stage for the lengthy process of affirming underlying values that all sides in this multifaceted issue might eventually find some version of common ground.

With its significant populations of immigrants and descendants of immigrants from the Middle East, it is no surprise that conflicts over the rights of Palestinians and the government of Israel should erupt at UIUC. Students for Justice in Palestine (SJP) is a determined interest group that pressures student governments to advocate for divestment from companies that trade with Israel. Pro-Israel advocates interpret these efforts and the rhetoric of SJP as anti-Semitic. As a result, incidents of both anti-Semitic and anti-Muslim speech have fueled the debate.

Jones has taken positive action to increase dialogue and change policy to ameliorate these conflicts. Like his response to the conflict over Native American imagery, Jones's message to the university community following anti-Muslim media posts by a university employee focused attention on what ought to be underlying values. He repeated an earlier message that "we are at our best when we engage in dialogue that encompasses the widest range of views and voices," affirming that "the university stands against Islamophobia, racism, and religious intolerance of any kind . . . we can always decide to place respect and tolerance above anger and resentment."[13]

Pandemic Recovery

As plentiful as crises driven by racial animosity have been in Jones's tenure as chancellor, they have been far from the only problems facing Jones and the University of Illinois. The World Health Organization declared the COVID-19 outbreak in Wuhan, China, a global emergency at the end of January 2020. The outbreak morphed into a full-fledged pandemic just over six weeks later and impacted UIUC along with every other institution on the globe. This public health crisis also revealed the breadth of Jones's ability to make a difference well beyond issues of racial injustice.

Jones and his colleagues realized that a research powerhouse like UIUC had the capacity to go beyond mask wearing and social distancing to take positive actions to reduce the spread of the virus. Jones supported a remarkable team of scientists and public health experts in creating a saliva-based test for the virus. The UIUC test had the advantages of being quick, cheap, and accurate. At the peak of the pandemic, UIUC administered the test to thousands of University of Illinois students each week. The university's supercomputer was key to timely analysis of test results. (Typically, they ran about .5 percent positive for the virus.) This fast turnaround in aggregating test results enabled the university to spot outbreaks in something close to real time. The Illinois test became widely used across the United States.

Jones remains proud of UIUC's ability to display the practical intellectual power of a comprehensive research university. In describing the achievement of researchers across disciplines, he credits his academic colleagues in chemistry, physics, landscape architecture, student affairs, and other departments.[14]

Budget Stalemate

Seasoned administrators know that if a problem can be fixed with money, you don't have a problem. Unfortunately, Illinois did not have the money when Jones took office in 2016. For years, state leaders of both parties had papered over Illinois's unfunded pension obligations and other liabilities with deferrals and unrealistic revenue projections. A year before Jones arrived, Republican Governor Bruce Rauner vetoed the spending plan presented by the state legislature, thus initiating a budget impasse that persisted for over two years. In August 2017, the legislature ended the stalemate by overriding the governor's vetoes.[15]

Few other public universities outside of Illinois experienced the sharp reductions occasioned by the state of Illinois's fiscal gridlock. Combining judicious reductions in spending, limited draws from the university's reserves, and some revenue enhancements, the university came through the fiscal crisis largely intact. Most important, Jones did not allow limited funding to detract from an aggressive fundraising campaign and his dedication to investing substantial resources in programs for low-income students.

Signature Achievements

On top of managing crises, and when possible, wrenching some good from them, since arriving at his chancellor post, Jones has pursued a positive agenda. He has made the University of Illinois Urbana-Champaign more affordable for low-income students, launched an innovative new medical school, and completed a record-breaking fundraising campaign.

Once a talented student from an economically strained background himself, Jones harbors special sympathy for students like him. He champions two important student aid programs: the Illinois Commitment and the Illinois Promise. The Carle-Illinois College of Medicine, initiated under his predecessor Phyllis Wise, became a reality under Jones's leadership. The new school was built on the confluence of UIUC's strengths in engineering and biology.

The Campaign for Illinois

Despite early fears that philanthropy would diminish during the pandemic, major universities like Illinois, and higher education as a whole, experienced gains in their annual giving and special campaigns.[16] The well-oiled machine that raises external support for UIUC was no exception, as it exceeded its ambitious $2.5 billion fundraising goal by the end of the campaign in June 2022. Of course, an immense scaffolding of professionals continually undergirds UIUC's multibillion-dollar fundraising enterprise regardless of who is at the top. Yet faculty leaders and top staff members have confirmed that Jones's personal contacts and reassuring public persona during the throes of the pandemic underpinned the university's record-breaking campaign.

"We Knew We Would Be OK with Robert in Charge"

Asked to identify what set Jones above previous leaders who also faced daunting challenges, professors, deans, and trustees consistently refer to Jones's "calming presence" in "emotionally charged situations." They respect his credibility as a scientist who performed at the highest level at the top-ranked University of Minnesota. Yet they most consistently cite his personal qualities as his greatest strength and the source of his most important accomplishment: restoring confidence in UIUC. One colleague states that he is "easily the best chancellor in my fifteen years at the university." This broad confidence in Jones's leadership on the part of faculty senate members, deans, vice chancellors, and trustees is captured in these words: "I knew we would be OK with Robert in charge."

His upbringing in a sharecropping family, the hard work in the fields of the Jim Crow South, and his perseverance in the face of blatant discrimination in the groves of the academy combined to nurture critical personal traits that would serve him, and the University of Illinois, so well. Grace, courage, and confidence are the hallmarks of Jones's leadership style—all nurtured by his family upbringing on a poor farm in rural Georgia.

Segregation and Sharecropping

Jones was born in 1951 in a sharecropper's shack on fourteen acres of land in Terrell County, Georgia, that his family worked but did not own. A forlorn well housing in the middle of a cotton field is all that remains of the Jones home today. That well supplied water for the family, their few chickens, hogs, cows, and a large garden.

A mile of dirt road separated the family home from the nearest paved highway. Young Robert, his older brother, and younger sister walked the road morning and night during the school year amid warnings from their parents about the dangers of walking alone at night. Young Black men and women were known to disappear, their bodies sometimes to be discovered a day or so later on the side of the road.

Jones's family worked hard to make ends meet, and his first formal educational experience took place in a plantation school for Black children. He says with his characteristic smile, "I am probably the last of a generation of folks who can say they are truly children of sharecroppers."

Slavery by Another Name

Economics and pride eventually drove the Jones family from their home in the cotton fields. Jones's father felt that he was being cheated out of his fair portion of the sale of the crops he raised, a common experience among sharecroppers. Adding insult to injury, the landowner took advantage of his power to seize some of the hogs Jones's father had raised. For a sharecropper like Jones, there was no way to safely dispute the thievery, so he moved his family out of the fields and into the town of Dawson. Their new home was in the "colored" part of town, near the main street named for the Confederate hero Robert E. Lee.

"Sharecroppers had to take the planter's word that the planter was crediting the sharecropper with what he was due," writes Isabel Wilkerson in her insightful study of the Black experience in America. She observes that by the time the planter subtracted the *furnish*—that is, the seed, fertilizer, clothes, and food—there was often nothing coming to the sharecropper at settlement.[17] According to one of the many sharecroppers Wilkerson interviewed, the planter was "as much master as any master during slavery, because the sharecropper was bound to him, belonged to him, almost like a slave."[18]

Sadly, violence against the Jones family had already gone well beyond cheating them out of a fair distribution of the income from sales of crops. When RJ Jones, Robert's father, was six years old, a drunk white landowner shot and killed his father (Robert's grandfather) in his front yard on his daughter's wedding day. The family knew it would be useless, even dangerous, to summon the police. "You must be kidding" was the unspoken response when family members were asked years later if they had ever considered reporting the crime.[19]

"Segregation Now, Segregation Tomorrow, Segregation Forever"

The past was very much alive in Georgia and the surrounding states as Jones grew up. Early in his teen years, he would have heard George Wallace, the populist governor of neighboring Alabama, declaring in his inaugural speech on January 14, 1963, "Segregation now, segregation tomorrow, and segregation forever."[20]

One can only wonder at the immense gap between Jones's upbringing in the often violent, repressive South of the 1950s and 1960s and the experience of many white, middle-class men who have historically dominated the ranks of college presidents. Those raised in more comfortable, safer circumstances likely come to the turbulence of the current era with far less preparation than a person like Jones, who experienced injustice and adversity from his earliest years.

"Very, Very Proud People"

"We were the Beverly Hillbillies of sharecroppers," Jones says in explaining that his father owned a car, albeit one that had accrued thousands of miles under at least three earlier owners. The Jones family was relatively better off than most of their neighbors, and they shared the fruits of their ingenuity and hard work generously. When other Black families in the small town of Dawson needed to borrow a cup of sugar or a bag of flour or corn, they came to the Joneses' door.

His father and mother did whatever was necessary, Jones says, to feed their three children and keep them in presentable clothes. Recalling life with his parents, Jones says, "My mother and father were very, very proud people."

RJ Jones, the family patriarch, was a resourceful and tough-minded man. He was determined that his three children would break through the bonds of sharecropping poverty. With only a grade-school education, he realized that continuing studies beyond high school would provide the best means of escape from a life of debt, grinding poverty, and disrespect guaranteed by the sharecropping system.

Energetic and multitalented, RJ found ways to increase the family income beyond what sharecropping their fourteen acres of cotton could yield. He also bequeathed those virtues to his children, especially Robert. If he had been born white or somewhere other than plantation country, RJ might have become a prosperous entrepreneur or successful tradesman. Lacking a high school degree and living in a county dominated by white landowners, his options were limited.

Jones's father was adept at finding economic opportunities within the severe limits available to a Black man in rural Georgia. A largely self-taught mechanic, he could operate and repair essential farm machinery, including the big cotton harvesters and the trucks that hauled cotton, corn, and peanuts. He held an after-hours, part-time job cleaning a butcher shop. As mentioned earlier, for a time, RJ owned and operated a three hundred-head hog farm, which he shut down after it became clear that the local landowner would demand more than RJ felt he was due.

RJ Jones's children grew accustomed to hard work and plenty of it if they wanted the necessities of life. Besides working in other men's fields, the family grew much of their own food in their large garden. "Once it is over an acre," Jones says, "it's really not a garden anymore." They raised chickens, dug earthworms to sell to fishers, and worked part time in local stores whenever they could. Jones recalls one year when only a single bale of cotton came out of the fourteen acres they farmed. There were no Christmas presents that year.

"More than a Denomination or a Community of Worshipers"

Jones's parents were serious churchgoing people, though they lived what Jones describes as a mixed marriage. His parents were members of different congregations. Jones recalls that his mother, Mamie, attended the Jerusalem Missionary Baptist Church, while his father was a member of St. Luke's African Methodist Episcopal Church. Mamie rose each Sunday morning, praying and singing joyfully in anticipation of church services. RJ was equally devout in his AME congregation, a largely Southern denomination composed mostly of the descendants of slaves.

Prayer and worship permeated the Jones household. Each meal began with giving thanks. Hymns and prayers and gospel music and preaching on the radio were part of family life in the sharecropper's shack and then in the small house in Dawson. Years later in Minnesota, Jones's powerful tenor would be added to an award-winning choral group, Sounds of Blackness.

Religion remains a central part of Jones's life. His sister and her husband established and maintain a small church in Dawson where Clifford Browner, Jones's brother-in-law, is the minister. Jones contributes generously to the Master's House Baptist Church, whose motto is "Everybody is somebody in the eyes of God." Jones attends services there when he returns to Georgia.

Jones's commitment to racial justice and equality could only have been made stronger in the religious atmosphere of his home and family. Speaking particularly of the AME church to which Jones's father belonged, Richard Newman, an expert on African American church history, writes, "The Black Church is a freedom church. It's a vehicle for the civil rights struggle. It's a fellowship. So, in a sense it's more than a denomination or a community of worshipers. It's a way of looking at the world."[21]

The quiet fervor that Jones brings to opening the doors of the great university he leads to low-income students, including many people of color and other minorities, surely is informed by the religious atmosphere of his upbringing.

A Plantation School on Stilts

Jones's educational career began humbly enough in a plantation school built on stilts. As a five-year-old, he attended the Laing School for the children of Black farmworkers. Laing, the owner whose land the Jones family worked, had founded the school to offer a rudimentary education with secondhand books to the Black children whose families worked his fields. Precocious from an early age, Jones, still too young to officially enroll, sat in on the first-grade class his brother attended.

Later, Jones earned the nickname "the professor" in the segregated high school where he proved to be a skilled student. After graduating, he enrolled in Fort Valley State College, some seventy miles away in Peach County, Georgia. Originally named the Fort Valley High and Industrial

School, the college (now university) was established in 1895 as a school of agriculture and mechanic arts for Negroes. Fort Valley was Georgia's 1890 land-grant college, the first of four land-grant institutions where Jones was a student, faculty member, research scientist, or chancellor.

Jones has fond memories of his four years at Fort Valley, where he graduated in 1973 with a degree in agronomy and enjoyed the support of faculty mentors who became lifelong friends. On the advice of his professors, Jones applied to and was accepted at several graduate schools. He settled on the University of Georgia (UGA), another land-grant institution and a product of the original 1862 Morrill Act.

Rainy Nights in Georgia

There were many rainy nights in Athens when Jones enrolled in the University of Georgia in 1973.[22] Jones's welcome to Athens offered more N-words than friendly greetings, which meant that he would have to draw deeply from the reservoir of emotional support received at Fort Valley to see himself through a rough time in the land of the Georgia Dawgs.

In 1961, twelve years before Jones arrived as a first-year graduate student, a federal judge ordered the very reluctant university to admit its first African American students. Charlayne Hunter, later the eminent journalist Charlayne Hunter-Galt, and Hamilton Holmes, who went on to become a distinguished physician and professor at Emory University, were greeted by a mob of white students and members of the Ku Klux Klan. The mob torched Hunter's dormitory, confronted the late-arriving police with rocks and bricks, and hurled racial slurs—including the N-word—at both students. It was widely believed that Georgia's segregationist governor at the time, Ernest Vandiver Jr., delayed calling in the state police, thus allowing the mob violence to escalate.[23]

The university, after suspending Hunter and Holmes, had them escorted off the campus. A court later overturned their suspensions, and both graduated from Georgia, Hunter with a degree in journalism and Holmes with a bachelor of science.

The attitudes of many whites on the UGA campus remained hostile by the time Jones enrolled in 1973. "Georgia was still not prepared to provide a welcoming environment for African American students," is Jones's understated appraisal of UGA's lack of readiness and interest in helping this new cadre of students to succeed. Overloading African American students with course schedules heavier than those of their white contemporaries and liberal use of the N-word by faculty and staff as well as visitors to the campus underscored the racist culture characteristic of the school during Jones's two years there. "It was almost as if they let us in then intentionally set us up to fail," says Jones. One of the few Black students enrolled in graduate programs at Georgia, Jones felt that he was a target for racist professors as well as students who used the N-word to attempt to intimidate him personally. He refers to the experience in Georgia as one of the most painful episodes in his life and "one that still hurts."

"A Crucible Moment"

Jones describes a critical moment in Athens that captures the animosity he and others, including Hunter and Holmes, faced. It also illustrates his resilience in the face of blatant racism. Jones had torn his anterior cruciate ligament, commonly known as the ACL, in a pickup basketball game during his first year at Georgia. A strained ACL will repair itself in a few days if augmented with physical therapy. But Jones's ligament was not just strained; it was torn. Jones was on crutches—a difficult maneuver anywhere, but especially challenging on the hills of the Athens campus. A few days earlier, he had received a disappointing grade in a course taught, he felt, by a bigoted instructor who disapproved of African American students studying at Georgia. Passersby repeatedly called out the N-word.

Hobbling down one of the campus's hilly streets on crutches, Jones recalls that he was at the end of his rope. "For a moment lasting less than half an hour," he says, "I toyed with the idea of leaving Georgia." He had a standing job offer from the Soil Conservation Service (since 1994, the Natural Resources Conservation Service), a federal agency within the Department of Agriculture dedicated to soil preservation, improving water quality, and safeguarding other natural resources. It was a firm offer from a worthwhile organization in a much more welcoming environment than Georgia offered.

Instead of taking a secure job with a federal agency in liberal New York State, Jones chose to stick it out in what he saw as an openly racist university. "I don't know where it came from," he says, "but I could hear the voices of all those who mentored and supported me." In his mind, Jones summoned his independent-minded father, his teachers and mentors from Fort Valley, and Hunter and Holmes, who first broke through the Georgia color barrier a few years earlier. He recalled how so many people "sacrificed and went the extra mile to encourage me to pursue my education."

In a moment of clarity—a moment that has repeated itself when he has faced other serious challenges—Jones determined that he and he alone would write his story. "I could hear the voices of displeasure if I allowed someone else to determine my destiny." In Jones's mind, that destiny meant seeking a doctorate, if not at Georgia, then at a more welcoming university. Turning in this lonely moment to his African American forbears, his family, and his contemporary mentors for strength and inspiration, Jones experienced what David Brooks describes as "a crucible moment."[24]

Despite taking some courses from highly competent and fair-minded professors, Jones had no intention of staying at UGA after his two-year struggle to a master's degree. A decidedly positive experience awaited him at the University of Missouri, where one of the best-known plant physiologists in the country recruited Jones for the doctoral program. Jones considers his time at the University of Missouri as a game changer for his career as an authentic scientist, not merely an African American scientist.

Jones found the Columbia campus largely free of the overt racism that punctuated his experience in Georgia. Although racial conflicts have erupted periodically at Mizzou, Jones's studies of plant physiology with top professors dominated his experience there. He completed his coursework in two years before engaging in his doctoral research project, which in turn opened the doors to the University of Minnesota.

"Environmental Perturbations"

Jones flourished as a scientist and an academic leader in the welcoming environment of Minnesota. His curiosity about the "environmental perturbations" governing plant growth drove Jones and his research team to solve a problem plaguing Minnesota corn farmers: what explained the difference between highly productive fields and those that failed to fully mature?

"I hooked up a bunch of corn plants in IV bags," Jones explains, in order to learn about the effects of rising temperatures caused by global warming. Jones tells people that growing corn is akin to child-rearing. With the right environment, they will reach a healthy maturity along a discernable "molecular physiological pathway." Whatever the analogies between plant and human growth, Minnesota provided a stimulating academic environment for Jones to come into his own as a scientist. He ascended from assistant professor in 1978 to full professor a decade later.

Although Jones felt productive in his professional life at the Twin Cities campus, as one of the few African Americans in his field, he also experienced environmental perturbations of his own. His discovery of the choral group Sounds of Blackness changed all that. Jones came from a family of gifted vocalists, and as such, he developed a powerful tenor voice. Jones's sister says of her talented brother, "He has music in his blood."

Sounds of Blackness, originally a Macalester College choral group, performed a varied repertoire, but always, according to Jones, served up "music with a message." In addition to numerous other awards, Sounds of Blackness has earned three Grammy Awards, four Stellar Awards, and an Emmy nomination. Jones's successful audition in 1980 led to his thirty-year membership in Sounds. His association with the group and the Black community surrounding it, says Jones, "anchored me as an individual."

Five years after his arrival in Minnesota, Jones was asked to serve in a program that provided scholarships to promising Black South Africans to study at US universities. What began as a two-year assignment scheduled for a few weeks each summer lasted an entire decade. It also began a close relationship with Archbishop Desmond Tutu, which endured until Tutu's passing in 2021.

During his first visit to meet with Tutu and administer the scholarship program, Jones returned to his hotel room to discover that his belongings were not as he had left them. As it turned out, Jones and his new friend, Tutu, were being spied on by the dreaded South African police, the group charged with enforcing apartheid. When Jones expressed his concerns, Tutu told him, "You are in South Africa now."

"An Accidental Leader"

Well into Jones's research stint as an associate professor with a laboratory of his own, University of Minnesota President Ken Keller asked Jones to take on an additional assignment as the director of a faculty mentorship program. One of the earliest programs of its type, the mentorship program was designed to support high-ability students of color. It continues to this day. The mentorship program was Jones's first administrative appointment. It was not to be his last.

Though Jones went on to accept subsequent administrative assignments, his heart remained with his research and his laboratory. Nevertheless, after decades researching how to grow healthier, more plentiful corn, Jones was asked to leave the laboratory he loved to join the senior administration of the University of Minnesota. "I am an introvert by nature," he says, "but all my life people saw in me things I did not see in myself." No one formally groomed Jones for a major university presidency, but clearly, Minnesota's president appreciated Jones's potential for leadership beyond the laboratory. One of his mentors in Minnesota says that Jones never actively sought higher positions, but he accepted them when offered, "almost out of a sense of duty." Jones may have been "an accidental leader" as another observer says, but the opportunities thrust upon him in Minnesota were ideal preparation for heading a modern research university.

By 2004, Jones had risen through a dozen positions and ad hoc assignments to become the university system's senior vice president for academic administration. This august title carried responsibility for oversight of the educational and research functions of the main campus, four coordinate campuses, extension, information technology, human resources, equity and diversity, and all international programs. For the eight years that Jones served as the chief operating officer of the university, he managed the internal functions of the institution so that the presidents he reported to could represent the outward-facing side of the university.

Few in the Minnesota hierarchy, including Jones himself, ever expected him to leave. Jones was not actively seeking a presidency, but one found him. Earlier in his career, as Jones was pulled away from his laboratory for administrative assignments, his friend Bishop Tutu suggested that perhaps "God has other plans for you."

Beginning in 2013, Jones served as the president of the University of Albany, a rising research-intensive university in the State University of New York (SUNY) system. Jones is credited with major achievements in Albany, including instituting the College of Engineering and Applied Sciences and securing two of the largest gifts in the university's history. However, agronomy is not among the 150 or so graduate programs offered at the University at Albany. And the politics surrounding the university in the state capital, where the subsequently deposed governor exercised great influence, was not entirely to Jones's liking.

By contrast, UIUC is the undisputed flagship of the Illinois system. It is truly a research powerhouse with strong programs in Jones's own field of plant science. Thus, when the search committee in Illinois tendered one nominee to be chancellor to Tim Killeen, president of the University of Illinois system, Killeen offered, and Jones accepted the position.

Resilience, Grace, and Class

Jones's reputation for exceptional leadership, like the other figures profiled in this book, rests on several interlocking bodies of evidence. Meeting challenges seems to come naturally to Jones. He joined the University of Illinois amid a severe budget crisis following years of scandals that derailed his two predecessors. He managed the budget problems without causing permanent wounds, and in so doing, helped restore credibility to the office of chancellor. Despite the disruptions that consume all the attention of many other leaders, Jones has delivered on several initiatives that would be counted as major accomplishments even in a more stable time.

In a cruel—but in some ways fortunate—irony, the challenging circumstances surrounding Jones's early years also engendered strengths that would prepare him well for the challenges of academic leadership. A resourceful and self-sufficient father, strong family bonds, the encouragement of teachers and mentors, the grit to persist in the face of adversity, and compassion for others from fraught backgrounds and a commitment to empower them were all gifts of his upbringing. These attitudes and his natural talents would serve him and the University of Illinois well some four decades later. They are also among the traits most needed by all college leaders in today's conflict-ridden environment.

CHAPTER 7

Kwang-Wu Kim
The College for Creatives

On an otherwise pleasant morning on the South Side of Chicago, a gang of Blackstone Rangers accosted a short, chubby Korean American a few blocks from his home. Dr. Kwang-Wu Kim, a young teen at the time, doesn't recall the exact date, but the incident is etched in his memory. He may have been heading toward a rehearsal with the Chicago Children's Choir or off to meet his piano teacher, the "little Korean lady" as he describes her, or simply running an errand. Whatever his destination, he had to pass through the gang's checkpoint first. The Rangers dominated crime and inspired fear on the streets surrounding the acclaimed University of Chicago, where Kim's parents were graduate students. At a few inches over five feet with a rounded physique, Kim was no physical match for the older boys. Few Asian American families lived on the South Side in those days. Kim was on his own.

Kim sensed that submissive behavior was unlikely to placate this tough crew. The gang made it clear that he would suffer a beating or worse. "Well," he announced, "if it takes this many of you to beat up one of me, go ahead." The unexpectedly adult voice and clever logic from the mouth of a diminutive boy might have amused the young toughs—or confused them. In any event, they let him go on his way. Kim says that he probably "freaked out" the gang. "After that, I never had any problems with gangs," he says. "I think the word spread that this little fat boy was strange."

Defying expectations became a hallmark of Kim's life and career, just as it still characterizes his leadership of Columbia College Chicago, where he became president in 2013. This school for creatives is located a few miles north of the neighborhood where Kim grew up. Countering intentions—whether threats from a street gang, the plans his Korean-born parents had for their talented son, or even his own career goals—has proven to be a recurring facet of Kim's life. His story is the journey of a man seeking to establish his sense of self as an individual, a performer, and a leader. Rejecting the limits imposed by others, realizing his own potential, and learning how to represent himself before diverse audiences are prominent goals in Kim's life. They also represent his vision for the students at the college he has led for a decade.

There is a paradoxical rhythm to Kim's development as a leader. Although his parents wanted Kim to pursue a traditional profession such as medicine or law, as many Korean immigrant parents do, he decided to forge his own career path. However, he embraces his Korean heritage in many other ways. His upbringing in a Korean American family shaped his sense of who he is, and the Korean values given to him by his parents also contribute mightily to his success as a college president.

Kim devoted years of his life to learning classical music performance at the most elite schools in the country. Yet he believes he found his true calling at an urban college with a welcoming admissions policy. His leadership style incorporates traits bequeathed by his Asian culture, habits formed by years of disciplined training in preparation for concert-level performance, and two decades of apprenticeship in enabling arts and education organizations to prosper in a changing marketplace.

Too Smart To Be a President

Kim is an unlikely college president, if for no other reason than there are so few Asian American college or university presidents. The American Council on Education's 2017 report on the presidency notes that in 2016, about 2.3 percent of college presidents represented themselves as Asian American.[1] This modest proportion contrasts with the numbers of Asian Americans in the total population, their enrollment in colleges and universities, and their degree attainment. Asian Americans are the fastest-growing racial or ethnic group in the country, totaling over 22 million, or about 6 percent of the population in 2020.[2] Asian American students represent over 7 percent of the national student population and are generally "over enrolled" at more elite and selective institutions.[3]

The dearth of presidents of Asian heritage is puzzling. Asian Americans are often characterized as "model minorities," who by dint of hard work succeed in realizing high social status and substantial income. Indeed, if talent and achievement were truly dominant criteria in selecting presidents, there would be many more Asian Americans in the president's office. Asians have more formal education than most Americans, judging by their accumulation of college and graduate degrees.[4] Asian American families also enjoy higher average incomes and have accrued greater wealth than typical Americans.[5]

Why then would search firms, committees, and boards of trustees be unable or unwilling to recruit and hire candidates from this pool of talented, high-achieving individuals? The truths and contradictions in the "model minority" construct provide part of the answer. In *Breaking the Bamboo Ceiling*,[6] Jane Hyun offers a guide for Asians striving to climb to the pinnacle of the corporate hierarchy. Her work also serves as a useful primer for non-Asians seeking to appreciate the special strengths Asians bring to organizations fortunate enough to hire them.

Among the characteristic (but by no means universal) traits embodied by Asian Americans, Hyun lists self-control and discipline, obedience to authority, humility, and a preference for collective decision-making. Hyun sees the centuries of Confucian teachings across Asia as a significant source of these traits shared by many in the Asian diaspora. She highlights a preference for "harmony and decorum" in human interactions,[7] especially in superior–subordinate relationships. She contrasts these behaviors with what have often become expected characteristics of executive behavior, including spontaneity, a willingness to question authority, self-promotion, and tough, individualistic, authoritative leadership.[8]

Asian Americans are often stereotyped as model minorities, which implies that they achieve success through unrelenting hard work, a knack for quantitative reasoning, and make-no-waves behavior. They make great analysts, technicians, and support staff, according to this stereotype, but are ill-suited for the rigors of the corporate C-suite or a college president's office. A mix of Asian and Western strengths, with some toning down of the exaggerations associated with the Western model and emphasizing the advantages of the Asian, would potentially yield an executive ensemble well equipped to lead in today's complex, multicultural world.

Kim's life story both reflects and transcends the "model minority" archetype. Like others considered members of a "model minority," Kim has been discriminated against for being "too smart" for the executive work of a college president. However, his leadership at Columbia College and elsewhere reveals a repertoire of talent richer and more complex than the confines of the Asian stereotype. Kim is highly intelligent to be sure, but as his success at revitalizing Columbia shows, he possesses other important strengths. One of these is the street savvy to thrive in a city like Chicago and convert a languishing art school for so-called misfits into a thriving environment for creatives.

A College for Creative Misfits

How did a man with a distinctly Korean name, who had served as dean of a school within a large public university in a faraway state, and had a less than fully satisfying presidency at a small school become the chief executive of Columbia College Chicago? Part of the answer lies in Kim's ability to impress the search committee with his energy and unique blend of talents acquired over his varied career. But his talents would not have mattered much without the open-minded and experienced board members who led the search.

"City of Big Shoulders," Carl Sandburg's famous moniker for Chicago, conveys a sense of the temperament of Columbia's trustees: smart, tough, successful Chicagoans steeped in the competitive worlds of business and the arts. They are astute judges of character as well, as evidenced by their selection of Kim.

"Diversity was never a problem for us," a trustee who served on the search committee says. Kim's predecessor was African American. The board itself is as diverse as the "second city." The trustee adds, "Many of our students would be considered misfits" in the mainstream of American education. It stands to reason that Columbia's search committee would be looking for a leader with an unconventional background "who could relate to our nontraditional students and persuade their parents that the college was a good choice."

More often than not, Columbia's students defy their parents' hopes that they will choose a practical degree leading to secure, steady employment. Like Kim in his early years, they seek to develop their own creativity while pursuing a career doing what they love most. Their aspirations and the challenges they need to overcome both at home and in society mirror those of the man who would become their new president.

Kim's academic background at Yale and the Peabody Conservatory at Johns Hopkins University guaranteed his credibility with the Columbia faculty. Being born and raised in Chicago was certainly a plus. Most important, though, his vision seemed to fit this college that celebrates its misfits, who Kim promptly recast as creatives.

Leading a College for Creatives

Columbia's search committee and then its board of trustees voted unanimously in favor of Kim as their new president in 2013. As impressive as his credentials were, they knew that, as with any presidential choice, they were taking a chance. In addition to his impeccable academic credentials, did Kim have the grit to lead this rough-around-the-edges college in downtown Chicago?

Kim had served as dean of the Herberger Institute for Design and the Arts at Arizona State University before moving back to Chicago. The contrasts between Arizona State and Columbia College could hardly have been more striking. Arizona State was well on its way to national preeminencc as an innovative public university under the leadership of its celebrated president Michael Crow. Yet it was a *public university*, sustained in part by state funding. And it was big. The school had an enrollment of 60,000 students when Kim arrived. How ready would he be to lead a tuition-dependent school with a tenth of Arizona State's enrollment and no state subsidy?

Kim's prior chief executive experience did not line up precisely with a school like Columbia either. It consisted of leading a small choral society in Texas and a small music school in Massachusetts. In Arizona, he carried out orders instead of issuing them. Kim was an attractive candidate but hiring him for the beleaguered college was still something of a gamble.

A College Adrift

Columbia was a college in trouble when Kim arrived. Enrollments were falling, budgets were out of balance, and a unionized faculty operated chronically at odds with the administration. Divided governance at the board and presidential levels also bedeviled the school. The board chair had styled himself as a co-president in the midst of an uneasy relationship with the actual president, who had been in office for more than a decade. While the leadership model combined the talents of two otherwise capable people, it proved dysfunctional for the work of reviving a school in decline.

Kim inherited three important assets along with these challenges. A remarkable new board chair, Richard Kephart, was one. Highly regarded in Chicago's arts and finance circles, Kephart proved to be a wise and energetic chair who had no need or intention of being co-president.

A second asset provided Kim with the financial resources to set the college on a positive course. In lieu of stock market investments that make up most college endowments, Kephart and other savvy trustees had amassed a lucrative inventory of real estate in the heart of downtown Chicago, acquired during a periodic slump in prices. The buildings proved to be the equivalent of an endowment, which would fund what the college called the "big gamble": a high-tuition, high-aid enrollment strategy designed to raise enrollment to a permanently higher plateau.

The college's progressive culture and history of welcoming a diverse student body represented the third important asset. Founded in 1890, the school that became Columbia attracted urban students of multiple races, ethnicities, and gender identities. Currently, about half of the students are of color, and an estimated 30 percent are members of the LGBTQ community.

Kim moved quickly to begin the turnaround. He embraced the advantages of his resourceful board of trustees, recruited a talented senior team who bought into Columbia's urban mission, and commenced the process of repositioning Columbia as a haven for creatives. Along the way, he managed the business of the enterprise to ensure the college's future.

A Board That Supports and Challenges

Making the most of a board replete with high-achieving Type A personalities requires a president with those same traits, plus the humility to recognize that he works for the board. A board that is clever enough to fund an endowment out of downtown property bought at bargain-basement prices would not tolerate anything less than an equally shrewd performance from its chief executive.

Though Kim's board is satisfied with his performance, its members regularly seek external appraisals and challenge him to achieve more. In these days of rapid presidential turnover, maintaining board confidence is something of an achievement in itself. That Columbia's board continues to extend Kim's contract is proof of this achievement.

A Talented and Diverse Team

Kim has assembled, supported, and occasionally pruned a brainy multicultural cabinet that includes his close advisors and the officers responsible for the academic, fiscal, and philanthropic goals of the college. One of his veteran advisors likened Kim's style of team leadership to that of an orchestra conductor: he expects top performance of each member of the team while also insisting that they work collaboratively. The cabinet is diverse across many racial, ethnic, and gender categories. Not surprisingly, Kim treasures variety in thought as well as experience. He recruits members who are street-smart, assertive, and unconventional, much like Kim and the students Columbia attracts.

Crisis Leadership

"The aftermath of a war zone" is how one observer described the destruction on Wabash Avenue and the area surrounding Columbia College following the demonstrations over the murder of George Floyd in Minneapolis in the summer of 2020. Kim ensured that the campus was as secure as it could be during the turbulent three days of rioting. He authorized protection for Columbia's most vulnerable building, a glass-walled student center at the epicenter of the violent demonstrations. It survived unscathed.

Kim may well have drawn strength from his mother during this time as he recalled hearing her account of her family's experiences amid the destruction of Seoul, Korea, in the 1950s.

A Practical Vision for Creatives

Kim's vision for Columbia and its students reads like a manifesto for a college committed to serving creatives in a diverse society. Kim has intensified Columbia's tradition of embracing diversity, equity, and inclusion. Diversity in the broadest terms has been one of Kim's priorities since long before it became a staple in college plans across the country. Like other presidents profiled in this book, Kim sets forth a vision for his college that offers striking parallels with his own circuitous journey as a creative performer.

Kim's most recent position paper addressed to the college and board commits Columbia to emphasizing "creative practice," instilling a "sense of agency" in its students and "discovering one's authentic voice" to navigate today's world. It calls upon students to "become authors of the culture of their times," which is also the centerpiece of the college's mission statement. He exhorts his colleagues to empower students to "understand, experience, and interrogate different viewpoints, narratives, and histories, and to recognize that difference has historically been suppressed and devalued in many fields of creative practice."[9]

Kim's emphasis on career preparation likely stems from his own struggles to find meaningful work that pays adequately. Practicality is part of Columbia's vision. Kim's admonition that "it is very hard to enjoy a meaningful life without a decent job" reflects his own sometimes painful experience. The part of his vision statement addressed to faculty and students alike asserts that "professional success almost always rests on the ability to put forward a cogent argument, pitch an idea or product, or sell a concept." Kim reinforces this idea of convincing the world of the tangible value of what one offers it by adding that "the key is the ability to frame an idea, develop a coherent narrative, and find optimal ways to tell a story." The first of eight pieces of advice in Kim's annual address to graduates is "show up on time."

"The Big Gamble"

Satisfied that the gamble of hiring Kim in the first place has paid off, the board has embarked on a second big bet. "Enrollment is our major concern," says a longtime trustee who served on the search committee that hired Kim. As with every independent college serving low-income students in a competitive marketplace, market-oriented leadership is critical. Under Kim's leadership, the college had experienced enrollment growth and the consequent budget surpluses up until the pandemic erupted in 2020.

Recognizing that COVID-19 and its variants will influence the market for colleges and universities for the foreseeable future, Kim and the board embarked on what they informally describe as the "big gamble." To achieve a sustainable level of enrollment and operating income, the college "harvested some of our unneeded real estate acquired in earlier years" to fund financial aid while at the same time raising tuition by 10 percent. The goal is to reach a continuing enrollment of 8,500 students, which has been deemed a financially sustainable plateau. Before the pandemic, the college experienced a 34 percent increase in first-year enrollment and the first head count increase in over a decade. First-year enrollments are again on the upswing—a key achievement that runs counter to downward trends nationally. Although it is too soon to declare victory, the second "big gamble" looks promising.

How did this Yale graduate trained to become a concert pianist develop the skills to redeem a gritty arts college in downtown Chicago? The answer begins in a Korean American home on the South Side.

A Formidable Korean Mother

Kim's mother, Sung Ok Kim, was the first and most influential of the several women whom Kim describes as "angels" in his life. As a young woman, she survived the waves of destruction of Seoul during successive attacks by opposing forces on the Korean peninsula. Early in the war, the invading North Korean troops commandeered her family home. She was forced to witness summary executions in the courtyard. Her well-to-do family "lost everything" in the violent pattern of advance, repulse, and retreat that defined the Korean War from 1950 to the armistice in 1953.[10]

This formidable woman was a force to be reckoned with. Kim says, "She literally knew no fear." She arrived in the United States in 1954, following her husband who had immigrated a few years earlier. After pursuing graduate work at the University of Chicago, she rose to be the first Asian-born senior administrator in the Chicago school system. She was as unsparing in her aspirations for her first-born child as she was for herself. Kim's name (Kwang-Wu) means "light of the universe." Astronomical expectations for her son's future started at birth.

In characteristic Korean fashion, Kim's maternal grandmother soon joined the family to help raise Kim and his sister, who was three years younger. The Korean family values ingrained in Kim and his sister from their earliest years were hard work, a passion for advanced education in fields with a practical purpose, the pursuit of a high-status occupation, and abiding respect for their distinctly Korean heritage and identity.

High Expectations

Being a dutiful son was a profound obligation in Kim's household. His parents expected him to apply his own remarkable intelligence to pursuing a prestigious and well-compensated career. Engineering, law, or medicine were the right occupations. Following suit, Kim's sister became a physician.

Much to his parents' dismay, however, Kim pursued the arts from an early age. His family tells the story about how a piano would attract young Kim like a powerful magnet. He would run toward it and immediately begin playing. Music might be fine as a hobby in the minds of his parents, Kim says, but a career in the arts was out of the question. Such a path represented "the lowest of the low," Kim notes. It was "on a par with being an entertainer—or even a prostitute." Imagine the concern of parents who named their son "light of the universe" when they learned that he was choosing what to them was a distinctly terrestrial career.

Kim's dedication at Columbia to the career success of his students certainly owes much to his mother's realism. Sometime in his teens, he surprised her by saying that he might like to become an actor instead of a musician. She replied with words to the effect that if he did so, he should also reconcile himself to life as "the Chinese busboy earning his living in the kitchen." Following this conversation, Kim chose not to pursue an acting career.

Success in their adopted country was always important in the Kim household. But equally so was respect for their Korean heritage. When Kim and his sister were in grade school, their mother took them for a monthlong visit to their cultural homeland. Kim describes this visit to Korea as transformative. He realized that he was no longer just another American teen in the diverse South Side; he was *Korean*. "If you ever think you are white," his mother told him, "look in the mirror" to see how others see you. Although he defied his parents' career expectations, Kim's sense of himself as a Korean American remains a core element of his identity.[11]

Conflict with His Cultural Heritage

Growing up in Hyde Park on Chicago's South Side prepared Kim for the multiracial and multilingual world he was to inhabit. Kim attended public schools then highly regarded for their ethnic diversity as well as their superior programs in art and music. As a youngster, Kim auditioned for the Chicago Children's Choir. The choir, "built on the premise of extreme inclusivity," recruited talented young people from each of the city's diverse communities. Kim quickly became the choir's star apprentice.

Kim's parents were proud of the accomplishments of their bright child, though not wholly comfortable with his taste for the arts. Likewise, Kim often felt conflicted in his efforts to reconcile his parents' expectations with his own emerging identity as a performing artist. "I felt at odds with my own cultural history because it didn't seem capable of embracing something that was so important to me," he recalls.

A self-identified teacher's pet, Kim was nevertheless one of the smartest kids in his class, and when he was accepted to Yale in 1975, his father and mother were pleased. He would graduate in 1980 after five years, having taken a year off during his sophomore and junior years. His proud parents were less than euphoric, however, when after switching majors seven or eight times, he finally opted to concentrate in philosophy. In addition to keeping up with his academic work, Kim practiced playing the piano ten or more hours a day. As much as he enjoyed immersing himself in the world of ideas embodied in Yale's philosophy curriculum, his enduring passion was music. But he knew that majoring in music would create a lifelong "conflict with my cultural heritage." When it came time for graduate studies, Kim's father agreed to fund law school. But if he pursued a degree in music, Kim would be on his own.

A Multicultural Upbringing

Kim credits growing up in Hyde Park, his experience with the Chicago Public Schools, and years in the Children's Choir with fostering his interest in the arts. His upbringing also fortified his comfort with individuals from various ethnic backgrounds. In processing his encounter with the Blackstone Rangers, Kim refused to frame it as a racial conflict. Instead, he describes it as one of "the tense moments" when he learned to think through fraught situations without anxiety. This mentality would serve Kim well in his life and career, especially years later during the riots in Chicago ignited by the murder of George Floyd.

Similar to his formative childhood experiences, at Yale, Kim was able to continue building relationships with members of the African American community. Yale's lottery system for assigning first-year students to dormitories placed Kim with a group of African American students. The only Asian in the group and one of relatively few at Yale then, Kim recalls how remarkable it was "to attend this elite white institution surrounded not by Asians but African Americans." These experiences with diverse classmates, as well as his growing up in a racially rich Chicago, prepared Kim well for advancing a diversity agenda at Columbia College.

A Classical Pianist

A full-ride scholarship to the Peabody Conservatory of Music at Johns Hopkins University solved Kim's post-Yale financial dilemma. He quickly became one of Peabody's stars. Kim studied with the famous Leon Fleisher then, and now, thanks to his recordings available in multiple media, he is regarded as among the foremost American classical pianists. Kim and Fleisher collaborated with renowned cellist Yo-Yo Ma in the filming of a master class. Fleisher played the teacher and Kim the precocious student. Kim developed a close relationship with the great pianist, eventually becoming his assistant.

Kim seemed to be on a trajectory to the highest levels of artistic performance. He enjoyed a close relationship with the enormously influential Fleisher. He won a handsome scholarship that funded his remaining graduate studies. He was widely regarded as among the most talented Peabody students. A self-assured performer, Kim expected that he would showcase his talents on the world's most prestigious stages.

Then, sometime in his later twenties, Kim discovered that "suddenly, things were not so easy."

"A Very, Very Dark Time"

"It looked like I was really going to break through into some kind of significant performing career," Kim recalls. Yet the breakthrough never came. Although he performed in several elite venues, the most desired invitations arrived less often. Other students—many with lesser credentials than Kim's—were getting the teaching jobs Kim aspired to. With more money going out than coming in, he was forced to seek financial support from his hard-working parents. It looked like their skepticism over a career in music was well founded. He gradually arrived at the painful realization that he was not going to achieve the heights of success as a concert pianist. Being the smartest kid in the room and working harder than anyone else was simply not going to be enough.

Why did a career on the concert stage elude him? Kim believes that he started serious training too late. His early training came under the tutelage of a piano teacher hired by his mother. Although music was his first love at Yale, he was forced to divide his piano time first with premed studies and then with philosophy. No amount of talent or hard work could compensate for starting relatively late in life to achieve the thousands of hours at the piano needed to become a pianist of the top rank.[12]

Kim's wilderness years persisted for nearly a decade from his later twenties to mid-thirties. The self-described very cocky young man was slowly coming to terms with a stark reality. Now, the wunderkind, the smartest in his class, the Yale graduate, and the student chosen to assist the master found his career stalled. In what he has described as "a very, very dark time," Kim needed to find a way to make a living outside of his chosen field.

Ironically, this nadir became the beginning of his ascent to the top levels of performance on another stage: the presidency.

Shedding the "Illusion of Superiority"

On the verge of accepting a teaching job on the West Coast, Kim received an invitation to become artistic director of the El Paso Choral

Society. Although Kim's only choral experience was with the Chicago Children's Choir over thirty years earlier, he had performed in El Paso, where board members were impressed with his virtuosity and engaging style. This inflection point in his career trajectory occurred when he was thirty-five years old.

El Paso, named for the pass where the Rio Grande descends from the Rockies to the great West Texas plain, would also become an important passage for Kim. There, he was to discover that he had a lot to learn about reaching audiences outside of classical music. "For starters," Kim recalls, "I had to shed the illusion of superiority." That lesson in humility would come in the delight he inspired among a class of fourth graders.

As artistic director, Kim's job was to build an audience from the largely Hispanic El Paso community, entice regional schools to host choral programs, raise money from affluent West Texas patrons, and erase the operating deficit he had inherited. Kim says that restoring the Choral Society to financial health is where he learned the importance of operations and finance in securing the survival of income-dependent organizations.

He learned something equally valuable as well: how to appreciate an audience and reach its members through attention to their culture and interests. He tells the story of appearing at a rural grade-school classroom filled with Hispanic kids, none of whom spoke English. Kim was to introduce the cellist then play the piano. No piano was available. Momentarily outraged when the children began to laugh at the huge stringed instrument that made strange noises, Kim suddenly realized that they were laughing with delight. "It felt like a hand touched my head," he says. "I realized my reaction was the sign of an angry, big-headed jerk." Witnessing the joy in the eyes of the children on hearing music they had never heard before was a revelation to Kim. He understood that his role in the art world could be much broader than solo performance before a sophisticated audience.

During his eight years in El Paso, Kim advanced the Choral Society from a troubled, deficit-ridden, white-dominated organization to a vibrant, diverse, community-centered enterprise. He and his team expanded the Choral Society from a community chamber chorus into a producer and presenter of chamber music whose work was highlighted by its internationally recognized chamber music festival.

As much as he loved the El Paso community and the respected position of the Choral Society within it, Kim felt that he had achieved his major goals for the organization. He let it be known that he was open to other opportunities.

"Places Attempting to Reinvent Themselves"

The Longy School of Music, a respected but challenged community music school in Cambridge, Massachusetts, was seeking to reposition itself as a more exclusive conservatory. The Longy board saw in Kim a candidate with the right combination of credentials and experience for the challenges they faced. He assumed the Longy presidency in 2001 and served until 2006. An accomplished pianist with an elite academic and musical background and the practical skills to turn around a beleaguered school, Kim impressed them with his knowledge of what needed to be done. Kim says of his many leadership posts, including Longy, "I seem to find myself in places attempting to reinvent themselves."

Facing serious competition from the better-known and much larger Berklee College of Music as well as the prestigious New England Conservatory of Music, Longy was suffering in a decidedly brand-conscious market. The task of transforming a community-centered music school into a conservatory whose reputation was based, in part, on whom it excluded would prove to be no easy task. As is often the case with a board that includes many alumni, trustees endorsed the idea of the more elite model but were not prepared to counter the opposition elicited by the proposed changes. The faculty felt that the changes Kim was asked to lead amounted to a repudiation of their credentials and commitment to serving the community.

Overall, Kim's experience at Longy was not a happy one. He reinvigorated a stalled capital campaign, improved facilities, refurbished the aging campus, and engineered curricular change. He developed some warm relationships with individual trustees and colleagues as well. However, his memories of the school are marred by several examples of strident racism and stubborn determination of some faculty and other stakeholders to oppose the changes he had been hired to produce.

He admits that he underestimated the trenchant opposition from faculty and the enduring fact that for all their rhetoric, many on the board were not committed to supporting change. Kim feels that his relationship with the board never achieved solid footing. While he focused on his change agenda and the faculty's role in it, he admits, "I should have been equally attentive to the board I inherited."

Painful as these lessons were, they prepared Kim to lead unpopular change in his next post as dean of a college of art at Arizona State University in 2006.

"Michael and I Have Decided"

Kim was pleased when President Michael Crow invited him to become dean of the Herberger Institute for Design and the Arts. If Arizona State represented a step down in title, Crow's invitation represented a step up in building Kim's experience in a public research university whose size and complexity dwarfed his earlier posts. With over 60,000 students and three sizeable campuses, at the time Kim was hired, Arizona represented a dramatic change from the world of the Choral Society and Longy. And he was hired by the celebrated Michael Crow, the avatar of a fresh model aspiring to combine high access with academic quality as described in his aptly titled book *Designing the New American University*.[13] Although their styles differed, Crow's vision of merging egalitarian values with a commitment to academic excellence mirrored Kim's. Crow's decisive exercise of leadership became one of Kim's hallmarks as well.

Kim was happy to return to the Southwest after his stint in Cambridge, but his timing was less than perfect. He arrived on the eve of the Great Recession, the consequences of which thrust upon him several unanticipated opportunities to excel as it did across all of higher education. The first wave of the Great Recession forced a 10 percent budget reduction midyear for all of Arizona State's deans and major units. More cuts soon followed.

Kim's challenges compounded when the provost informed him in 2009 that "Michael and I have decided" that the art and design programs would be merged, and there would be less funding than in the past. Kim was to be dean of the merged entity. The faculty members of both colleges were outraged. Caught between the angry professors (most of whom were tenured) and nonnegotiable orders from Crow and his provost to merge, the new dean was faced with a singularly difficult problem, albeit no less of one than he had faced in his earlier efforts to introduce unwelcome change.

Caught between the mandate from on high and his own mostly tenured faculty, Kim needed to exercise a different mode of leadership. He called the faculty together, saying, "Look, none of us asked for this merger. And it is not going to change. What you think of me doesn't matter. What does matter is that we are not going to allow this merger to affect our students' education." Disgruntled as they may have been, Kim says, his colleagues rose to the occasion and kept their unhappiness largely outside their classrooms and studios.

End of All His Exploring

T. S. Eliot's lovely poem "Little Gidding" reads in part "and the end of all our exploring / will be to arrive where we started / and know the place for the first time."[14] Kim's return to Chicago following his circuitous journey echoes the spirit of "Little Gidding." His explorations were cultural, geographic, and very personal as well.

Kim's inner journey is inseparable from his external one. Its central themes are his evolving relationship with his Korean heritage, which began with a partial rejection only to mature into a lifelong embrace. Kim flourished personally and professionally as he forged expectations of himself built on his family's Korean values. He gradually realized that as talented and dedicated to unrelenting hard work as he might be, he would not attain fortune and fame as a classical pianist. Paradoxically, this sense of failure stirred the metamorphosis that led to his superior performance as a leader of institutions of higher education. The sum of his experiences turned an unlikely president into one ideally suited to advancing Chicago's school for creatives.

CHAPTER 8

Mary Marcy
The Intentional Leader

G rowing up on a cattle ranch and attending class in a one-room
schoolhouse are rarely requirements for the college presidency; yet
many of the values and skills that these experiences engender are essential attributes for transformational leadership. Picture this encounter
that Dr. Mary Marcy, president emerita of Dominican University of California, often shares.

A serious snowstorm was imminent. If the herd was going to survive,
it needed to be brought from the pasture to the barns around the main
house. Marcy, about twelve at the time, and her father saddled up and
headed out to the pasture. Unfortunately, the blizzard arrived before
they reached the herd. Marcy explains, "The winds were blowing away
from the barn, and it's really hard to drive cows directly into the wind,
snow, and ice; but that was the only way they were going to survive." As
she remembers that day, she says, "I was cold, my horse was just miserable, and I probably started sniffling a little bit. My dad came over,
looked me directly in the eyes and said, 'Look, Mary, we're cold, you're
miserable; but for these cattle it's a matter of survival. We *have* to get
them in.'" Marcy and her dad, cold and miserable, just kept working at
it. Eventually the herd reached safety. Lesson one: when others are depending on you, failure is not an option.

Marcy acknowledges that many of the persistent themes in her life
and career started on the ranch. In her early years, Marcy learned to

prepare for unpredictable crises ranging from rattlesnake bites to fires. She developed the laser sharp focus required to lasso cattle, and she cultivated the sense of caring and responsibility that comes from raising her own foal at a young age. Each of these qualities was evident throughout her decade of leadership at the Dominican University of California, where she transformed it, in the words of a presidential colleague, "from an unknown third-rate institution with no direction to a vibrant university." In the process, Dominican became widely recognized as a model for small-college transformation.

Marcy is committed to developing programs and policies to ensure that higher education becomes an equity engine. In an increasingly diverse higher education landscape, she has fostered the development of an education model *intentionally* designed to enable every student to find a unique calling, identify distinctive talents, and live a meaningful, engaged life regardless of their background. This model has been informed by Marcy's knowledge of evidence-based pedagogy and her recognition of the importance of mentorship. It has been further honed by the sensitivities that emerge from her personal experience as "an outsider." Dominican University of California provided the perfect venue for this strategic leader to live out her commitment.

When Marcy, who retired in 2021, recalls her time at Dominican, she is most proud of the advances the institution made with regard to equitable student success. Located in an exclusive residential area in the hills of San Rafael, California, Dominican University boasts a highly diverse student body. Two-thirds of the undergraduate population is composed of students of color, most from groups underrepresented in higher education; 35 percent are Pell-eligible; and 23 percent are the first generation in their families to attend college. Over an eight-year period (2011–2019), the institution improved its four-year graduation rate by 94 percent, and the six-year graduation rate by 45 percent. At the same time, the ethnic diversity of Dominican's student body increased by nearly 30 percent.

Dominican University also garnered external recognition for its work. In the fall of 2020, Dominican University of California was recognized with the American Council on Education/Fidelity Investments Award for Institutional Transformation. The Stanford University Equality of Opportunity Project revealed that Dominican ranked eleventh in the nation out of 578 selective private colleges for student social mobility, defined as moving students from the bottom socioeconomic quartile to the top quartile.[1]

Marcy's book, the *Small College Imperative*, has become required reading in higher education classrooms, as well as among college presidents and boards of trustees.[2] She currently serves as president-in-residence at the Harvard University Graduate School of Education.

LGBTQ+ Leaders

Mary Marcy is uncommon in several ways. Not only did she grow up on a cattle ranch, but she is also one of a growing number of openly lesbian leaders in American higher education. In an earlier presidential search approximately fifteen years ago, Marcy made a very favorable impression at the initial off-site interview. She was invited to campus as a finalist and the search committee requested that she also bring her husband. Reflecting on this incident, she notes, "During the initial interview I had worn rings, as I do now, including a ring on my wedding finger." When the search consultant conveyed the invitation for the finalist visit, Marcy took a deep breath and said, "I'm really interested. But I don't have a husband, I have a same-sex partner. I'll talk to her and see if she's available." Marcy recollects, "The search consultant paused for quite a bit and then said, 'Thanks for telling me. I'll call you back.' " Within the hour she was informed that she was welcome to come to campus for the interview, but she was no longer a serious candidate.

Marcy's personal experience is representative of the obstacles that LGBTQ+ candidates have encountered, and, in some instances, continue to encounter. When she began her career in higher education administration in the early 1990s, she was silent about her sexual orientation. She and her partner resided in different parts of the country. To protect their professional lives, their relationship was private. As she describes it, "I didn't highlight it or hide it." As she began to consider opportunities for presidency, even though she surmised that being a lesbian would be an impediment, she decided that the cost of living in-authentically was unsustainable. Marcy determined that she would be open about it in any searches that came her way. From her perspective, her sexual identity was not at the forefront of her considerations. She was much more focused on the match between her talents and the mission and needs of the institution.

Marcy notes, "I'm very aware that gays and lesbians are in an interesting liminal space. It's a continuum for most folks where they can make choices about how public they are and how they present in the world." Trying to quantify the presence of LBGTQ+ presidents and chancellors in American higher education is a complex matter. As the LGBTQ Leaders in Higher Education website explains, "The academy has long been richly blessed with LGBT folk both in and out of the closet."[3] Current membership in the organization founded in 2010 includes eighty-six active and seventeen retired leaders.[4]

The increased presence of openly gay and lesbian presidents indicates a greater openness in the academy; however, anecdotal evidence suggests many capable LGBTQ+ individuals continue to be excluded from serious considerations in presidential searches based on their sexual orientation. As cultural norms incorporate broader conceptions of sexual orientation and gender identity, perhaps we will be able to quantify more accurately the representation of LGBTQ+ individuals among American college and university presidents and better understand and address the barriers they face.

Becoming President Marcy

In many ways, Marcy's professional journey has been the perfect training for a university presidency. She served on the senior leadership teams of three institutions, two public and one independent. Her portfolios have included government relations, strategic planning, and managing a president's office. She directed a think tank on the future of higher education, and she taught a few political science courses at the undergraduate level. Despite this breadth of experience, Dr. Marcy felt her unconventional pathway might actually be an impediment. She had not followed the normal faculty route of becoming tenured, and she lacked a significant publication record. Keenly aware that the majority of college presidents had progressed through the academic ranks, she questioned whether a presidency was within her reach.

More insightful people thought otherwise. Impressed by her grasp of the challenges facing higher education, her commitment to student success, and her strength of character, a former president and professional colleague began to nominate her for presidential positions. Search firms also saw potential in her profile. "You just have to find the right fit," a wise search consultant assured her. "You will be a remarkable president at the right place."

Given her commitment to being fully authentic, Marcy laughed out loud when, after six years as provost and vice president of Bard College at Simon's Rock, she was approached by a search consultant regarding the presidency at Dominican University of California. Clearly this was a long shot. Despite her many years in higher education, she had never heard of the place. More importantly, from her perspective, a non-Catholic woman married to a same-sex partner was hardly a fit for a formerly Catholic institution, even in the California Bay Area. At the outset, she was very clear with the consultant that she was openly gay. She insisted that this had to be acceptable to the search committee and the board before she would even consider the opportunity.

Good search consultants can be persistent when they have the time to look deeply for the right fit. In this case, the consultant was convinced that Marcy's commitment to the liberal arts, diversity, and student success coupled with her collaborative leadership style were precisely what the institution needed. She strongly encouraged her to consider the opportunity. Marcy was intrigued by the potential she saw as learned more about Dominican. She was excited about the broad range of ethnic diversity at the institution and impressed with the desire of faculty and staff to reclaim the institution's founding values of study, community, reflection, and service.

However, she remained concerned about the issue of sexual orientation. In response, the consultant reminded her that Dominican had been independent of the Catholic Church and the religious order of the

Dominican Sisters for over fifty years. The institution was ecumenical and progressive, and it even offered same-sex partner benefits. The consultant assured Marcy that based on her interactions with the committee, she did not think issues of sexual orientation would be a consideration in the search. In fact, on several occasions during the search process, the chair had canvassed the search committee about its readiness to consider candidates representing various identities inclusive of race, ethnicity, gender identity, and sexual orientation. In each instance, the search committee members affirmed (theoretically and in the absence of a specific candidate) their openness to a broad range of identities.

But unconscious assumptions and biases can interfere with well-intentioned efforts. In this case, bias was based on presentation of self. When Marcy's colleagues describe her, in addition to sharing tales about lasso twirling in administration building hallways, they observe that upon entering a room she "exudes confidence and competence." Others note that she is always "impeccably dressed." For many on the search committee, Marcy's presentation of self was inconsistent with their assumptions about how a lesbian would present herself. During its interaction with the candidate, the search committee assumed it was interviewing a straight white woman. So, when she was offered the job and asked about any specific needs her family might have, there was some surprise when Marcy indicated that she had a same-sex partner.

As she describes this incident, Marcy notes, "I think people were operating in good faith. There was a little startle effect, but it didn't last long. I feel fortunate that Dominican was not an institution or a culture that assumed that my personal life was a violation of their notion of a good ethical, moral leader. Jan, my spouse, is a mathematician and math educator. The board and the faculty embraced her. It worked out quite well."

Neither the search committee nor the candidate addressed the issue of sexual identity as fully as they thought they had. Marcy assumed that she had addressed it through her conversations with the consultant. She notes, in retrospect, that she probably should have been more direct with the committee. The search committee attempted to broadly address issues of identity independent of specific candidates and, as a result, failed to recognize the unconscious assumptions that various members had. Luckily for the school, and for Marcy and her partner, good intentions prevailed. Looking back, Marcy thinks that she and the search committee failed to fully recognize the complexity of such issues.

Those who have worked most closely with Marcy as members of her leadership team or as trustees repeatedly note that "her moral compass is never in doubt." Many observe that her commitment to ethical leadership is one of her most outstanding qualities. Apparently, the Dominican Sisters who served on the search committee recognized this immediately. Although she worried that the nuns might find it unacceptable that she is a lesbian, this was far from the case. The sisters appreciated the apparent alignment of her values with those of their Dominican founders. Institutional legend has it that the sisters, who resided in the convent across the street from the university, were so excited about the potential of a president who shared their values that they sent her a card displaying a group of nuns lighting candles and praying to encourage her to accept the position.

Having completed her own due diligence, Marcy accepted the presidency of Dominican University of California in 2011, becoming the ninth president in its 121-year history. From her perspective, given its diverse student body, its committed faculty, and its lack of stellar student outcomes, Dominican University represented the perfect setting to develop an educational model intentionally designed to foster the success of all students. The promise of significant philanthropic support from members of the search committee was a definite plus. However, Marcy realized that there were also challenges to overcome.

Marcy's predecessor, Dominican University's eighth president, served for twenty-four years and is credited with having saved the institution early in his tenure. However, over the course of his presidency, he focused increasingly on the external aspects of the job. When the institution began to experience enrollment declines, the faculty and the administration had conflicting views regarding resource allocation. Faculty feared that the institution was abandoning the values established by the founding Dominican Sisters.

Given the level of conflict between her predecessor and the faculty,

Marcy was particularly concerned about determining whether conflict with the administration was engrained in the culture and whether the faculty was amenable to innovation and change. She had several extensive conversations with the two faculty members on the search committee prior to accepting the position. Based on these conversations she concluded that the faculty was open to the possibility of innovations that could move the institution forward.

In the poem "Working Together," poet David Whyte declares,[5] "We shape our self/to fit this world//and by the world/are shaped again." Marcy's approach to leadership, both what she tries to accomplish and the methods she employs, was shaped by intersecting forces, including her upbringing on a cattle ranch, her educational and professional experiences and expertise, and a prevailing sense that she was "an outsider."

When professional colleagues and friends describe Marcy, the accolades are innumerable. A few recurring words include courageous, compassionate, intellectually curious, humble, and funny. One longtime associate observes, "Mary loves nothing more than being confronted with a problem of significance for society to which she can bring data, research, and human sensitivity, while engaging a community in developing a solution. Most of all, she loves implementing the solution." Others report that her courage manifests in multiple ways: her willingness to accept the risks associated with innovation, saying what she means in a direct yet kind way, entertaining difficult conversations, and being authentically herself regardless of the pushback. She rarely takes credit for the accomplishments at Dominican without acknowledging the work of dedicated faculty and staff members, as well as an accomplished leadership team. She also emphasizes the support of the board.

Growing Up on the Ranch

Marcy, the last of five children and quite a bit younger than her siblings, was born on a cattle ranch in northwestern Nebraska. With her eyes dancing and a not a little bit of pride, she recollects, "I could ride a pony before I could walk, had a horse by six, and was given a foal to raise at about twelve."

According to Marcy, her childhood was far from boring. She rode to the pastures alone, equipped with a wire cutter and bolts so she could repair a fence or a windmill. She understood that if the windmill wasn't working, the cattle would quickly run out of water—a possible death sentence. Aware of the danger posed by rattlesnake bites, she was prepared to attend to an animal that may have been bitten. Dinners in the family home were filled with banter as Marcy and her older siblings engaged in lively debates about current events, an activity that was encouraged by her mother. Even though she was the youngest, she learned to hold her weight in family discussions quite early. This skill would prove beneficial years later.

Although life on the ranch emphasized the importance of individual effort, she particularly appreciated those aspects of ranch life when the community came together for a common purpose such as fighting fires and branding cattle. She realized quite early that she enjoyed working with others to accomplish important tasks.

A strong work ethic and persistence in the face of difficulty are just a few of the lessons from the ranch. "As much as I rely on, value, and believe in community, I never assume that anybody will take care of something that I have to do," she admits. It was on the ranch that Marcy developed a unique combination of resilience, scrappiness, and pragmatism that predisposes her to "make do" with whatever she's given. She wastes little time hoping that a situation is different. Instead, she accepts a situation as it is and asks what she should do about it. She appreciates the importance of having the necessary tools in her toolbox before attempting a project, an essential attribute in leading transformations. Most importantly, she learned that failure is never an option. It's a luxury that you cannot afford on a ranch.

Marcy began her education in a one-room schoolhouse and rode her pony approximately six miles to the school if her parents could not provide transportation. When she was in the third grade, her family relocated to the town of Hay Springs (population 599) so that her older siblings would not have to endure the long drive from the farm to the high school, a trip that was especially hazardous in the winter. There were thirty-two people in her high school graduating class. She showed horses and cattle in the summer and, like most of her peers, played volleyball and basketball during the school year.

Unlike many in the area, her parents stressed the importance of higher education and set an expectation that each of their five children would attend the University of Nebraska and major in an agriculture-related field. From their perspective, higher education would make the children better ranchers. An avid reader who was curious about current events and the outside world, Marcy excelled academically; but she wanted more from higher education than the opportunity to study agriculture. She saw academics as her ticket to get out of Nebraska on the "next train north," perhaps to Northwestern University to study journalism.

The Calling of Higher Education

When you ask Marcy about the genesis of her commitments, she responds, "I found my calling through higher education. Higher ed helped me figure out how to contribute to the world." She believes that every student should have such an opportunity, regardless of background. Reflecting on her own higher educational experience, she notes, "I realized the opportunities that I had were less about my own drive or the way the institutions were designed. It was simply luck. The luck of having the right mentor, the right faculty member, or the right experience. I was aware of other students who didn't have that." Thinking about this much later, she realized that the undergraduate program had not been intentionally designed to ensure that every student had an experience as rewarding as hers had been. She felt this was definitely something that could be fixed.

When Marcy arrived at the University of Nebraska, she brought the conservative values and beliefs of her community: all people are equal and should be treated with respect; people should pull themselves up by their bootstraps; and the American dream is accessible to anyone who works hard enough. She also brought a sense of confidence and a willingness to challenge ideas, which came from competing on the debate team and in sports.

As a first-year student, she was troubled by the existence of a women's center and a diversity center. She marched into the student union to ask the staff advisor why these were needed. As she explains, "I was like, 'We're all equal. What's the problem? Why segregate?' " The advisor encouraged her to come back for a more substantive conversation. Although Marcy can no longer recollect the specific details, she remembers that the interaction changed her worldview, and the staff person became an influential lifelong mentor. "She helped me see the world through the eyes of people who may not have felt at home at the University of Nebraska. Given the fact that I had often felt like an outsider in my own hometown, it was easy for me to empathize."

Although her experience at Nebraska was positive, like many undergrads, Marcy was in a state of panic about life after graduation. Her distress was exacerbated by the fact that she was "clueless" about her sexual identity. "Relationships didn't work for me, and I was pretty sure I wasn't going to be good at being married. But I also had no template for anybody doing anything else. I was quite panicked." From her perspective, college was the one thing she was good at. As her senior year began, she was fearful about what she would do if she didn't stay in school.

Several faculty members encouraged her to consider graduate school. An attorney who had followed her success in the local hometown newspaper encouraged her to apply for a Rotary Scholarship. Given her record of student leadership activities and outstanding academic performance, it was no surprise that Marcy had multiple options for graduate study: Harvard, Wisconsin, Berkeley, Oxford, and the London School of Economics. However, she lacked sophistication when it came to academia, and she had no criteria for making the decision about graduate school. "I did think you probably didn't turn down a Rotary Scholarship to Oxford, so I went," she says.

In many ways, the University of Oxford was Marcy's ultimate outsider experience. Laughing at herself, she shares another story.[6] Upon arriving at Oxford, Marcy was given her room assignment by the Trinity College porter. She entered the 10-by-12 space, where she encountered a desk, chair, bench, and bookcase, but no bed. With a twinkle in her eye, she confesses that she thought, "Wow, they take academics seriously here. I guess I am not supposed to sleep very much." Armed with the "deal with what you are given" philosophy of the ranch she began to unpack her suitcase, storing her clothing on the bench. At this point, a fellow graduate student sauntered into her room and asked in amazement, "Do you really plan to sleep here?" He then explained that graduate students received both a study and a bedroom. Her bedroom, he informed her, was up the stairs. Marcy admits, "I was the laughingstock of the grad students for a good few months."

Whenever Marcy wants to understand the experience of a first-generation college student, all she has to do is remember Oxford. She embarked on her international academic experience having never traveled beyond South Dakota, Kansas, and Iowa. She did not own a passport and had never used international currency. She arrived at Oxford with no understanding of the British educational system. Why were there no classes each week? What was a tutorial? Why were there no midterm exams or other forms of feedback? She was without any of the academic markers that she had previously used (quite successfully) to track her progress. She was, in her own words, "completely unmoored and confounded by everything." So, she did what she had always done best and immersed herself in her studies.

At the end of the academic year, she successfully completed her first-year examinations in politics. But during the summer, without the structure that her academic routine had imposed, the Nebraska native found herself without any grounding. She suffered a serious depression and was hospitalized for about six weeks. During this period, a good friend bicycled out to see her weekly, and others stayed in touch. Her advisor assured her that she was going to be fine. "When you're ready, we can talk about reading and what you will do next, but don't feel you need to do it now," he counseled. The concern of her friends and her advisor underscored the significance of the relationships in academic and personal success, a lesson she would carry with her many years later when thinking about important elements in undergraduate education.

Returning for her second year, Marcy joined the Oxford women's basketball team, an international conglomerate of women whom she remembers with great fondness. The team gave her community and structure beyond academics. While working on her master's exams and preparing her thesis, trauma struck again in the form of a sexual assault that ended up in court. In retrospect, she observes, "The one thing that came out of the assault was my understanding, finally, of my own resilience." Recounting the situation over thirty years later, she recalls that her primary concern was staying on track academically. Although an awful thing had happened, she reasoned that people had given her a scholarship. She was determined to complete her studies. Marcy did extremely well on her exams, noting that there were thirty-six students when she started that master's program in politics, eight completed the degree, and only two were women. Marcy credits part of her success to her great advisor, which was another lesson that would impact her approach to higher education.

Marcy, who finished her doctorate in politics with no further travails, credits her Oxford experience for teaching her to think. It was at Oxford she recognized that she was, in fact, a scholar. "I loved my discipline and my research. I loved sharing it with others and learning what they were doing," she reports.

On the Outside

Marcy admits that as far back as the ranch she had a persistent feeling that she did not fit in. She felt she was odd but did not know why. While growing up, she attributed it to the fact that she wanted more out of life than the ranch. She had and still has great respect for ranchers and farmers. She honors the work and the land, saying that whenever she is back at the ranch, she grabs a horse to ride to the pastures. "It just wasn't for me," she says. "The problem was, I didn't know *what* was for me. I read more than others; I was interested in more than sports. I liked current events and things happening all over the world." It never occurred to the perplexed adolescent that some of her discomfort may have been related to sexual orientation. That possibility was intellectually inaccessible and completely foreign at the time.

While at the University of Nebraska, she immersed herself in student government, becoming president of the student union, yet she admits it was much easier for her to figure out where she didn't belong than to understand where she did. "I was clueless about my own identity. I wasn't consciously avoiding the notion that I might have a different sexual orientation; it honestly didn't occur to me. I had strong friendships, male and female. But when I would start dating seriously, it usually ended badly."

Lack of exposure and limited social capital were other aspects of her experience as an outsider. This was perhaps most apparent at Oxford where most of the other Americans were much more sophisticated than she was. Many had attended elite undergraduate institutions, had traveled abroad previously, and were familiar with the British educational system. Upon graduation from Oxford, they had various networks in the academy, the public sector, and the business world that enabled them to leverage their Oxford degrees.

Marcy lacked such a network. Nothing in her upbringing provided a framework for understanding academia. She admits that she really didn't understand the significance of an Oxford degree or what she could do with such credentials. She comments, "I didn't really feel like I was part of a selective group. Even with an Oxford degree, as shiny as it is, if you're not particularly networked, you can be lost." She found herself, much as she had at the beginning of her senior year at Nebraska, almost freaked out. She wondered, "Have I run out of education? What happens next?"

Mentors and advisors play a critical role for those who do not understand the way a system operates. They enable one to envision unimagined possibilities and design pathways to reach these opportunities. Mentorship played a seminal role in Marcy's career trajectory, including the faculty and staff at Nebraska who encouraged graduate school and the hometown lawyer who suggested the Rotary Scholarship. Upon completing her studies at Oxford, a baffled Marcy again sought guidance from faculty and staff members at the University of Nebraska.

Marcy wanted to be in higher education, but policy and politics were her interests. She began to apply for jobs advertised in the *Chronicle of Higher Education*. At twenty-eight years old she was hired as director of governmental relations at the University of Central Washington, where she was, by far, the youngest person on the president's cabinet. The position was perfect for her. She could teach a few undergraduate courses while representing the institution at the state government level.

After Marcy served in a variety of administrative roles, each of which included a seat on the president's cabinet, the policy wonk assumed a leadership role at Antioch University's Project on the Future of Higher Education. As Marcy engaged with higher education leaders, policy experts, and demographers, she began to grapple with a serious question. What was required for higher education to fulfill its responsibility to serve as an engine of opportunity for all students, particularly those who have historically been underrepresented or underserved? She also recognized the impact that presidential leadership might have on an institution and on the lives of students. She was particularly intrigued by mission-focused, small liberal arts colleges where she believed it would be possible to work in collaboration with others to enact meaningful change.

Challenges at Dominican

By her own admission, Marcy was not looking for a turnaround opportunity when she accepted the presidency at Dominican. She was in search of an institution that was open to innovation, a place where she might collaborate with others and bring her lasso-twirling focus to student opportunity and success. However, she inherited an institution in need of significant transformation in the areas of governance, administration, culture, and programs. Equally challenging, she would need to address these simultaneously. Dominican University of California needed a turnaround, requiring that Marcy tap into her perseverance, insightfulness, and calm external presence.

As she considered the challenges and opportunities before her, Marcy recalled a cautionary tale from her participation in the Harvard University Institute for New Presidents, which she had attended in 2005 shortly after assuming her responsibilities at Bard College at Simon's Rock. Dr. Judith McLaughlin, the director of the program, gave a fireside chat on why presidents fail within their first two years. She observed that many new presidents had introduced too much change too quickly without sufficient appreciation for the history and culture of the institution. The result was "rejection of alien tissue."

This caution resonated with Marcy on multiple levels. As a self-defined outsider, she was highly sensitive to various forms of rejection. As a trained political scientist, she assessed organizations through their various constituent groups, ever conscious that "the same constituents who vote you in can vote you out." What were the expectations of the board, administration, faculty, staff, students, alumni, and the Dominican Sisters whose convent was across the street from the university? Prior to her arrival Marcy had had very limited exposure to Dominican's faculty and staff or students. The search had been closed. All the meetings had taken place off campus. Only two faculty members were on the committee—a perfect set-up for tissue rejection. She recalled one of the most important lessons she had learned growing up on the ranch. Failure was not an option. She would beware.

A keenly self-aware leader, Marcy constantly grappled with the question of how much change an institution can handle and when. She observes, "My leadership style was quite different from my predecessor. I was moving into a community that had been fighting over identity, culture, and resources. I was the outsider—a non-Catholic and a lesbian." During her first year she often found herself asking which of the multiple issues she faced would generate the formation of alien tissue.

Marcy's concern about tissue rejection may have consciously or unconsciously informed her approach to change management. Marcy had intended to spend her initial year getting to know the community and becoming known. But Dominican needed a governance overhaul, new forms of team leadership, a coherent vision and strategy, and a cultural shift. Marcy had learned long ago on the ranch that you take what you are given and deal with it. The self-proclaimed pragmatic optimist got to work.

Timing is everything in leadership and Marcy had three significant intersecting institutional challenges:

1. Enhancing the senior leadership team's capacity to innovate
2. Reimagining the institution's founding principles of study, service, reflection, and community in support of a diverse student body
3. Enhancing the board's capacity to govern effectively

While some of these were addressed with ease, others were far more challenging.

Those most familiar with Marcy report that her superpowers are her ability to galvanize people around a vision, to develop a strategy, and to serve as a moral compass as the strategy is implemented. Her joy comes from designing a strategy to resolve a presenting challenge. She is less interested in tactics and delegates appropriately while holding her colleagues accountable. If Marcy was going to be an effective leader, she required a committed team that could work collaboratively to implement change.

In the absence of strong leadership, clear vision, and accountability, senior leadership teams adopt dysfunctional behaviors such as withholding information from one another, cultivating divisional fiefdoms, and developing patterns of competition rather than cooperation. This behavior had emerged at Dominican prior to Marcy's arrival. Each unit of the institution was focused on protecting its turf. Stability rather than innovation was the guiding principle. In the face of enrollment declines and significant budget cuts, the strategy had been to expand program offerings rather than to improve student retention and success.

Marcy placed a premium on collaboration, transparency, and positive student outcomes. Her expectation was that senior leadership would collaborate effectively and work as a team. Moreover, her priorities meant that the team would need to shift from a focus on continuous expansion and growth to a focus on serving current students more effectively. In some cases, this might result in program closure rather than expansion. It was a radical change.

Despite this, Marcy's inclination was that she would spend her initial year listening, learning, and carefully assessing the team. However, she very quickly learned that the provost and the chief financial officer were at war and incapable of the level of collaboration she expected. Additionally, Marcy's emphasis on innovation to improve student opportunity and success met resistance from some of the senior leaders. By the end of the year, three of the five vice presidents had left the university. Several took other jobs, and one retired.

Marcy recalls, "This was much more change at the senior level than I had anticipated, and I was really nervous about it." She worried that these major transitions early in her presidency might produce anxiety among trustees, faculty, and staff. Several of the vice presidents had developed strong relationships with board members, and she was anxious about the board's reaction. Although a few trustees expressed concern, the leadership team changes posed no major problems for the board. Surprisingly, the transitions had little discernible impact on faculty and staff.

It took almost three years for Marcy to develop the team she needed. Once assembled, she invited the group into a thought partnership. She often held cabinet meetings around the kitchen table in her home, fostering community and demonstrating that these were intimate and important conversations. To surface the best ideas, she encouraged intellectual disagreement (but not conflict) within the group, intentionally allotting time for all to express their thoughts. She promoted taking risks, provided it was consistent with the mission. Several team members observed that while Marcy seemed to work nonstop, she did not demand this of others. She delegated, did not micro-manage, and invested in the development of each member of the team. She also maintained a respectful distance. The president was a trusted colleague and partner, friendly but not a friend.

Team members note that she was "gracious, humble, clear minded, focused, dedicated, and kind." Her sense of humor knew no bounds as she regaled them with stories of varmints and critters or falling off the horse on round-up day. Through her interactions with the leadership team, Marcy modeled the type of leadership she hoped would permeate the university. Her rules were clear: honesty, respect, collaboration, gracious listening, and absolutely no backroom dealing.

Reimagining Dominican University

Marcy hoped to spend much of her first year at Dominican engaging the community around a new vision while gaining trust and instilling hope. She quickly ascertained that any form of innovation would be impossible unless the community replaced deficit thinking with a mindset based on an appreciation for the school's unique student body and for the potential to create an educational model to support its needs. Faculty and staff would need to acquire the knowledge required to enable them to re-envision educational programs informed by research on learning, pedagogy, and high-impact practices.

She explains, "When I asked faculty and staff to describe the university, they would tell me what we were not: we're no longer Catholic; we are located in Marin, but we are not wealthy." There was limited understanding of the ways in which students' intersecting identities (employment, first generation status, and race/ethnicity) impacted their ability to take advantage of what the institution offered or to succeed academically.

She began to engage faculty and staff across the university in an effort to learn what was held in common. Whenever she heard common threads from different divisions, ranging from health sciences to the humanities and the business school, she would begin to share these ideas with the community. She heard a commitment to:

- the rigorous exploration of ideas,
- engaged student learning,
- leveraging the diversity of the student body in support of learning, and
- the Dominican values of scholarship, reflection, service, and community.

These commitments informed Marcy's analysis of the board-endorsed Dominican University Strategic Plan, which had been developed prior to her arrival. The wide-ranging plan included over thirty priorities. Aware of the dangers of alien tissue, Marcy did not reject the plan outright.

Instead, she encouraged the university to focus on those initiatives that were institution-wide and related to student success. She had already determined that only five priorities met this threshold. "I didn't say we wouldn't do anything else. I said we can't do all this at once. We're not that large. We don't have the infrastructure. Let's focus on students and on those priorities that are institution-wide rather than serving one niche of the campus."

To catalyze these efforts, Marcy engaged the community in sustained conversations. After sharing data on student diversity and student outcomes with the board, the leadership team, and faculty and staff, she asked each group to consider how the institution might better fulfill its mission to students. She asked what responsibility they each had in this process. Marcy exposed the community to information on student success and high-impact practices and then asked how Dominican could provide these for every student regardless of background. To move the campus from thought to action, she reallocated resources to create a fund for strategic initiatives. Faculty and staff were invited to propose grants related to student engagement and success. Many of those programs are still operative.

Marcy also opened her home to multiple groups of faculty and staff for what she called "presidential listening sessions," which focused on those aspects of the strategic plan related to student success. As is the case at many colleges and universities, the Dominican faculty and staff were not particularly aware of the emerging research on student learning. Marcy identified one faculty member and one staff member to lead each of these discussions.

It was very important that the president's role in these conversations was listener-in-chief. Centering the voices of faculty and staff garnered the investment, engagement, and trust required for innovation. The president, faculty, and staff got to know one another, and the entire campus began to take ownership for student learning, engagement, and success. A common language was emerging. The groundwork for curricular and program redesign was in play.

From 2011 to 2017, the Dominican faculty and staff worked collaboratively to create the Dominican Experience, a distinctive undergraduate program that ensures every student receives personalized coaching, takes part in community engagement, completes signature work, and develops a digital portfolio. This effort required that the faculty redesign the general education program and revise undergraduate and graduate programs. As a result, Dominican was able to reduce the institution's reliance on adjunct faculty and streamline the time students needed to complete the requirements for their degrees.

Reimagining the Board

When Marcy arrived in 2011, the Dominican University board structure and its operations reflected practices more common in the 1980s. There was no governance committee and no system for ongoing presidential or board assessment. Trustees jockeyed to be in the small group that the president invited for post-meeting dinner and drinks, creating the perception of an "in" group and an "out" group. Board meetings included long reports from administrators with limited opportunity for strategic engagement. There was a lack of clarity regarding shared governance, conflict of interest, the board's role in policymaking, and the authority of the full board versus the authority of individual board members. In many ways, the board had come to serve as a rubber stamp for a long-serving and well-respected president.

Marcy determined that board development would be essential to any institutional transformation strategy. The savvy president began by changing the agenda and structure of board meetings, reducing reports, and engaging the board in data-informed strategic conversations. She recommended the board work with external consultants to improve policies, procedures, structure, and bylaws.

In the fourth year of her presidency, in the midst of these governance reform efforts, the behavior of a few board members with significant financial capacity became untenable. They attempted to garner influence by leveraging their philanthropic intents, which was a clear violation of fiduciary responsibility. Without consulting the board, they began to make demands on the president in areas completely unrelated to the board's authority or to institutional priorities. It appeared these individuals assumed that a pledge agreement of a significant amount provided license to interfere with the administration of the university independent of the president or the board. Several individuals familiar with the situation observe, "It was essentially a fight over who was president." When Marcy held her ground, these trustees attempted to orchestrate intensely personal attacks.

In typical rancher style, she "sucked it up" and got on with running the university. She did not complain. Those with knowledge of the circumstances credit Marcy for handling these issues "masterfully." She understood that the resolution of this issue was not the responsibility of the president; it rested with the board. She outlined the situation to a few trustees, encouraging them to see it as another opportunity for further board development, particularly related to the clarification of trustee responsibilities, donor expectations, and conflicts of interest. "It was never about her," one trustee noted. "It was always about making the board better."

Checking the less than appropriate behavior of trustees (particularly significant donors) is not for the faint of heart. The Dominican board rose to the occasion. Ever gracious, Marcy credits board members for taking on the difficult situation. A former trustee admits, "At one point the Dominican board was the weakest board I had ever served on. Now, it is one of the best, by far."

In retrospect, the self-aware leader confesses that she may have allowed the situation to fester too long before bringing it to the board's attention. She truly believed she could rectify it herself, that she could reason with the individuals given their commitment to the university. "Was it hubris?" she asks herself.

Because of her very calm demeanor, a distinguishing aspect of her personality, few trustees were aware of the depths of the problem or the degree to which Marcy was negatively affected. Conflict with board members in whom one has placed trust is personally hurtful and possibly harmful professionally. Above all, it is problematic for the institution. A long-serving trustee familiar with the situation described it as an intensely painful experience for the president. "She does not show her vulnerability at work and yet she feels it deeply."

In fact, it was so painful that she considered seriously entertaining one of the many job inquiries that were beginning to come her way. But her commitment to the Dominican University mission and to the innovations underway was stronger than her conflict with a few trustees, no matter how problematic and painful. To leave in the middle of such potentially impactful work would have been unforgivable, a bit like leaving the cattle to fend for themselves during the storm because she was cold and miserable.

Marcy continued to serve for another five years, ensuring that the Dominican University innovations were institutionalized, while providing crisis leadership related to the COVID-19 pandemic and the recurrent fires in the adjacent Napa and Sonoma counties. As she navigated these crises, the president inspired the university to demonstrate its commitment to service and community. Dominican became a staging area for the Red Cross during the fires and provided housing for displaced students, faculty, staff, and alumni. During the pandemic, nursing students assisted local health care providers, and the institution provided personal protective equipment from its laboratories. Although the campus was physically closed for more than a year, all staff were retained and communication with the community was both consistent and constant.

One of Marcy's closest colleagues remarks, "Mary is energized by designing solutions. She's an innovator, not a caretaker." When she was confident in the capacity of the senior leadership team, satisfied that the institution had weathered the pandemic, and convinced that Dominican's approach to personalized education represented an educational model that resulted in success for all students regardless of background, Marcy stepped down as president in 2021. She leaves behind a legacy of innovation and a model of courageous, compassionate leadership.

Faith in Higher Education

As she reflects on her experience, Marcy encourages boards and search committees to critically assess the unconscious assumptions they may harbor regarding candidates who present any form of "outsider" status.

She recommends that boards clarify their expectations. Does the board expect the individual to assimilate to its current culture? Is there openness for new forms of engagement, leadership, and presentation of self? Marcy also advises LGBTQ+ and gender non-conforming candidates to talk candidly with the search firm and the search committee regarding their needs and concerns.

Marcy's sense of mission is informed by personal experience, her knowledge of policy, and her belief that higher education programs that are properly designed and delivered can advance equity. "A leader doesn't simply want to please people, she wants to take them somewhere," she says. For her, that somewhere is rooted in a belief that, as Horace Mann noted long ago, "Education, then, beyond all other devices of human origin is the great equalizer."[7] She is the first to acknowledge that higher education, in many of its current iterations, often serves as a source of stratification. However, with a broad smile, she says, "Despite its imperfections, I deeply believe in higher education."

CHAPTER 9

Recruiting Exceptional Leaders
A Forensic Approach

Recruiting a successful, much less exceptional, president via traditional search methods requires a lot of luck. William "Brit" Kirwan describes the odds of recruiting a successful first-time president as a "crapshoot."[1] A mathematician by training, former president of the University of Maryland College Park and Ohio State University, and chancellor of the University System of Maryland, Kirwan has plenty of experience to back up his estimate.[2] Second-time presidents are more likely to be successful, but as the job becomes more difficult there are no guarantees that a veteran will flourish.

We agree with Kirwan's grim assessment of first-time presidents but suggest an additional reason why so many searches fail to secure highly effective leaders. The search process itself is the problem. As usually practiced, presidential searches often work against recruiting a leader with the right combination of temperament and talent to lead in today's disrupted environment.

To be sure, many underprepared first-time presidents learn how to survive in the precarious terrain of a new presidency. They develop into capable leaders if they are quick learners, if they have the savvy to manage unexpected troubles, and if their boards and faculty grant them the room to grow into the job. Thanks to luck and astute members of search committees, most of the superb leaders profiled in this book were selected via the traditional search model. We argue, however, for a more systematic and penetrating approach that will bring better prepared leaders into candidate pools and into the presidency.

The forensic model calls for a deeper and more analytic style of recruiting leaders whose abilities are so critical to institutional success and, sometimes, survival. The approach devotes substantially more time to recruiting top talent and more effort to freeing the committee of self-defeating assumptions. Though initially more expensive than conventional methods, the forensic approach is highly cost effective when compared to the costs of an underperforming or failed presidency. This method substantially increases the odds of identifying and hiring a truly superior president in the same league as the leaders profiled in this book.

The first step in justifying the change in the search process is to answer a fundamental question. What should "success" mean when seeking a new college or university president?

The Consensus Choice May Be the Wrong Choice

"It's time to declare victory," announced an exhausted search committee chair after a majority of her committee finally agreed on a final candidate. Search fatigue is a powerful tool for bringing closure to a serpentine process that invites much deliberation and debate along the way. Unfortunately, the consensus choice often represents the lowest common denominator among candidates.

A successful search is usually defined as hiring a widely acceptable candidate after months of deliberation and the expenditure of hundreds of thousands of dollars in direct and implicit costs. Unfortunately, declaring "mission accomplished" is often premature. Hiring the consensus candidate may well represent a failure, although that misfortune may not be fully apparent for months, or even years.

The North Star for a truly successful search is selecting the candidate best equipped to lead the institution in these most challenging times. This standard of excellence is different than securing agreement from up to twenty or so individuals of varying experience and sometimes conflicting interests. The latter is a political process, and the former is a matter of well-informed judgement. As we shall see, the trick is to design searches that result in hiring the most able and talented candidate, even if they are not the immediately obvious choice or initially the most appealing.

Flawed Searches Produce Failed Presidents

This case of a search gone wrong leading to a failed presidency illustrates common mistakes in the conventional approach to presidential selection. Throughout this chapter, we will refer to this cautionary tale, a hypothetical composite narrative drawn from several actual searches. Inviting a search committee to discuss this case at their first meeting will alert them to many of the common pitfalls to avoid.

The Case of President Smith

Within three weeks of the new president's arrival on campus, several search committee members began to feel their choice of Bob Smith might have been a mistake. Within three months, nearly everyone on campus knew they had picked the wrong person.

Before he was hired, Smith seemed to be an ideal candidate. True, he had lasted less than two years in his former presidency, but his explanation was persuasive: apparently, he just didn't click with several influential trustees. Smith said, "We disagreed on the mission of the university." The search consultant confirmed that explanation. Smith had very strong references. His former board chair was clearly in his corner. Colleagues around the country were eloquent in describing his strengths. Smith gradually emerged as the leading candidate. Of the thirty-five applicants who responded to the usual notices of a presidential vacancy, Smith seemed the best. Beyond a few checks with individuals not listed among his references, deeper background checks seemed unnecessary.

"At last, we have a true academic in the pool," a faculty member exalted, after noting Smith's doctorate and teaching experience in classical music. In sharp contrast to his predecessor, Smith came across as just plain likable. Running the gauntlet of interviews, he impressed nearly everyone with his good humor and humility. Someone joked that perhaps Smith had much to be humble about. It helped that he fit the part of a college president—tall, well-spoken, with a touch of grey. He reminded some faculty members of the actor George Clooney in his more self-effacing roles. Affirmative action principles were honored by including a woman and an African American among the finalists. So, without rigorous questioning about what made Smith so attractive, a consensus formed around him as the right choice.

The board chair, a corporate executive and strong figure in his own right, dominated the search. He and Smith hit it off. Search committee members later said they had lingering doubts about Smith but failed to raise their concerns. They were relieved to have the chair take responsibility for the search.

It quickly became clear that the new president had at least one very serious flaw—he just couldn't make a hard decision. He looked the part of a president, and he was congenial and seemed to enjoy the job's many ceremonial obligations. Increasingly pointed advice from the board didn't help. The more difficult the situation calling for action, the more he dithered.

Within two years he retreated to a well-paid professorship (a sinecure guaranteed in his contract), and another search began.

What went wrong?

A serious mistake likely predated the search itself. Without considering the alternatives, search committees often unconsciously adopt a legacy archetype of what an American college or university president should look and sound like. The president in this case appeared to fulfill this creature of imaginations and social conditioning. The power of the archetype was so strong that the committee and its chair never took a hard look at what leadership strengths Smith might possess. The firmly etched prototype of a college president also meant they never really considered what less conventional, but perhaps more capable, candidates might have to offer.

The committee and the search process itself share much of the blame for the failed search. The members warmed to Smith's pleasing personality and thus mistook likability for leadership. As the consensus formed around Smith as the choice, the committee took less interest in other candidates who might have shown superior potential. Allowing one strong personality to dominate the selection despite some misgivings represents a major mistake. In this case, the board chair's leadership of the committee may have stifled dissent.

The search consultant failed on several counts as well. Lack of aggressive recruiting led to a weak pool of candidates. A perfunctory background investigation never uncovered Smith's weaknesses of character, or if it did the consultant chose not to share this information with the committee. Endorsing a dubious explanation for a short tenure in a prior presidency would seem a betrayal of the client's best interests. As we will see, the pressures on search firms to conduct multiple searches in a condensed time frame contributed in this case to hiring the consensus candidate.

The Presidential Search Business

"Round up the usual suspects," says the world-weary Captain Renault in the classic 1942 romantic film, *Casablanca*. Rounding up the usual candidates is often the recourse of fatigued and overworked search consultants in a business that thrives on fast turnover. The irony of the modern search business is that the financial success of the search industry comes at the cost of making it more difficult to secure truly exceptional candidates such as those featured in this book.[3]

Recruiting talent is a very big business, with revenues exceeding $12 billion in 2021, according to one estimate.[4] Search firms dominate presidential recruiting in higher education, although the field accounts for only a small portion of the global talent search industry. In the mid-'90s, less than a third of presidential searches involved a firm. By 2015, more than 90 percent of searches were conducted by external consultants or firms.[5] The going rate can be upwards of $200,000 per search contract. The fee will be less for a pared down, low-bid contract, and it could be much more if the cost is based on the percentage of a substantial salary.

Executive searches in higher education are profitable and growing enterprises. The Great Resignation of college presidents has placed unprecedented demands on search firms as they respond to requests from boards of trustees and search committees. Whether officially organized as profit-making or nonprofit, they operate like businesses in every sense of the word. The formula for success in the search business is to multiply the number of searches, reduce the time devoted to each, and control the costs of service by passing time-consuming work on to lower paid staff. This ensemble of strategies makes economic sense in the short run, but it also impedes the search for truly exceptional candidates who take more time to identify and recruit.

Shootouts and Rainmakers

Choosing a search firm usually begins with a shootout, which is the term used in the industry to describe the contest among competing firms to gain the contract. A rainmaker pitches the search firm's virtues in contrast to rival companies. The rainmaker is the face of the search firm, yet the star may play a very modest role in the early stages of the search itself. A large part of filling the pool of candidates falls to lower-paid associates with limited experience of the work of a president.[6] They canvas the market through phone calls and email requests for suggestions and nominations, sift through responses to advertising, and comb the vitae of recent unsuccessful candidates in the firm's digital rolodex. Candidates who show at least *initial e*vidence of being qualified for the job are poured into the pool.

Experienced consultants do have much to offer when they have the time. They typically possess a roster of potential candidates, often those who came up short in earlier searches. A veteran consultant will have developed an instinct for the "fit" between a candidate and a particular institution. The best of the principal consultants serve as trusted advisors to the committee and its chair on search protocols, how to handle disagreements on the committee, and practical matters such as candidate confidentiality.

Alas, the intensely competitive nature of the search business demands that the victor of the shootout moves on quickly to the next contest. There is little precious time remaining to give individual attention to the client, much less to identify and cultivate potentially high-performing candidates who don't fit a conventional mold.[7] The traditional search process worked well enough when solid candidates lined up to for a chance to interview for a presidency, but the multiple challenges facing presidents in today's environment, plus the Great Resignation, has changed all that. In-depth recruiting of untraditional candidates is time consuming, and time is a limited commodity in the competitive search business.

Shallow Background Checks

Personal recruiting of nontraditional candidates and passive candidates not actively hunting for a new job takes a back seat to advertising and scanning the digital rolodex on the front end of a search. Unfortunately, in-depth vetting of finalists receives short shrift as well. As one critic told us, vetting as it is usually practiced "leaves many stones unturned." The predictably positive reviews of candidate-selected references, a few "off-reference-list" phone calls, and checks of databases like LexisNexis are poor substitutes for thorough investigations.

This style of a light once-over leaves two important questions unanswered. The first being: does the top candidate, or the top few if the vetting includes them, really possess the leadership qualities that they claim? The hapless president in the case that begins this chapter passed all the tests for criminal behavior. Deeper probing could have revealed that he lacked the backbone required in modern presidents.

The second question asks if there are less visible but equally damning behaviors to be discovered that extend beyond criminality or legal entanglements that might show up in police files or court records. Egregious examples of a candidate's misbehavior are apt to be noticed, while less obvious lapses often remain undetected for a time. Resignations of university presidents and system heads that follow belated discoveries of failing to act in cases of alleged sexual harassment point to shallow background checks. Title IX violations and allegations of misbehavior, including indifference to complaints of unwanted sexual advances and harassment, are endemic in higher education. They deserve, but are only beginning to receive, special scrutiny in background checks.

Search professionals genuinely care about securing the best available leadership for their clients. They have multiple incentives to do so. Highly publicized failures of short-term presidencies raise embarrassing questions about the quality of the consultants and their firms. Contracts typically offer guarantees of resuming the search at no or lower cost should the president leave within a year or two of appointment. Even the most well-intended consultants, however, are pressured by the business dynamic that results in too little attention to recruiting truly exceptional candidates and vetting that relies on easily accessible information rather than deeper inquiry. The dearth of hard evidence of a candidate's strengths and weaknesses leads to overreliance on the popular but unreliable tool—the interview.[8]

Interviews Are Not to Be Trusted

Interviews provide entertaining conversation for search committee members and, if open to the public, stir up lively discourse across campus and beyond. Unfortunately, these Q and A sessions are unlikely to reveal much about how a candidate will perform as president. These mainstays of the search can harbor three serious flaws. First, search committees and other interviewers tend to believe that candidates' words are consistently truthful presentations of their values, accomplishments, and leadership styles. In many cases, they are not. Second, a candidate's desire to appear better than they may really be motivates them to present an image pleasing to the committee. That image is never an entirely accurate picture of how the candidate will perform as president. And third, interviewers and candidates often fail to realize that the event is a quasi-theatrical performance. As an experienced search consultant told us, the interview is really an audition for the role of president.

For a deeper understanding of the limitations of interviews, we turn to a sociologist who has made the study of deception his life's work. Timothy R. Levine, a distinguished professor and chair of communications at the University of Alabama at Birmingham, has devoted twenty-five years to the study of truth and deception and is the author of *Duped: Truth-Default Theory and the Social Science of Lying and Deception*. We also consult a brilliant essayist, Malcolm Gladwell, who draws on Levine's work to suggest how even intelligent academics can mislead themselves when it comes to detecting truth for falsehood.

The Default to Truth

Most of us believe that what we hear is truthful, although the era of fake news is breeding greater skepticism. In the environment of the interview, at least, we like to believe that all parties are telling the truth, at least as they understand it. Levine describes this habit as "the default to truth." The flaw in our thinking, according to Levine, is the bad habit of believing people to be honest.

Levine writes that we "can be astonishingly gullible," because "we uncritically accept virtually all communications messages we receive as 'honest.' "[9] According to him, we habitually persist in this belief even when the facts discredit the speaker.[10] Levine offers multiple examples based on his own and others' experiments and analysis of real-life situations to confirm that even skilled interviewers can only separate truth from fiction about half of the time. On average the chances of correctly assessing honesty ranges from 44 percent to 64 percent, with a consistent average of 54 percent.[11] We interviewed a police detective who admitted that there was no sure way to separate truth from falsehood in an interview. Evidence would reveal the truth, he said, but words expressed in an interview were unreliable.

Gladwell relies on Levine's research to illustrate the misplaced reliance on interviews in a variety of settings from polices stations, to courtrooms, to college campuses. He profiles a host of dishonest characters, such as Adolf Hitler, Bernie Madoff, and an infamous Cuban spy named Ana Montes. He also features the university-based sexual predators Larry Nassar at Michigan State and Jerry Sandusky at Penn State who persuaded otherwise intelligent people to believe their protestations of innocence.[12]

Gladwell concludes that the ability to lie with a straight face succeeds less because of the liar's skill and more due to our gullibility. He argues that interviewers ought to know better. Indeed, liars such as the ones he identifies are completely untrustworthy. But buying into their lies, Gladwell writes, "is not that there is something brilliant about *them*. It is that there is something wrong with *us*."[13]

In the world of academic searches, bold-faced lies may be few, though shades of deception are plentiful in the forum of the interview. Even the most intentionally honest and straightforward candidates host blind spots of which they are unaware. Without any conscious intention of misleading, many candidates are truly blind to their leadership flaws. Savvy presidential aspirants and candidates for other posts work to communicate the most positive interpretation, or "spin" as politicians would call it, on their qualifications and accomplishments. The president in the hypothetical case explained his early departure from a prior job as the result of a personality conflict. No one checked to see what exactly that conflict might have been.

Appearances Really Are Deceiving

First impressions and appearances may also contribute to a search committee's inability to detect a candidate's mistruths. Levine discovered in an experiment that people are more likely to believe a person if they are well-dressed and appear self-assured.[14] A winning candidate may show up for the interview with an amiable appearance, a ready smile, and a direct gaze. These are appealing qualities in a candidate for president, but they reveal nothing about leadership ability.

Another of Levine's corollaries, common enough in human experiences, is that "people typically lie for a reason."[15] Levine gives ten reasons why people turn to lying as a tactic to achieve their ends or avoid painful consequences. Four of the ten offer motivations for misrepresentations in presidential (and other) interviews. They may be hiding a personal failure or transgression, seeking economic gain, seeking non-monetary gain, or trying to appear favorably to others.[16]

Interviews Are Theatre

Interviews occur in the space somewhere between acting, storytelling, and creative nonfiction. An interview is a conversation housed in a drama. The most successful finalists play a role featuring gravitas, charm, and sincerity—attributes we like to see in presidents. Sophisticated protagonists seek to portray themselves as capable, experienced, and most important of all, trustworthy individuals. Their dramatic struggle is to prevail in the quest for an offer of the presidency.

Long before opening night candidates, like actors, rehearse their parts to test out various narratives. Their lines may include language designed to explain away embarrassing actions or outright failures, as well as illustrations of their competence. A president fired for being tone-deaf to the politics of the academy can be cast as a hero who paid the price for his courage in making hard decisions. Candidates role-play the interview conversations on the stage of their own imaginations and with a friendly audience, or occasionally a communications professional, hoping to gauge their plausibility and confirm their accuracy.

The theatrical element of interviews, indeed the whole drama encompassing the search, is not lost on search professionals. After an inexperienced candidate floundered through his interview, a search consultant observed that "he didn't realize the interview was an audition for the role of president."

Dubious References

If a candidate's own testimony should be viewed agnostically, references deserve even more scrutiny. Someone may have written over the top testimonials for friends and colleagues they wish to support, as well as for characters they would like to make someone else's problem. Off-reference list calls are suspect, as well. A call from a stranger seeking an appraisal of a candidate is not likely to produce dependable feedback.

Of course, few presidential candidates are outright liars, and fewer still are criminals. (Although there are examples of both). The "default to truth" habit, however, occurs whenever we unquestionably rely on our ability to judge character and veracity based on what people say and how they say it.[17] We fail to doubt, or question enough, our own tendency to believe what people say.

Search committees must combine open-mindedness with skepticism. Openness to the potential strengths of candidates, particularly non-traditional candidates like those profiled in this book, creates the possibility of hiring a truly exceptional leader who might otherwise be overlooked. Wariness of the claims of all candidates, pending evidence confirming their virtues and accomplishments, is a healthy counterweight to an uncritical "default to truth."

The Forensic Model

The interview as a form of personal testimony is a staple of the presidential search ritual that is here to stay. What should be set aside, however, is the naïve belief that the public performance is a sure guide to a candidate's leadership potential. The entire search process stands to be improved with steps that bring stronger candidates to the forefront and enable search committees to distinguish truly exceptional leaders from those who talk a good game.

We call this superior alternative the forensic model.

The goal of this fresh approach is to turn the search for exceptional leaders from a crapshoot into more of a sure thing. The term forensics signals a deeper and more analytic style of selecting truly high-performing leaders. In its modern usage, forensics is associated with law, accounting, and psychology to probe beneath appearances to get at the reality of candidates' potential. We use the term in precisely that sense.

The forensic method includes basic elements of the conventional approach but improves upon them in several important ways. Forensic searches feature wide-ranging reconnaissance for superior candidates well before the official start of the search. A quiet phase of two months or so allows time to intrigue strong applicants without allowing so much time that they succumb to other offers. Superficial vetting is replaced by more penetrating scrutiny of the personal leadership styles and professional accomplishments of top candidates. Because the first year of a new presidency is so critical, this model calls for intensive coaching and support beginning shortly after the selection.

These strategies are not new in the business of presidential searches, but they are not practiced as often as they should be. This integrated effort that blends forensic elements with conventional practices produces more well-equipped leaders than either can alone. They demand more effort, time, and cost as the price for recruiting truly exceptional leaders. As a practical matter, the added expense is far less than an underperforming or outright failed presidency and yet another search.

How the Model Works

1. *The confidential recruiter.* Recruiting begins two months ahead of the official start of the search. The limitations of the typical thirty- to sixty-day application and nomination window is captured in these words from a veteran search consultant: "We advertise for a month or two and see what we get." The combination of advance recruiting during a quiet phase and conventional advertising in the relevant media is a powerful tool for building a well-qualified pool of candidates. Ideal choices for this recruiter role could be a recently retired or semi-retired academic with a network developed over years or a veteran search consultant working independently of a firm.

In a recent exercise of this strategy, a skilled recruiter secured eight highly competitive candidates for a research university. Charged to seek out unconventional candidates whose personal stories revealed strengths absent in the usual suspects, this individual cultivated promising candidates not actively seeking a new post to accept nominations. The recruiter earned the nickname "sleuth," since the entire process was conducted confidentially between the recruiter, each potential candidate, and the committee chair.

2. *A culturally sophisticated search committee.* An effective search committee is composed of truly open-minded and experienced members who appreciate what nontraditional, as well as conventional, candi-

dates have to offer. Members receive serious instruction in the perils of bias including the tendency to underestimate the talents of candidates who do not fit the traditional mold. The committee includes members diverse in thought and background who commit to seeking a truly exceptional president over a merely acceptable one. The appointing authority, likely to be a board chair or a system head in the case of public universities, may choose not to be a member of the committee to avoid pressures to select a consensus candidate. The size of the committee is less important than its composition and leadership.

3. *Strengths of character.* Seeking candidates with strengths of character, as illustrated by the seven presidents profiled in this book, should be the top priority. Academic credentials and experience are important both for credibility with the faculty and to demonstrate familiarity with the business side of higher education. Yet, as our seven profiles illustrate, personal leadership strengths are as important as academic credentials for leadership in these conflicted times.

Because these personal qualities are more difficult to identify than academic degrees, publications, and administrative positions, personal traits typically receive less scrutiny than they deserve. A veteran search consultant says that too often "formal credentials served as an unreliable proxy for competence." He goes on to say that academics in particular rely on credentials alone to narrow the field, thereby unintentionally eliminating many nontraditional and potentially superior candidates.

Recommendations from trusted friends and colleagues offer insight on how close associates regard the candidate, but they should not be fully trusted. Verified examples of critical incidents when the potential leader displayed courage, political sensitivity, and practical intelligence, or other essential leadership qualities, provide more useful evidence. Early life experiences, those crucible moments that forge character, signal the presence of traits like resilience and persistence and reveal the candidate's own sense of their personal strengths.

Personality and leadership assessments, common in corporate human resources practices, can help both search committees and candidates become more aware of their inner strengths and weaknesses. The Humanex assessments described earlier in this book identify leadership strengths of value to everyone involved in the search process. A link to Humanex is provided on the last page of this book.

4. *Critical interviews.* Committee orientations should stress the unreliability of interviews and encourage members to question their own first and second impressions of candidates. Overreliance on lists of predictable questions, avoiding incisive follow-ups, accepting performative responses, and failure to demand evidence of whatever accomplishments the candidate asserts are common flaws. Assigning one question to each member of a large committee all but ensures shallow responses and truncates the time available for follow-ups and clarifications.

Where open-meeting laws and the politics of the committee allow, subsequent private discussions between top candidates and search leaders should be pursued. These sessions provide the occasion for a candid back-and-forth conversation more likely to reveal a candidate's strengths and weaknesses.

Shannon McCambridge, an experienced search consultant who contributed to this chapter, offers effective anti-bias training, though she reports that only one in five committees seek such training. When skillfully presented, we have found that most committee members will accept and learn from the experience. Frequent reminders to maintain an open-minded appraisal of candidates, especially when selecting finalists, will help prevent backsliding to old habits of thought. Those who refuse to participate should not be in the business of selecting a president.

5. *Coaching unconventional candidates.* This book has argued that unconventional candidates often possess the qualities most needed to address today's complex challenges. What the Bjorks termed the "advantage of disadvantage" may account for their rise to the top in the search,[18] but people of color, those with English as a second language, and anyone crossing class lines face special challenges in presenting themselves in interviews. Coaching can help these candidates in communicating their potential to an unfamiliar or even prejudiced audience.

Jane Hyun in *Breaking the Bamboo Ceiling* recommends leadership assessments to her Asian American clients seeking higher positions. These tools enable candidates to better understand their own "temperament, organizational abilities, and relational style" before they take the interview stage.[19]

A well-regarded search consultant observed two Asian candidates with different but equally dysfunctional behavior during the interviews. One defied the passive model minority stereotype by delivering a boisterous interview, while the other was highly self-effacing. Neither were hired. "Both were excellent candidates," she said. "I just wish I had coached them better." Hyun's advice to her Asian clients applies to all other candidates as well.

6. *Deeper background investigations.* Some hyperbole is expected as candidates make their case. Careful background investigations should explore the facts behind the claims. Did the candidate lead in developing the big new facility, or were they just there at the ribbon cutting? Is the strategic plan heralded by the candidate exceptional, or is it the more prosaic exercise? Does the candidate accept responsibility for collective failures instead of blaming circumstances, staff, or the trustees? Is the candidate truly a collaborative and transparent leader, as virtually all claim to be? Positive responses to questions like these can confirm that a top candidate would be a good choice for president.

There are a host of surprisingly common flaws that don't receive the attention they deserve in the normal vetting process. Almost six percent of American adults suffer from alcohol use disorder (7.6 percent of men and 5.3 percent of women).[20] These figures suggest that about an equal proportion of presidential candidates either abuse alcohol or are full-fledged alcoholics. Some may also struggle with opioid and other addictions. Otherwise capable presidents from a variety of institutions have been dismissed following DUI (driving while intoxicated) charges. The alcohol abuse was often known to former colleagues but never thoroughly investigated prior to their hiring.

The frequency of Title IX violations demands focused investigation of aspiring candidates. It may be necessary to secure a candidate's permission to talk with their institution's legal counsel and campus security office. Other potentially embarrassing issues include lavish entertainment expenses, misuse of employees for personal business, mysterious absences, questionable relationships with subordinates, and conflicts of interest. These investigations can be relatively straightforward once the candidate's name becomes public. They must be managed with great care by a skilled researcher if the candidacy must remain confidential.

To get a solid read on the candidate's personality, leadership style, and the validity of their claims to accomplishments, there is no substitute for a personal representative visiting the campus or other place of work. The sleuth-like recruiter from the start of the search process may be a good candidate for this investigative work. Individuals who are knowledgeable of the institution and trusted there, former investigative reporters adept at pursuing clues, and experienced recruiters not employed by the firm assisting in the search are potential agents, as well. A board representative, the chair, or the head of a system who meets personally with their counterpart is much more likely to receive a candid appraisal of the candidate than if a search consultant makes a cold phone call.

7. *Intensive first-year support.* Every president needs a coach, mentor, or trusted advisor they can go to in confidence for counsel. This is especially important for unconventional candidates who are less familiar with the customs, expectations, and taboos of academic culture and the attitudes of the surrounding community. New presidents face some common challenges including learning the political terrain, managing multiple and conflicting expectations, sizing up the current senior team, and building support for a fresh agenda. An experienced former president can help the neophyte avoid missteps associated with all these tasks. A shepherd or two of the president's own choosing to guide them through the first critical month and year should be mandatory and paid by the institution. Mandating this service in board policy or the president's employment agreement will take the sting out of whatever prejudice remains about coaching.

It is more important than ever to transition away from the traditional methods of recruiting candidates for university presidents. The processes suggested here are tools for recruiting, selecting, and launching an exceptional and long-serving president. The willingness to question one's own preferences, assumptions, and biases regarding candidates, combined with an open-minded stance toward the qualities that unconventional persons can bring to the presidency, are key to a truly successful search.

Afterword
The Next Generation of Exceptional Leaders

The Great Resignation of college presidents presents an unparalleled opportunity for higher education to bring on board a new generation of leaders whose backgrounds have prepared them for the rigors of the office. The most important task of boards of trustees and presidential search committees is to recognize the reservoir of talent available from individuals hitherto set aside. Candidates invited to interview "just for show" may well possess the strengths of character and other leadership qualities most needed in today's turbulent environment.

Several of the presidents profiled here have stepped down, and others are approaching an age that invites consideration of the next chapter in their lives. Freeman Hrabowski has resigned after a remarkable thirty years as president. Following nearly a decade at Dominican, Mary Marcy has gone on to other influential work in higher education. Able new presidents have taken their places. But there are many other colleges and universities searching for new leaders. The individuals profiled in this book will be tough acts to follow, but their journeys to exceptional leadership light the way.

We began this book with twin desires: to get to the core of the essential qualities of exceptional educational leaders in today's fraught environment. Our second desire has been to enable boards of trustees and search committees to recognize these leaders and develop more effective ways of attracting them to the presidency.

Our narratives of seven exemplary leaders illustrate the following interlocking dimensions of their lives and careers. Early experiences charged with adversity have engendered strengths of character that underpin leadership styles, resulting in the ability to provide exceptionally effective direction during challenging times. It sounds simple.

However, there is nothing automatic about the journey through hardship to superb leadership. As our profiles reveal, the pathways are anything but linear. Inevitably, the routes are circuitous, mysterious, painful, and baffling to their travelers. Several of the profiles illustrate the damaging effects of systemic racism. In no way do we condone such injustice. Undoubtedly, the love and support these individuals have received from their families, mentors, and communities enabled them to meet and overcome the hardships they endured. In the process, they developed a unique combination of toughness and empathy.

The themes summarized below are intended to alert readers to important features higher education should be seeking in the next generation of college presidents.

Upbringing

Hardship painfully experienced and overcome is a common theme in the lives of the presidents profiled here. Adversity beginning in their early years continued in a variety of guises throughout their careers. In every interview, our subjects described harsh experiences that lingered in their memories and became sources of both strength and empathy. They told stories of "crucible moments," to use David Brooks's term, that illuminated much that went before in their lives and forged a fierce determination to make a difference in their own futures and the lives of their students.

These pivotal experiences crystalized a previously inchoate sense of purpose. For Freeman Hrabowski, the critical experience unfolded over five "unspeakable" days in a Birmingham jail. For Mary Marcy, it came in her father's words about spending long, cold hours in the saddle in order to save their cattle from perishing in a Nebraska blizzard. The juxtaposition of the lives of young prostitutes, thieves, and addicts on the mean streets of Seattle with Jeffrey Bullock's experience with his loving foster family inspired a sense of purpose in that future president.

Both adversity and affection had a significant impact on the development of these leaders. Their ability to overcome hardships fostered the toughness and determination that are major aspects of their styles of leadership. These leaders' capacity to empathize, especially with students, is informed by the difficulties they experienced coupled with the support they received. Many of their students endured challenges similar to their own. Waded Cruzado captured the experience of several when she told us that she grew up "without much money but with a lot of love."

Character

These presidents exhibit a similar ensemble of strengths of character. Courage, resilience, tenacity, mental toughness, intercultural competence, and emotional and practical intelligence appear as prominent leadership traits embedded in their personalities and revealed in their performances. As an independent check on our impressions, we asked each president to complete a leadership assessment conducted by the professional staff of Humanex Ventures. According to its designers, the HUMANeX In-Depth Leader Assessment is "designed to identify those talents that are consistent with top performers and inconsistent with low(er) performers."

The assessment showed that our presidents share several important leadership traits. They are driven by a sense of mission often described in religious terms as a *vocation* or *calling*. Dedication to values such as honesty and integrity, characterized as "doing the right thing" in every instance, was another common feature. They accept personal responsibility and hold themselves accountable for successes and failures alike. If a staff member fails at a task, one told the assessor, "it's because I put them in the wrong position" or "I didn't help them to develop the skills they needed." They use the pronoun *we* much more often than *I*. Each one's sense of vision for the future of their institution begins with a collective commitment. One president characterized her college's vision for the future as a "co-creation" with the academic community. Finally, we were told that these leaders just "can't slow down . . . they are driven to look for what's next."

These results place the presidents in the top 10 percent of all business, nonprofit, and higher education executives in Humanex's portfolio as high achievers. The vocabulary differs slightly, but the attributes uncovered in the external assessment correlate with the character strengths described in each of the profiles.

Challenges

Confronting difficulties from their earliest years, each of the presidents developed confidence that would empower them to address serious challenges in colleges and universities later on. For Jeffrey Bullock, Kwang-Wu Kim, and Mary Marcy, the enterprise itself was in jeopardy. If they failed to attract a critical mass of students, the institution would not survive. The University of Illinois and Hollins University experienced what might be called cultural crises. Illinois suffered from lost trust in its leadership before Robert Jones arrived. Cultural dysfunctions at Hollins demanded the sensitivity and attention of Mary Hinton. The different kind of problem facing UMBC and Montana State might be characterized as a crisis of unrealized potential. "It ain't broke" is how a Montanan described the University in Bozeman to Waded Cruzado before she assumed the presidency. Indeed, MSU functioned well enough prior to her arrival. However, the dramatic growth in enrollment, the development of the campus as a modern learning and research venue, and its stellar reputation all highlight the unrealized potential that preceded her. Freeman Hrabowski led the transformation of a middling urban public university into one with a nationally recognized track record for enabling all of its students to achieve at higher levels than they or many others expected.

Leaders who have contended with arduous circumstances, developed strengths of character including toughness and empathy along the way, and offer a track record of succeeding in overcoming major challenges represent a good starting point for recruiting presidents in today's environment. Rounding out these personal strengths with academic and administrative accomplishments completes a bouquet of attributes to be sought in twenty-first-century college and university leaders.

ACKNOWLEDGMENTS

We wish to recognize and express our appreciation to these individuals, who contributed valuable perspectives, information, and insights:

Javaunne Adams-Gaston	Nancy Gray	Laurent Pernot
Michael Babcock	Jim Gunn	Susan Pierce
Sheyonn L. Baker	Al Guskin	Nicola Pitchford
Carina Beck	Tom Hogan	Lawrence Rosen
Brad Black	Mike Hope	Philip Rous
Clifford Browner	Douglas Horstmann	Barry Sabloff
Mary Browner	Richard Ice	William Schneider
Bob Bruininks	Michael Joseph	George Smith
Deborah Buol	Robin Kaler	Yvonne Sode
Mary Jane Burke	Charles Kimball II	Michael Summers
John Butler	Scott Knapp	Tim Terrentine
Joseph Chlapaty	James Kopp	Jerry Terrer
Betsy Cossaboon	Larry Ladd	Alexandra Trower
Marcella David	Terry Leist	Amber Vestal
Jennifer Edminster	Denise Leslie	Annalee Ward
Kerry Edmonds	Sandra Ludescher	Mark Ward
Tracy Ellig	Shannon McCambridge	Barbara Wheeler
Katherine Enke	Peter McPherson	Hugh Williams
Chris Fastnow	Suzy Mink	Alicia Wilson
Walter Fleming	Bob Mokwa	Charon Wilson-Taylor
Kevin Foley	Derek Musgrove	Tom Woodward
Sean Garrick	Stacey Ortman	Robert Zimmer
Laura Glower	Steve Parrot	

Eileen B. Wilson-Oyelaran wishes to give special thanks to Dr. Rose Simon for her gift of time and her editorial suggestions and to Dr. Carol Spigner for her support throughout this project.

Chapter 1. The Great Resignation Presents a Great Opportunity

1. Ian O. Williamson, "The 'Great Resignation' Is a Trend That Began Before the Pandemic—and Bosses Need to Get Used to It," *The Conversation*, November 12, 2021, https://theconversation.com/the-great-resignation-is-a-trend-that-began-before-the-pandemic-and-bosses-need-to-get-used-to-it-170197.

2. For readers looking for a more detailed commentary on the modern presidency from the viewpoints of veterans who have held the job, we recommend three books (all from Johns Hopkins University Press). The earliest is *Presidencies Derailed: Why University Leaders Fail and How to Prevent It* (2013) by S. J. Trachtenberg, G. B. Kauvar, and E. B. Bogue. The second is a compilation of essays by presidents entitled *Leading Colleges and Universities: Lessons from Higher Education Leaders* (2018), edited by S. J. Trachtenberg, G. B. Kauvar, and E. G. Gee. *The Empowered University: Shared Leadership, Culture Change, and Academic Success* (2019), by F. A. Hrabowski, with P. J. Rous and P. H. Henderson, is the third. Hrabowski is one of the seven presidents profiled in this book. These authors offer insights on the challenges of the contemporary presidency, but they only hint at the origin stories of exceptional leaders, which is our major theme. In a sense, this book rounds out these three commentaries on the contemporary presidency.

3. Jennifer Hedlund has a useful definition of practical intelligence: "the ability that individuals use to find a more optimal fit between themselves and the demands of the environment through adapting, shaping, or selecting a new environment in the pursuit of personally valued goals." Jennifer Hedlund, "Practical Intelligence," in *The Cambridge Handbook of Intelligence*, ed. Robert J. Sternberg, 2nd ed., vol. II (New York: Cambridge University Press, 2020), 736–55. Drawing on Robert J. Sternberg's *Beyond IQ: A Triarchic Theory of Human Intelligence* (New York: Cambridge University Press, 1985), Hedlund notes that practical intelligence is commonly understood as "common sense" or "street smarts" as contrasted with "book smarts." For a helpful definition of cultural intelligence, see Soon Ang, Kok Yee Ng, and Thomas Rockstuhl, "Cultural Intelligence," in Sternberg (2020) above, 820–45. Soon Ang and colleagues characterize this trait as the ability to operate effectively in culturally diverse situations (820). Speculating on the roots of this brand of intelligence, the authors suggest, based on their own research and the research of others, that multicultural identity—defined as identifying with two or more cultures, as would all the individuals profiled in this book—is likely an "antecedent" (828) of this capacity, along with personality and international experience.

4. Barbara Wheeler et al. researched the role of character in determining the success of presidents of theological schools. Their conclusions coincide with our findings. See Barbara G. Wheeler et al., "Leadership That Works: A Study of Theological School Presidents," *Auburn Studies* (December 2010). In describing the purpose of their research, Wheeler says their "goal was to discover the ingredients of executive leadership that make institutions both durable—as in fit for the long haul—and visionary—that is, moving forward in ways the future is likely to require" (1). These are among their findings: "Character is a better predictor of executive leaders' success than credentials and interview performance" (2); "The findings of this study suggest that the focus on credentials is misplaced. There is no correlation between resume and presidential success." (30); traits of successful presidents include "personal strength . . . powerful intelligence, confidence, persuasiveness and persistence . . . firmness and the capacity to withstand criticism . . . where the right answer is 'No' and that response will disappoint or even anger some powerful constituency." (4).

5. Georg Simmel, "The Stranger," in *On Individuality and Social Forms* (Chicago: University of Chicago Press, 1971), 143–149. Described "as one who comes today and stays tomorrow," Simmel's stranger "may be attractive and meaningful" (145) and able to conduct special tasks that community members are unable to perform. Simmel's archetype for the stranger is a person who was Jewish in pre–World War II Europe.

6. The average tenure of presidents is listed as 6.5 years. Jonathan S. Gagliardi et al., *American College Presidents Study 2017*, Washington, DC: American Council on Education, 2017, https://www.acenet.edu/Documents/American-College-President-VIII-2017.pdf.

7. Angela Duckworth in *GRIT: The Power of Passion and Perseverance* (New York: Scribner, 2016), employs the word *grit* to capture several of these attributes. She defines grit as being composed primarily of passion and perseverance (56).

8. Doug Lederman, "Diversity on the Rise among College Presidents," *Inside Higher Education*, February 14, 2022.

9. Timothy Egan, *The Worst Hard Time: The Untold Story of Those Who Survived the Great American Dust Bowl* (Boston: Houghton Mifflin Company, 2006), 130.

10. Malcolm Gladwell, *David and Goliath: Underdogs, Misfits, and the Art of Battling Giants* (New York: Little, Brown and Company, 2013), 102.

11. Elizabeth Bjork and Robert Bjork, "Making Things Hard on Yourself, But in a Good Way: Creating Desirable Difficulties to Enhance Learning," in *Psychology and the Real World: Essays Illustrating Fundamental Contributions to Society,* ed. Morton Ann Gernsbacher, Richard W. Pew et al. (New York: Worth Publishers, 2011), 55–64.

12. Gladwell, *David and Goliath.*

13. Gladwell, *David and Goliath,* 6.

14. Gladwell, *David and Goliath,* 6.

15. Elizabeth Bjork and Robert Bjork, "Making Things Hard on Yourself," 55–64.

16. Elizabeth Bjork and Robert Bjork, "Making Things Hard on Yourself," 58.

17. Jay Belsky et al., *The Origins of You: How Childhood Shapes Later Life* (Cambridge, MA: Harvard University Press, 2020).

18. Belsky, *The Origins of You,* 25.

19. Belsky, *The Origins of You,* 25.
20. Belsky, *The Origins of You,* 25.
21. Belsky, *The Origins of You,* 25.
22. Belsky, *The Origins of You,* 25.
23. Belsky, *The Origins of You,* 25.
24. Isabella B. Cho, "Bacow Joins a Growing List of Higher Education Leaders Who Are Heading for the Exits," *The Harvard Crimson,* June 9, 2022, https://www.the crimson.com/article/2022/6/9/wave-of-departures/
25. The requirements of the law (known simply as "Title IX" in higher education circles) may need further explanation for readers outside the academy. The Office of Civil Rights of the U.S. Department of Education is a good place to start. Title IX of the Education Amendments of 1972 prohibits discrimination based on sex in any education program or activity that receives government assistance. Sexual harassment falls under Title IX and is the first example of discrimination listed on the OCR website: www2.ed.gov/about/offices/list/ocr/sexoverview.html.
26. Kevin Reilly, personal note to the author, August 28, 2022.
27. Mark Jackson, "Evaluating the Role of Hans Selye in the Modern History of Stress," in *Stress, Shock, and Adaptation in the Twentieth Century,* ed. David Cantor and Edmund Ramsden, Chapter 1 (Rochester, NY: Rochester University Press, 2014), https://www.ncbi.nlm.nih.gov/books/NBK349158/. Selye argues that the response to stress occurs in a three-part sequence: the alarm reaction, resistance behavior, then exhaustion. It seems fair to say that this sequence explains how many presidents responded quickly to the unexpected arrival and spread of COVID-19, but after two years of intense maneuvering to manage the crisis experienced Selye's third stage: exhaustion.

Chapter 2. Jeffrey Bullock

1. This characterization of UD's commitment to students comes from item six of seven in the first half of the university's Student Success Commitment document; the words also appear in other university literature. The Commitment is signed personally by the president and each undergraduate student.
2. For an informed description of Elon University's transformation from an average institution to one of the most highly regarded schools in the Southeast, see George Keller's *Transforming a College: The Story of a Little-Known College's Strategic Climb to National Distinction* (Baltimore: Johns Hopkins University Press, updated edition, 2014).
3. *U.S. News & World Report* 2022–2023 edition of *Best Colleges* ranks Macalester College number 27 in a tie with Colorado College among national liberal arts colleges; see https://www.usnews.com/best-colleges/rankings/national-liberal-arts-colleges.
4. Lily Denehy, "Way Back at Mac: A Look at Mac Football's Historic Losing Streak," *The Mac Weekly,* April 21, 2021, https://themacweekly.com/79618/sports/way-back -at-mac-a-look-at-mac-footballs-historic-losing-streak/.
5. *Streetwise,* directed by Martin Bell (United States: Angelika Films, 1984; available on the Criterion Channel, https://www.criterionchannel.com/streetwise).
6. William James, *The Varieties of Religious Experience: A Study in Human Nature* (New York: Penguin Books/Penguin Classics, 1985), 189.

7. Alvin J. Straatmeyer and Joel L. Samuels, *Child of the Church: The University of Dubuque 1852–2008* (Cedar Rapids, IA: WDG Publishing/the University of Dubuque, 2008), 231.

8. Terrence MacTaggart, ed., *Academic Turnarounds: Restoring Vitality to Challenged American Colleges and Universities* (Washington, DC: ACE-Praeger, 2007), 3.

9. The AAUP report "Academic Freedom and Tenure: University of Dubuque," published in the September–October 2001 edition of *Academe*, led to the censure of the University of Dubuque. AAUP's lengthy document concludes that "the board of trustees and the administration of the University of Dubuque violated the 1940 Statement of Principles on Academic Freedom in terminating the tenured appointments" of the two professors who sought the association's investigation.

10. Douglas J. Schuurman, *Vocation: Discerning Our Callings in Life* (Grand Rapids, MI: William B. Eerdmans Publishing Company, 2004), 4.

11. Martin Buber, *I and Thou*, trans. Walter Kaufman (New York: Charles Scribner's Sons, 1970), 178.

12. Annalee R. Ward, "Character and Crisis," in *Character and . . . Crisis*, 8 (2022): 2–11. https://digitalud.dbq.edu/ojs/index.php/character/article/download/104/78.

13. The document signed by Bullock and each student is grounded in educational psychology, as well as Christian principles. A footnote reads "adapted from the Gallup-Purdue Index research on the impact of college experiences and a meaningful life."

Chapter 3. Waded Cruzado

1. Barrett is quoted at some length in "Montana Voices: 10 Years On, MSU President is a Montanan and State is Grateful," *Missoula Current*, December 30, 2019, https://missoulacurrent.com/waded-cruzado.

2. *The Oxford Companion to English Literature* characterizes the literature of "magic realism" (commonly labeled "magical realism") as having "a strong narrative drive, in which the recognizably realistic mingles with the unexpected and the inexplicable, and in which the elements of dream, fairy story, or mythology combine with the everyday." Margaret Drabble, ed., *The Oxford Companion to English Literature* (Oxford: Oxford University Press, 2000), 629–630.

3. Barrett, "Montana Voices."

4. For commentary on the threats to institutional integrity posed by Division I Athletics, see Howard L. Nixon II, *The Athletic Trap: How College Sports Corrupted the Academy* (Baltimore: Johns Hopkins University Press, 2014).

5. Bobcat Quarterback Club website: https://www.bobcatquarterbackclub.com.

6. Niccolo Machiavelli, *The Prince and Other Writings*, trans. Wayne A. Rebhorn (New York: Barnes and Noble Classics, 2003), 25.

7. According to Montana State Legislature's records, since 2001, Republicans have controlled both the House and the Senate nine times as compared to Democratic control occurring twice. See https://Leg.mt.gov/civic-education/facts/party-control.

8. Tribune editorial board, "Wittich, Cruzado Spar over Projects at MSU," *Great Falls Tribune*, Sept. 11, 2015, https://www.greatfallstribune.com/story/opinion/tribune-editorials/2015/09/11/wittich-cruzado-spar-projects-msu/72097032/.

9. Data provided by Office of Planning and Analysis, Montana State University, December 13, 2022.
10. Jonathan R. Krakauer, *Missoula: Rape and the Justice System in a College Town* (New York: Penguin Random House, 2015).
11. Waded Cruzado, "Empowering People, Transforming the World: Today's Land-Grant University," Montana State Inaugural Address, September 10, 2010: 8.
12. Jorge Luis Borges, *The Garden of Forking Paths*, trans. Donald A. Yates, Andrew Hurley, and James E. Irby (London: Penguin Random House UK, 1998).
13. Stephanie Burt, "A Critic at Large: The Never-Ending Story," *The New Yorker*, November 7, 2022: 77.

Chapter 4. Mary Dana Hinton

1. "Black Enrollments in Post-Pandemic Higher Education," *The Journal of Blacks in Higher Education*, January 2, 2023, https://www.jbhe.com/2023/01/black-enrollments-in-post-pandemic-higher-education/.
2. *American College President Study 2017* (Washington, DC: American Council on Education, 2017), https://www.aceacps.org/.
3. Jennifer Oast, " 'Faithful and Valuable': Slavery at Hampden-Sydney College, the University of Virginia, and the Hollins Institute," chapter 5 in *Institutional Slavery: Slaveholding Churches, Schools, Colleges, and Businesses in Virginia, 1680–1860* (Cambridge: Cambridge University Press, 2015), 159–202, https://doi.org/10.1017/CBO 9781316225486.006.
4. Ethel Morgan Smith, *From Whence Cometh My Help* (Columbia: University of Missouri Press, 2000), 4.
5. Sheyonn Baker, email message to Eileen Wilson-Oyelaran, January 31, 2023.
6. "Hollins University Working Group on Slavery and Its Contemporary Legacies," Hollins University, updated July 19, 2022, https://wgscl.press.hollins.edu/.
7. Mary Dana Hinton, " 'All of Us Must Do the Work. All of Us Must Begin Now.': President-Elect Hinton Calls for 'Lasting, Meaningful Cultural Change' at Hollins," Hollins University, June 19, 2020, https://www.hollins.edu/all-of-us-must-do-the -work-all-of-us-must-begin-now-president-elect-hinton-calls-for-lasting-meaning ful-cultural-change-at-hollins/.
8. The Opportunity Atlas (website), US Census Bureau, https://www.opportunity atlas.org/.
9. The construct of "sense of shame" is used to describe the internalization of the negative messages that an individual has received, resulting in feelings of inadequacy for which the individual holds themselves responsible. This internalized oppression presents a series of barriers the individual must overcome in order to self-actualize.
10. Mary Dana Hinton, "The Genuine Authenticity It Takes to Lead" in *Thriving as A Woman in Leadership in Higher Education: Stories and Strategies from Your Peers*, ed. Elizabeth Ross Hubbell and Daniel Fusch (New York: Academic Impressions, 2021), 13.
11. Ellen Hunter Gans, "Lighting the Way Forward: A Look Back at the Legacy of Dr. Mary Dana Hinton," *Saint Benedict's Magazine*, June 2020, 4, https://cdm.csbsju .edu/digital/collection/CSBArchives/id/9777/.

Chapter 5. Freeman Hrabowski III

1. Freeman Hrabowski III, "4 Pillars of College Success in Science," TED video, April 8, 2013, https://www.youtube.com/watch?v=9EglK8Mk18o.
2. Freeman Hrabowski III, *Holding Fast to Dreams: Empowering Youth for the Civil Rights Crusade to STEM Achievement* (Boston: Bacon Press, 2015), 36.
3. For additional information on the Children's Crusade, please see Taylor Branch, *Parting the Waters* (New York: Simon & Schuster, 1988), 754–59; Henry Hampton and Steve Frayer, *Voices of Freedom* (New York: Bantam Books, 1990), 131–132.
4. Hrabowski III, *Holding Fast to Dreams*, 38.
5. Freeman Hrabowski III, "Oral History Interview, Part 1," interview by Joseph Mosnier, University of North Carolina at Chapel Hill, Southern Oral History Program, July 14, 2011, www.c-span.org/video/?83852-1/freeman-hrabowski-oral -history-interview-part-1.
6. While some may find this choice of words offensive, this is a direct quote. The word choice is reflective of the racial, cultural, and linguistic norms of that era. While Connor's word choice was racist and intentionally demeaning, Hrabowski's word choice was essential for survival.
7. James M. Washington, ed., *A Testament of Hope* (San Francisco: Harper & Row, 1986), 221.
8. Hrabowski III, *Holding Fast to Dreams*, 59.
9. Freeman Hrabowski III, Philip J. Ross, and Peter H. Henderson, *The Empowered University* (Baltimore: Johns Hopkins University Press, 2019), 95.
10. Marlene Ross et al., *The American College President* (Washington, D.C.: American Council on Education, 1993), 17, 23.
11. Megan Hanks Mastrola, "UMBC Leads Nation in Producing African-American Undergraduates Who Pursue M.D.-Ph.D.s," University Of Maryland, Baltimore County, January 2, 2018, https://umbc.edu/stories/umbc-leads-nation-in-producing -african-american-undergraduates-who-pursue-m-d-ph-d-s/.
12. Mastrola, "UMBC Leads."

Chapter 6. Robert Jones

1. Hannah Max, "4 of Illinois' Past 10 Governors Went to Prison," *Illinois Policy*, April 11, 2022, https://www.illinoispolicy.org/4-of-illinois-past-10-governors-went-to -prison/.
2. Jodi S. Cohen et al., "Madigan Swayed U. of I. to Admit Relatives, Donors," *Chicago Tribune*, May 5, 2010, https://chicagotribune.com/mews/ct-met-madigan-admissions -20100505-story.html.
3. Wise initiated plans for an innovative model of medical education, which became the Carle-Illinois College of Medicine. Jones oversaw the opening of that college in 2017.
4. Scott Jaschik, "Phyllis Wise Fires Back at U of Illinois Board," *Inside Higher Education*, August 13, 2015, https://www.insidehighered.com/quicktakes/2015/08/14 /phyllis-wise-fires-back-u-illinois-board.
5. Mike Helenthal, "Chancellor Search Committee Creating Candidate Profile, Forming List," *Illinois News Bureau*, March 17, 2016, https://news.illinois.edu/view/6367

/339829. John V. Lombardi, an experienced research university president, observes that major research universities carry an internal momentum that sustains them in spite of the occasional ineffective executive. He adds, however, "If ineffective leadership becomes the norm, then over time the unit will eventually decline as its faculty, staff, and students respond to the poor management." John V. Lombardi, *How Universities Work* (Baltimore: Johns Hopkins University Press, 2013), 196–197. According to faculty leaders, the University of Illinois had been trending downward for a decade before Robert Jones became chancellor.

6. Andy Thomason, "As George Floyd Protests Rock U.S. Cities, Students and Presidents Condemn Systemic Racism," *Chronicle of Higher Education,* May 31, 2020, https://www.chronicle.com/article/as-george-floyd-protests-rock-u-s-cities -students-and-presidents-condemn-systemic-racism.

7. Robert Jones, "Being Black in America," *News-Gazette,* July 5, 2020, https://www .news-gazette.com/news/being-black-in-america-ui-chancellor-robert-jones /article_1b42a91b-d795-5f36-938c-131257e306a9.html.

8. Robert Jones to University of Illinois Massmail, "A New University Call to Action to Address Racism and Social Injustice," July 27, 2020, https://massmail.illinois .edu/massmail/1982189843.html.

9. Michael Gorra, *The Saddest Words: William Faulkner's Civil War* (New York: Liveright Publishing, 2020), 20. Gorra analyzes Faulkner's novels to illustrate the persistence of a romanticized view of the Civil War divorced from its racist origin into the twentieth century.

10. Ronald Heifetz, *Leadership Without Easy Answers* (Cambridge, MA: Harvard University Press, 1994), 35. Heifetz's classic work suggests that reframing divisive issues from a values perspective can be a fruitful approach to problems over which leaders can exert little direct control.

11. Lee V. Gaines, "The Retired University of Illinois Mascot Still Lingers on Campus," *Illinois Newsroom,* July 30, 2020, https://illinoisnewsroom.org/a-retired-university -of-illinois-race-based-mascot-still-lingers-on-campus/.

12. Eric J. Jolly and Stu Levenick, "Report of the Chancellor's Commission on Native Imagery: Healing and Reconciliation," May 13, 2019, http://chancellor.illinois.edu /NativeImageryReport.html. See also Robert J. Jones, "Implementation Plan on Native Imagery," Office of the Vice Chancellor for Diversity, Equity and Inclusion, December 4, 2020, https://diversity.illinois.edu/2020/12/04/implementation-plan -on-native-imagery/.

13. Robert Jones to University of Illinois Massmail, "Our Commitment to Respect and Inclusivity," November 12, 2020, https://massmail.illinois.edu/massmail/915781880 .html.

14. Robert Jones and Andreas Cangellaris, "Chancellor, Provost Offer Reflections on 1 Million COVID-19 Tests at Illinois," Illinois Featured Content, University of Illinois Urbana-Champaign, December 14, 2020, https://blogs.illinois.edu/view /6231/966702854.

15. Susana A. Mendoza, Office of the Illinois Comptroller, *Consequences of Illinois' 2015–2017 Budget Impasse and Fiscal Outlook,* September 18, 2018, https://illinois comptroller.gov/__media/sites/comptroller/Consequences%20of%20201520 17%20Budget%20Impasse2.pdf.

16. Michael T. Nietzel, "Several Colleges and Universities Report Record Fundraising in 2021–2022," *Forbes*, August 3, 2022, https://www.forbes.com/sites/michaeltnietzel/2022/08/03/several-colleges-and-universities-report-record-fund-raising-in-2021-22/?sh=4e80da837df9.

17. Isabel Wilkerson, *The Warmth of Other Suns: The Epic Story of America's Great Migration* (New York: Random House, 2010), 53.

18. Wilkerson, *Warmth*, 53–55. Wilkerson points out that the economics of sharecropping often ensured that perpetual debt carried over from year to year, from one generation to the next. Not only did the landowner who also owned the local farm store charge for the "furnish" that Wilkerson describes, he also controlled the market price for the crop in many cases. Often, only the landowner was permitted to purchase the farmer's crop, resulting in below-market prices and too little money to pay off the sharecropper's debt to the man who owned the land and controlled the price of supplies. In one of Wilkerson's interviews (54), a sharecropper reports that after the costs of the furnish were subtracted from the controlled-price crops, the best the tenant farmer could do was break even. Breaking even reduced the sharecropper to bare subsistence living.

19. Douglas A. Blackmon, *Slavery by Another Name: The Re-Enslavement of Black Americans from the Civil War to World War II* (New York: Doubleday, 2008), 6. This book chronicles the widespread use of what he characterizes as neo-slavery, wherein courts sent dissident Black people "into slave mines or forced labor camps." Convicts could be, and often were, leased to landowners until their fines and court costs had been met. As Blackmon points out, the Deep South justice system was designed to criminalize attempts of poor Blacks to stand up for their rights. Although the threat of incarceration that Blackmon describes largely ended with World War II (402), the well-justified belief that the Georgia court system, like that in other Southern states, would not render justice to Black people persisted.

20. Anyone believing that Wallace's histrionics were about states' rights should read his speech delivered in what he described as the "Cradle of the Confederacy . . . the very heart of the great Anglo-Saxon Southland." For major excerpts of Wallace's 1962 inaugural speech, see "(1963) George Wallace, 'Segregation Now, Segregation Forever,' " *Blackpast*, January 22, 2013, https://www.blackpast.org/african-american-history/speeches-african-american-history/1963-george-wallace-segregation-now-segregation-forever/.

21. Henry Louis Gates cites Richard S. Newman's biography of the founder of the AME Church, Richard Allen. Richard S. Newman, *Freedom's Profit: Bishop Richard Allen, the AME Church, and the Black Founding Fathers* (New York: New York University Press, 2009), 169–175. Henry Louis Gates Jr., *The Black Church: This Is Our Story, This Is Our Song* (New York: Penguin Press, 2021), 49.

22. For the "rainy night" reference, see Brook Benton, vocalist, "Rainy Night in Georgia," by Tony Joe White, recorded 1969, Cotillion/Atlantic, 45 rpm.

23. Eddie R. Cole, *The Campus Color Line: College Presidents and the Struggle for Black Freedom* (Princeton: Princeton University Press, 2020), 1–2. The University of Georgia seems to have been more deeply steeped in racism than its rival, Georgia Institute of Technology (Georgia Tech), located seventy miles from Atlanta. Cole notes that desegregation was handled peacefully at Georgia Tech one week after

the UGA riots aimed at forcing Hunter and Holmes to withdraw. Cole credits the leadership of Tech President Edwin D. Harrison for "leading Georgia Tech to become the first Deep South university to desegregate *without violence or a court order*" (8–9).

24. David Brooks, *The Road to Character* (New York: Random House, 2015), says that "the road to character often involves moments of moral crisis, confrontation, and recovery" (13). Brooks captures something of Jones's experience when he writes that at these moments of personal crises, "they didn't have to flail about, because hands were holding them up" (14).

Chapter 7. Kwang-Wu Kim

1. American Council on Education, *American College President Study 2017* (Washington, D.C.: 2017), 34.

2. Abby Budiman and Neil G. Ruiz, "Key Facts about Asian Origin Groups in the U.S.," *Pew Research Center*, April 29, 2021, https://www.pewresearch.org/short-reads/2021/04/29/key-facts-about-asian-origin-groups-in-the-u-s/. There is some controversy over the "model minority" concept as a universal descriptor of Asian attitudes and behavior. The construct masks the diversity among Asian cultures and Asian Americans. Drawing from US Census Bureau data, Budiman and Ruiz list, in order of their population in the United States, Chinese, Filipino, Indian, Vietnamese, Korean, Japanese, Pakistani, Cambodian, Hmong, Thai, Laotian, Bangladeshi, and Burmese as significant groups. These groups "differ significantly by income, education," and other characteristics. The authors go on to say that "these differences highlight the wide diversity of the nation's Asian population and provide a counterpoint to the 'model minority' myth and description of the population as monolithic." While the authors characterize the "model minority" construct as a myth, many Asian Americans do not. For example, erin Khuê Ninh offers a well-researched, highly personal account of the power of the traits embodied in the "model minority" construct. In *Passing for Perfect: College Imposters and Other Model Minorities*, this Vietnamese American argues that the stereotypes embodied in the "model minority" idea "are demonstrably false for many Asian Americans," while they are "demonstrably true for others." Ninh presents cases of Asian American students whose obsession with honoring the "model minority" mandates led to tragic results. "Where I come from," she writes, "the model minority is not a myth." Ninh defines the "model minority" as "an *identity*: a set of convictions and aspirations regardless of present socioeconomic status or future attainability." (See erin Khuê Ninh, *Passing for Perfect: College Imposters and Other Model Minorities* [Philadelphia: Temple University Press, 2021], 4, 5.) She credits Jennifer Lee and Min Zhou with coining the term *success frame*, which is defined as "earning straight A's, graduating as the high school valedictorian, earning a degree from an elite university, attaining an advanced degree, and working in one of four high status professional fields: medicine, law, engineering, or science." (See Jennifer Lee and Min Zhou, *The Asian American Achievement Paradox* [New York: Russell Sage Foundation, 2015], 6.)

3. Melanie Hanson, "College Enrollment & Student Demographic Statistics," Education Data Initiative, July 26, 2022, https://educationdata.org/college-enrollment

-statistics. For commentary on Asian American academic achievements, see also Robert VerBruggen, "Racial Preferences on Campus: Trends in Asian American Enrollment at U.S. Colleges," Manhattan Institute, April 28, 2022, https://www .google.com/url?sa=t&rct=j&q=&esrc=s&source=web&cd=&ved=2ahUKEwiX2IL 9iYWAAxUUrYkEHSVgBwEQFnoECAsQAQ&url=https%3A%2F%2Fmedia4 .manhattan-institute.org%2Fsites%2Fdefault%2Ffiles%2Fverbruggen-trends -in-asian-enrollment-at-us-colleges.pdf&usg=AOvVaw1lHfUJv6264im4fSjy2 Nrx&opi=89978449.

4. New American Economy Research Fund, "Examining Educational, Workforce, and Earning Divides in the Asian American and Pacific Islander Community," May 13, 2021, https://research.newamericaneconomy.org/report/aapi-examine-educational -workforce-earning-divides/. For commentary on the influence of a home environment on schoolwork conducted at home among various groups, see Michael Hansen and Diana Quintero, "Analyzing 'the Homework Gap' among High School Students," Brookings Institution, August 10, 2017, https://www.brookings.edu /articles/analyzing-the-homework-gap-among-high-school-students/.

5. New American Economy Research Fund, "Examining Educational, Workforce, and Earning Divides."

6. Jane Hyun, *Breaking the Bamboo Ceiling: Career Strategies for Asians* (New York: HarperCollins, 2005), 7.

7. Hyun, *Breaking*, 6.

8. Hyun, *Breaking*, 24–25.

9. Kwang-Wu Kim, "Distinctiveness, Value, and Purpose: Building Our Brighter Future" (position paper, Columbia College, Chicago, April 2021).

10. Bruce Cummings, *The Korean War: A History* (New York: The Modern Library, 2010), 21. The narrative offers grim statistics that provide a sense of what Kim's mother experienced during the battles for Seoul. Cummings writes, "The war for the south left 111,000 South Koreans killed, 106,000 wounded, and 57,000 missing; 314,000 homes were destroyed, 244,000 damaged."

11. See Hyun, *Breaking*, 15. In "The Perpetual Foreigner Syndrome," she writes, "Asian Americans, by virtue of their physical features, face the challenge of being considered foreigners in social and professional circles—outsiders in the land they call home."

12. Malcolm Gladwell, *Outliers: The Story of Success* (New York: Little, Brown and Company, 2008), 40. *Outliers* cites Daniel J. Levitan's *This Is Your Brain on Music: The Science of a Human Obsession* to confirm the importance of very long hours of practice in order to achieve exceptional levels of performance. Levitan writes, "In study after study, of composers, basketball players, fiction writers, ice skaters, *concert pianists* (emphasis added)," it takes about ten thousand hours "to achieve true mastery." See Daniel J. Levitan, *This Is Your Brain on Music: The Science of a Human Obsession* (New York: Dutton, 2006), 197.

13. Michael M. Crow and William B. Dabars, *Designing the New American University* (Baltimore: Johns Hopkins University Press, 2015).

14. T. S. Eliot, "Little Gidding," in *The Complete Poems and Plays 1909–1950* (New York: Harcourt, Brace and Company, 1952, orig. 1943), 145.

Chapter 8. Mary Marcy

1. "Economic Diversity and Student Outcomes at Dominican University of California," *The Upshot* (webpage), *New York Times,* accessed October 2022, https://www.nytimes.com/interactive/projects/college-mobility/dominican-university-of-california.
2. Mary Marcy, *The Small College Imperative* (Sterling, VA: Stylus Publishing, 2020).
3. "About Us," LGBTQ Leaders in Higher Education (website), accessed July 25, 2023, https://www.lgbtqleaders.net/about.
4. Jim Berg, email correspondence to author, October 31, 2022.
5. David Whyte, "Working Together," poem in *The House of Belonging* (Moorhead, MN: Many Rivers Press, 1996).
6. Mary Marcy, interview with Jeff Selingo and Michael Horn, "The Opportunities for Small Colleges," *Future U Podcast,* podcast audio, March 2, 2020, https://futureupodcast.com/episodes/the-opportunities-for-small-colleges/.
7. William Mathis, "The Purpose of Education: Being the Great Equalizer," Opinion Columns, *Stowe Reporter,* June 30, 2016, https://www.vtcng.com/stowe_reporter/opinion/opinion_columns/the-purpose-of-education-being-the-great-equalizer/article_8fd76944-3ece-11e6-9e14-93ae4dcb0da0.html.

Chapter 9. Recruiting Exceptional Leaders

1. William Kirwan, "Becoming a President," in *Leading Colleges and Universities: Lessons from Higher Education Leaders,* eds. Stephen Joel Trachtenberg, Gerald B. Kauvar, E. Gordon Gee (Baltimore: Johns Hopkins University Press, 2018), 3.
2. Stephen Joel Trachtenberg, Gerald B. Kauvar, and E. Grady Bogue, *Presidencies Derailed: Why University Leaders Fail and How to Prevent It* (Baltimore: Johns Hopkins University Press, 2013), 97. The uncertainties associated with searches are widely recognized, though little has come forth to improve their effectiveness in identifying capable leaders. The authors comment in a short but valuable section on improving academic searches that producing high-performing leaders is often "a matter of luck rather than the outcome of a sound process" (97). They go on to say, "After the audition—the interrogations, the checking, the interviews, and the hazing—they have no way of knowing how good the last woman or man left standing will really be. The institution only learns that much later" (97).
3. Jean A. Dowdall, *Searching for Academic Leadership: Advice for Candidates and Search Committees, ACE/Praeger Series on Higher Education* (Westport, CT: Praeger Publishers, 2007); Joseph Shackford Johnston Jr. and James P. Ferrare, *A Complete Guide to Presidential Search for Universities and Colleges* (Washington, DC: AGB Press, 2013). Two guides published by respected professional associations propose what we call the conventional model as *the* model to adopt in searching for a president. An alternative model employs a much smaller committee, sometimes composed solely of board members, who make the choice before presenting a stranger turned president to the campus. This approach occurs occasionally among independent colleges, and rarely in the case of public universities and systems.

4. Association of Executive Search and Leadership Consultants, "The Past, Present, and Future of Executive Search," *Executive Talent,* downloaded January 31, 2023, https://www.aesc.org/insights/magazine/article/past-present-and-future-executive -search.

5. Judith Wilde and James Finkelstein, "A Fundamental Change in Hiring College Presidents is Unfolding," *Higher Ed Dive,* November 15, 2021, https://www.higher eddive.com/news/a-fundamental-change-in-hiring-college-presidents-is-unfolding /609978/. These figures come from professors Wilde and Finkelstein of the Schar School of Policy and Government at George Mason University.

6. Judith Wilde and James Finkelstein, "The People Hiring College Presidents Don't Have Experience as College Presidents," *Higher Ed Dive,* November 16, 2021, https://www.highereddive.com/news/the-people-hiring-college-presidents-don't -have-experience-as-college-presidents/609980. According to Wilde and Finkel-stein, junior staff are not the only ones in the search business lacking experience. Wilde and Finkelstein report that of nearly two dozen heads of higher education search firms, few "had experience in the big chair on campus" and fewer still "had higher education experience of any type."

7. Suzanne Teer and Karen Burg, "How Higher Education Can Reinvent the Lead-ership Search," *The Chronicle of Higher Education,* July 20, 2020, chronicle.com /article/how-higher-education-can-reinvent-the-leadership-search. Search firms shift some of the burden of recruiting onto campus search committees. In the words of a senior partner with a major search firm, "This is no time for people on the hiring committee to sit back and expect consultants to do all the outreach." Seeking nominations from the campus community, as this consultant suggests, is a worthy idea, so long as your expectations of the returns are low.

8. Peter Cappelli, "Your Approach to Hiring Is All Wrong," *Spotlight Series, Harvard Business Review,* May–June 2019, 4. According to Peter Cappelli writing in the *Harvard Business Review,* corporate recruiters are turning to "voice recognition, body language, clues on social media, and especially machine learning algorithms" to speed recruitment. Cappelli finds scant evidence that these technologies pro-duce better results.

9. Timothy R. Levine, *Duped: Truth-Default Theory and the Social Science of Lying and Deception* (Tuscaloosa, AL: University of Alabama Press, 2020), 93–100.

10. Levine, *Duped,* ix.

11. Levine, *Duped,* 10.

12. Malcolm Gladwell, *Talking to Strangers: What We Should Know about People We Don't Know* (New York: Little, Brown, 2019) 123–131.

13. Gladwell, *Talking to Strangers,* 68.

14. Levine, *Duped,* 242. Levine draws a pertinent distinction between the appearance of honest and honesty itself. He writes, "Differences in how honest different peo-ple seem to be are a function of a combination of eleven different behaviors and impressions that function together. Honest demeanor has little to do with actual honesty."

15. Levine, *Duped,* 166.

16. Levine, *Duped,* 166.

17. Levine, *Duped,* 93–100.

18. Elizabeth Bjork and Robert Bjork, "Making Things Hard on Yourself, but in a Good Way: Creating Desirable Difficulties to Enhance Learning," in *Psychology and the Real World: Essays Illustrating Fundamental Contributions to Society,* ed. Morton Ann Gernsbacher et al. (New York: Worth Publishers, 2011), 55–64.

19. Jane Hyun, *Breaking the Bamboo Ceiling: Career Strategies for Asians* (New York: Harper Collins, 2005), 41.

20. National Institute on Alcohol Abuse and Alcoholism, "Alcohol Facts and Statistics," February 2020, https://www.niaaa.nih.gov/alcohols-effects-health/alcohol-topics /alcohol-facts-and-statistics.

academic programs, elimination and expansion of, 30–31
affirmative action, 35
African Americans: access to education, 62, 63, 76, 98; and church culture, 81, 111–12; civil rights movement, 76–79, 102; and Historically Black institutions, 85, 86, 87, 89; and inclusion, 61, 65, 91–93, 103; segregation and desegregation, 62, 76, 79–80, 85, 109–10, 113–14, 196–97n23; and slavery legacy, 59–60, 109, 196n19; in STEM, 84, 85, 90, 91, 92–93; underrepresented in higher education leadership, 55, 66, 89–90
Alabama A&M University, 85
alcohol abuse, 178
American Association of University Professors, 100
Ang, Soon, 189n3
anti-Muslim behavior, 99, 105
Antioch University, Project on the Future of Higher Education, 153
anti-Semitic behavior, 99, 100, 105
appearances and first impressions, 172
archetypes, of leaders, 66–67, 166
Arizona State University, 124–25, 136–37
Asian Americans: foreigner status, 198n11; high enrollment in higher education, 121–22; Korean heritage, 120, 121, 129–31; "model minority" construct, 122–23, 197n2; underrepresented in higher education leadership, 121, 122
athletic programs, building projects, 42–43, 45–46, 47–48
authenticity, of leaders, 67–68, 73, 95–96

background checks, 169–70, 178–79
Bard College at Simon's Rock, 143, 153
Barrett, Steve, 39–40

Bell, George, 82
Bell, Martin, *Streetwise*, 25
Belsky, Jay, 7
Birmingham, Alabama, 76–79
Bjork, Elizabeth and Robert, 6–7, 177
Blackmon, Douglas A., 196n19
Black people. *See* African Americans
Blackwell, Erin "Tiny," 25
Blagojevich, Rod, 99
boards of trustees, relations with presidents, 15, 126, 135, 136, 156, 159–61
Bodner, Seth, 47
booster clubs, 42–43
Brooks, David, 115, 182, 197n24
Brown v. Board of Education, 85
Buber, Martin, 32
Budiman, Abby, 197n2
building renovations, repurposing, and construction, 42–43, 45–46, 47–48, 70
Bullock, Dana, 26, 29
Bullock, Jeffrey, 17–34; conversion experience and sense of calling, 25, 32; educational background, 20–22, 26; mentors to, 22–23, 24; as minister, 26; passion for Christian mission, 29–30, 33; signature initiatives at Dubuque, 33, 192n13; transformative work at Dubuque, 30–31; values instilled in during upbringing, 18–19; work with troubled teenagers, 24–25

calling, 32, 51, 81, 183
campus renovations, repurposing, and construction, 42–43, 45–46, 47–48, 70
Cappelli, Peter, 200n8
Carle Illinois College of Medicine, 107, 194n3
Carnegie Foundation Community Engagement Classification, 91

Catholic educational values, 50–51, 55
character strengths and leadership qualities: overview, 1–2, 4, 11–12, 183–84; in forensic model of presidential searches, 176–77; shaped by hardship, 2–3, 4, 6–8, 182–83
Chief Illiniwek (University of Illinois Urbana-Champaign mascot), 99, 103–4
Children's Crusade (1963), 76–78, 81, 82
Christian, Clay, 39–40
citizenship, 36
civil rights movement, 76–79, 102
class inequality, 59–60, 62, 65, 76–78, 108–10, 196nn18–19
coaching, for candidates, 177–78
Cole, Eddie R., 196–97n23
collaboration, 70, 127, 146, 155–56, 158, 183–84
College of Saint Benedict, 55–58, 66, 70–71
Columbia College Chicago: challenges and advantages at, 125–26; presidential search, 123–24; transformation under Kim, 126–29
communication: capacity for hard conversations, 23; and cultural fluency, 50; rhetorical skills, 81–82; transparent, 68–69
compassion and love, 1, 11, 23, 24, 32, 67–68, 71, 72–73, 95–96
Connor, Bull, 77–78
consultants and search firms, 167–69, 170, 200nn6–7
conversion, defined, 25
Coppin State University, 85, 86
COVID-19 pandemic, 15, 58, 61, 71, 99, 105–6, 128, 161
Crow, Michael, 124, 136
Cruzado, Waded, 35–53; booster club relations, 42–43; educational background, 50–52; faculty relations, 43–44, 52; obstacles to presidential candidacy, 35–36, 37–41; passion for land-grant mission, 35, 38, 39, 41, 48–49; Puerto Rican background, 36–37, 49–50; signature initiatives at MSU, 47–48; state leadership relations, 44–46
cultural intelligence: benefits of, 50; defined, 189n3; as virtue of character, 1, 11, 183
Culture of Care (Hollins University), 71
Cummings, Bruce, 198n10

Denehy, Lily, 21
desegregation, 62, 76, 85, 113–14, 196–97n23
desirable difficulties, 6–7
diversity. *See* inclusion and diversity
Dominican University of California: board dynamics, 159–61; challenges at, 145–46, 153–56; presidential search, 143–45; transformation under Marcy, 140–41, 157–59
donations and fundraising, 46, 70, 72, 107
Duckworth, Angela, 190n7
Dunedin Multidisciplinary Health and Development Study, 7–8

Easter, Robert, 99
Eliot, T. S., 137
Elon University, 18
El Paso Choral Society, 133–35
enrollment growth, 44, 46, 47, 90, 128–29
enslaved individuals, 59–60
Environmental Risk Study (E-Risk), 8
ethnicity. *See* racial and ethnic identity
exceptional leadership, criteria for, 10–12

facility renovations, repurposing, and construction, 42–43, 45–46, 47–48, 70
faculty: dismissal of, 30–31, 192n9; relations with presidents, 31, 43–44, 52, 88, 137, 145–46; role of, in student success, 84–85, 86; unionization of, 27–28
Faulkner, William, 103, 195n9
Fawcett, Henry Eli, 22–23, 24, 26
Fawcett, VeNita, 23
federal funding, 35, 48, 91
financial strength: dismissals and program eliminations to achieve, 30–31; fundraising and donations, 46, 70, 72, 107; and land-grant status, 35, 48; real estate investments, 125, 128; research funding, 91; scholarships and financial aid, for students, 72, 92–93, 107, 116, 128; state funding, 44–45, 98, 106, 124
Finkelstein, James, 200n6
first-generation students, 51, 65, 140, 150
first impressions and appearances, leaders, 172
Fleisher, Leon, 132
Floyd, George, 61, 99, 101–2, 127, 132
forensic model, of presidential searches, 164, 174–80

Fort Valley State College (now University), 112–13
fundraising and donations, 46, 70, 72, 107

Gamble, Geoffrey, 38
Georgia Institute of Technology (Georgia Tech), 196–97n23
Gladwell, Malcolm, 6, 171–72
Gorra, Michael, 103, 195n9
graduation rates, 46, 88, 90
Great Recession (2007–2009), xv, 15, 136–37
Great Resignation: impact on search firms, 168, 169; as phenomenon, 1, 14–15

Hampton Institute, 83
Harrison, Edwin D., 196–97n23
Harvard University Institute for New Presidents, 153–54
HBCUs. *See* Historically Black institutions
Heatherington, Laurie, 63
Hedlund, Jennifer, 189n3
Heifetz, Ronald, 104, 105, 195n10
Herberger Institute for Design and the Arts, Arizona State University, 124–25, 136–37
Herman, Richard, 99
Hinton, Mary Dana: educational background, 62–64; embracing marginality, 66–67, 73–74; leadership philosophy, 67–69, 72–73; leadership potential, 64–66; mentors to, 63, 64; obstacles to presidential candidacy, 55–57, 59; passion for inclusion, 57, 61, 67–68, 71–72, 73–74; transformative work at College of Saint Benedict, 57–58, 70–71; transformative work at Hollins University, 71–72; values instilled in during upbringing, 61–63
Hispanic heritage, 36–37
Historically Black institutions, 85, 86, 87, 89
Hollins community, 60
Hollins University: challenges at, 58, 61; historical overview, 59–60; presidential search, 58–59; transformation under Hinton, 71–72
Holmes, Hamilton, 113
Hooker, Michael, 85, 86, 87–88, 89
Howard Hughes Medical Institute (HHMI), 75

Hrabowski, Freeman, III, 75–96; accolades, 75–76; civil rights movement involvement, 76–79; educational background, 82–84, 85; leadership lessons, 81–82; leadership philosophy, 94–95; obstacles to leadership appointments, 86–88, 89–90; passion for student success, 84–85, 88–89, 91–93; transformative work at UMBC, 90–94; values instilled in during upbringing, 79–81
Hrabowski, Jackie, 87
Humanex leadership assessment, 12, 176–77, 183
Hunter-Galt, Charlayne, 113
Hyun, Jane, 122, 177–78, 198n11

Illinois politics, 98, 99
immigration status, 36
inclusion and diversity: in institutional mission and identity, 57, 61, 91–92, 127–28; in leadership teams, 67–68, 126–27; programs to support, 71–72, 92–93, 102–3; recognition for, 140–41; as value instilled in during upbringing, 131–32
intelligence, cultural: benefits of, 50; defined, 189n3; as virtue of character, 1, 11, 183
intelligence, practical: defined, 189n3; as virtue of character, 1, 11, 183
interviews, unreliability of, 170–74, 177
Iowa State University, 21

James, William, 25
Jones, RJ, 98, 109, 110–11
Jones, Robert, 97–119; educational background, 112–16; leadership potential, 117–18; mentors to, 115, 117; response to COVID-19 pandemic, 105–6; response to racial conflict, 101–5; sharecropping background, 97–98, 108–10; signature initiatives at UIUC, 107; values instilled in during upbringing, 110–12

Keller, Ken, 117
Kephart, Richard, 125
Killeen, Tim, 118
Kim, Kwang-Wu, 120–38; educational background, 124, 131, 132; Korean background, 120, 121, 129–31; leadership experience at Arizona State, 124,

Kim, Kwang-Wu (*cont.*)
136–37; leadership experience at music institutions, 133–36; musical background, 130, 131, 132–33; obstacles to presidential candidacy, 123, 124–25; transformative work at Columbia, 126–29; values instilled in upbringing, 131–32
Kim, Sung Ok, 129
King, Martin Luther, Jr., 76, 79, 102
Kirwan, William "Brit," 163
Korean heritage, 120, 121, 129–31
Krakauer, Jon, 47
Ku Klux Klan, 78, 113

Laing School, 112
land-grant institutions, 35, 38, 39, 41, 48–49, 113
Lawrence, Pareena G., 58
leadership. *See* character strengths and leadership qualities
Lee, Jennifer, 197n2
Lee, Robert E., 109
Levine, Timothy R., 170–71, 172, 200n14
Levitan, Daniel J., 198n12
Lewis, John, 102
LGBTQ+ individuals, 126, 141–42, 143–44, 151–52, 162
LGBTQ Leaders in Higher Education, 142
Lombardi, John V., 195n5
Lombardi, Vince, 16
Longy School of Music, 135–36
love and compassion, 1, 11, 23, 24, 32, 67–68, 71, 72–73, 95–96

Ma, Yo-Yo, 132
Macalester College, 20–21, 191n3
MacDowell, Michael A., 64
Mackin, Kevin, 55, 64–65
magical realism, 38, 51–52, 192n2
Mandela, Nelson, 104
Mann, Horace, 162
Marcy, Mary, 139–62; cattle ranch background, 139–40, 146–47; educational background, 147–51; leadership lessons and experience before Dominican, 152–54; mentors to, 149, 150, 152; obstacles to presidential candidacy, 141–45; passion for collaboration, 145–46, 154–56, 158; response to COVID-19 pandemic, 161; *Small College Imperative*,

141; transformative work at Dominican, 140–41, 157–59; trustee relations, 159–61
Mary Baldwin College, 59
Mayagüez, Puerto Rico, 49–50
McCambridge, Shannon, 177
McLaughlin, Judith, 153–54
McNair, Cynthia, 78–79
Meade, Paula, 60
Meyerhoff Scholars Program (UMBC), 92–93
minority status. *See* outsider status
Misericordia University, 64
"model minority" construct, 122–23, 197n2
Montana State University (MSU): building projects, 42–43, 45–46, 47–48; faculty-president relations, 43–44; land-grant status, 35, 38, 39, 41, 48–49; presidential search, 35–36, 37–41; state funding, 44–45; student success, 46, 48; versus University of Montana, 46–47
Morrill, Justin, 48
Morrill, Rich, 64
Morrill Act (1862), 35, 48, 113
Mount Saint Mary's College, 64
multilingual skills, 50

National Academy of Sciences (NAS), 75
National Education Association, 28
National Labor Relations Board, 28
Native American imagery, 98–99, 103–4
Newman, Richard, 112
New Mexico State University, 36, 37, 38
Ng, Kok Yee, 189n3
NICHD Study of Early Child Care and Youth Development, 8
Ninh, erin Khuê, 197n2

outsider status: and bias, 8–10, 144–45, 161–62, 176, 177; defined, 4; and desirable difficulties, 6–7; and disadvantage paradox, 5; embracing, 66–67, 73–74; as obstacle to presidential candidacy, 36–37, 39, 54, 55–57, 59, 86–88, 89–90, 123, 141–45; and self-awareness, 154

Palestinian-Israeli conflict, 99, 100, 104, 105
passion for mission, 2, 11, 183
Peabody Conservatory at Johns Hopkins University, 124, 132

people of color: and educational potential, 84–85; and inclusion, 61, 65, 91–93, 103; underrepresented in higher education leadership, 55, 66, 89–90, 121. *See also specific groups*

Pittsburgh Theological Seminary, 26

political relations, 44–46, 98, 99

Porter, Reverend, 81

poverty, 62, 78. *See also* socioeconomic inequality

practical intelligence: defined, 189n3; as virtue of character, 1, 11, 183

presidency challenges: capacity to confront, as mark of exceptional leadership, 10–11, 184; overview, 13–16; and support system, 179

presidential searches, 163–80; background checks, 169–70, 178–79; bias in, 8–10, 144–45, 161–62, 176, 177; cautionary tale, 165–67; and consensus choice, 164–65; forensic model, 164, 174–80; interviews, 170–74, 177; power dynamics, 40; search firm business model, 167–69, 170

Puerto Rico, 36, 49–50

racial and ethnic identity: and inequitable economic and social systems, 59–60, 62, 65, 76–78, 108–10, 196nn18–19; as obstacles to presidential candidacy, 36–37, 56–57, 86–88, 89–90; social justice initiatives, 102–5. *See also* inclusion and diversity; *specific groups*

racism and racial conflict, 76–79, 99, 101–5, 113–15, 120, 127, 132, 196–97n23

Randolph Macon Women's College, 59

rankings, 34, 47, 71, 141

Rauner, Bruce, 106

real estate investments, 125, 128

reconciliation language, 104

recruitment, advance, 175

references, questionable, 173–74

religion: conversion experiences, 25, 73; and educational values, 50–51, 55, 81; in institutional mission and identity, 27, 29–30, 33; and racial justice values, 112; vocation and calling, 32, 51, 81

research institutions, 44, 91, 101, 195n5

resilience, virtue of, 1, 7, 11, 183

retention rates, 46

reverse discrimination claims, 93

Rockstuhl, Thomas, 189n3

Romney, George, 45

Roosevelt, Theodore, 6

Ruiz, Neil G., 197n2

rural state dynamics, 48–49

Saint John's University, 57, 70

Saint Mary's High School, 63, 65

Sandburg, Carl, 123

scholarships and financial aid, 72, 92–93, 107, 116, 128

Schuurman, Douglas, 32

search committees, effective, 175–76

searches. *See* presidential searches

search firms, 167–69, 170, 200nn6–7

Seattle, Washington, 24–25

Seattle Pacific University, 26

segregation and desegregation, 62, 76, 79–80, 85, 109–10, 113–14, 196–97n23

self-awareness, 66–67, 154

Selye, Hans, 16, 191n27

sexual misconduct, 14, 47, 169–70, 178, 191n25

sexual orientation, 141–42, 143–44, 151–52, 162

shame, sense of, 62, 65, 193n9

sharecropping, 97–98, 108–10, 196n18

Simmel, Georg, 2, 190n5

16th Street Baptist Church bombing, 78–79

slavery legacy, 59–60, 109

Smith, Ethel Morgan, 60

social justice initiatives, 102–5

socioeconomic inequality, 59–60, 62, 65, 76–78, 108–10, 196nn18–19

Sounds of Blackness (choral group), 112, 116

South African students, 116–17

Southern Christian Leadership Conference (SCLC), 81

state funding, 44–45, 98, 106, 124

Stearns, Sheila, 39–40

STEM: inclusion and student success in, 84, 85, 90, 91, 92–93; president background in humanities versus, 38, 39

stereotypes, of leaders, 66–67, 166

stranger archetype, 2, 190n5

Streetwise (documentary), 25

strength of character. *See* character strengths and leadership qualities

stress, stages of, 16, 191n27

Students for Justice in Palestine (SJP), 105

Leader

FOUNDATION 5

humanex
ventures

Discover the Leader Within You

Find your top 5 leadership talents by taking our **free** online assessment!

Visit: pathway.humanexventures.com or scan the QR code.

Sample Leadership Report

Mission	You are intrinsically motivated to help others. You demonstrate a commitment to serve and derive personal and professional satisfaction from being supportive of others.
Orchestrator	You coordinate the right people and non-people resources to effectively execute plans. You align these resources and manage multiple moving parts in a systematic way to ensure objectives can be carried out by your team.
Courage	You stand up for what you believe is right. You proactively voice your opinions and will push an agenda you feel strongly about. You confront obstacles head-on and are not afraid to stand alone on matters that are important to you.
Networker	You are good at meeting new people. You establish connections with others to develop mutually beneficial relationships. You intentionally build and maintain contacts who share common backgrounds, interests, and goals.
Vision	You are energized by thinking about the future. Able to clearly visualize what this will look like in the long-term, you articulate this vision with such conviction that others often want to follow.

With over 40 years of experience partnering with top organizations, Humanex Ventures takes the guesswork out of selecting top candidates via our suite of research-based structured interviews. These interviews evaluate the key strengths necessary for success in critical roles, such as leadership.

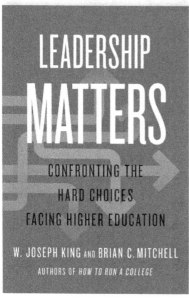
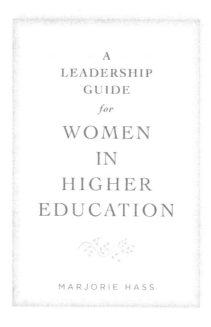
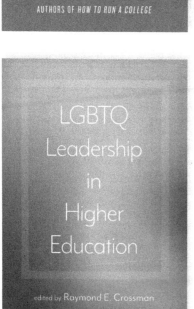
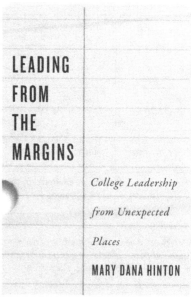